Italians Then,
Mexicans Now

ITALIANS THEN, MEXICANS NOW

IMMIGRANT ORIGINS AND SECOND-GENERATION PROGRESS, 1890 TO 2000

JOEL PERLMANN

RUSSELL SAGE FOUNDATION
NEW YORK, NEW YORK

THE LEVY ECONOMICS INSTITUTE OF BARD COLLEGE
ANNANDALE-ON-HUDSON, NEW YORK

The Levy Economics Institute of Bard College

The Levy Economics Institute of Bard College, founded in 1986, is a nonprofit, nonpartisan research organization devoted to public service. Through scholarship and economic research it generates viable, effective public policy responses to important economic problems that profoundly affect the quality of life in the United States and abroad.

Library of Congress Cataloging-in-Publication Data
Perlmann, Joel.
    Italians then, Mexicans now : immigrant origins and second-generation progress, 1890 to 2000 / Joel Perlmann.
        p.   cm.
    Includes bibliographical references and index.
    ISBN 0-87154-662-0
        1. Mexican Americans—Social conditions—20th century.   2. Immigrants—United States—Social conditions—20th century.   3. Children of immigrants—United States—Social conditions—20th century.   4. Mexican Americans—Economic conditions—20th century.   5. Immigrants—United States—Economic conditions—20th century.   6. Children of immigrants—United States—Economic conditions—20th century.   7. Assimilation (Sociology)—History—20th century.   8. United States—Race relations—History—20th century.   9. United States—Ethnic relations—History—20th century.   I. Title.

E184.M5P427   2005
330.973′0089′6872—dc22   2005048999

Text design by Genna Patacsil.

RUSSELL SAGE FOUNDATION
112 East 64th Street, New York, New York 10021
10 9 8 7 6 5 4 3 2 1

For Rivka

CONTENTS

About the Author ix

Acknowledgments xi

Introduction 1

Chapter 1   Toward a Population History:
A Basis for Comparisons 7

Chapter 2   Immigrant Wages Then and Now 37

Chapter 3   Second-Generation Schooling 60

Chapter 4   Second-Generation Economic Outcomes 90

Conclusion 116

Appendix 126

Notes 163

References 175

Index 183

ABOUT THE AUTHOR

JOEL PERLMANN is senior scholar at the Levy Economics Institute of Bard College and the Levy Institute Research Professor at Bard College.

ACKNOWLEDGMENTS

I AM GRATEFUL to Christopher Jencks for an extensive, illuminating, and selfless email correspondence conducted intermittently over the years; those exchanges helped me to think through many methodological and substantive issues. Seminar presentations to the Bard College faculty and at Bard's Levy Economics Institute helped me more than participants probably realize, as did peppering my colleagues with questions. I am especially grateful to Asena Caner, Sanjaya De Silva, Michael Donnelly, Yuval Elmelech, Dimitri Papadimitriou, Andrew Pearlman, and Ajit Zacharias. Presentations at the CUNY Graduate Center and the Radcliffe Institute helped in the same way. Other conversations helped as well—some extensive, some brief but reorienting—with Alejandro Portes, James Rebitzer, Joseph Stiglitz, Mary Waters, and William Julius Wilson. Robert Margo and Roger Waldinger not only exchanged long, thoughtful emails with me over a long period, but they—as well as Richard Alba and Stanley Engerman—read an early draft of the entire manuscript; the four sets of comments on that draft greatly improved the later drafts.

The Levy Economics Institute of Bard College has supported me financially and has given me a place to work independently in peace, a place where I can also draw on a helpful support staff—a boon whose value anyone who aspires to research will understand. I am especially grateful for the staff work of Linda Christensen and Rae Ann Moore, and the incomparable administrative skills of Susan Howard. This particular project grew out of a Russell Sage Foundation grant, administered with sensible flexibility and much patience by project officer Stephanie Platz. Genna Patacsil and David Haproff of the Foundation's Publications and Communications divisions shepherded the transformation of manuscript into book. And I owe a special debt to Suzanne Nichols, director of publications at the Foundation; in early stages she went far beyond the call of duty to help this transformation along. All in all, it is a pleasure to thank both the Institute and the Foundation for such sustained aid, and more personally the presidents of each, Dimitri Papadimitriou and Eric Wanner.

Of course, I alone am responsible for what I made of all this help.

INTRODUCTION

WE SAY COMPLACENTLY that "America is a land of immigrants" only because we also say that "America is the land of opportunity." When confidence in upward mobility dims, so too does confidence that immigrants and their descendants will enter the mainstream. And because upwards of twenty million immigrants are once again coming to America in the course of a generation, it is natural to ask whether the conditions relevant to immigrant progress in the past are the same today. The stories of immigration and social mobility are tightly linked not only in American mythology, but as well in American history. The immigrants typically started out at or near the bottom and climbed, or clawed, their way to something better—to something vastly better in the mythology, to something at least appreciably better in the eyes of both those doing the climbing and the historians. Above all, those immigrants anticipated a better life for their children. And rightly so, for whatever they had to endure, their children seemed generally to be doing better and their grandchildren—or was it their great-great-grandchildren?—could hardly be differentiated from the descendants of the Mayflower arrivals (Lieberson and Waters 1988). More precisely, these generalizations hold for the immigrants from Europe, for most of American history the overwhelming majority of all immigrants—not least because America restricted immigration from Asia. But will this upward mobility continue to be the American immigrant story? Accepting all the reminders that the climb in the past was slow and painful, can American society today continue to provide immigrants and their descendants a reasonably similar rate of improvement?

The past, even in the United States, covers a long time. The most useful way to sharpen the question of immigrant prospects in past and present is to restrict "the past" under discussion to the last mass immigration prior to our own time, the immigrations of the 1890 to 1914 period. One practical reason for doing so concerns the records: we can say much more about this last wave of immigration because the statistical evidence covering the immigrants and their descendants is much fuller than for earlier periods. There are also many strong substantive reasons for choosing this last immigration wave of 1890 to 1914 as the point of comparison to the present. America at the end of the nineteenth century seems much more familiar to us than the America of earlier times; by the late nineteenth century, large-scale industry was transforming the country and while over half the population still lived in places smaller than 2,500, ever larger numbers lived in, or at least near, large cities—some of them among the largest in the world. The immigration of 1890 to 1914 involved a new set of origins: the peoples of southern, central, and eastern Europe, particularly the Italians, Poles and other Slavs, and the east-European Jews. During the 1890s these became the majority of all arrivals. They arrived poor, typically with few industrial skills, and took up low-skill work in industry, construction, and mining. They spoke languages new to the United States and settled together in immigrant neighborhoods where poverty and cultural distinctiveness were pronounced. Contemporary native-born Americans of the time distinguished these immigrants from their predecessors by calling them "the new immigrants," a description that stuck among historians until the designation was applied instead to immigrants of our own time. At the time their influx appeared to be a serious social challenge—to cities, class structure, mobility patterns, schools, and the political system. It was not long before popular animosities and elite theorists arose to distinguish between the new and old immigrant stocks in racialized terms. There was much reflection, too, about whether America could absorb so many new immigrants (Higham 1955; Archdeacon 1983).

Following Stanley Lieberson (1980), I refer to these southern, central, and eastern Europeans as SCE immigrants; and in comparing past and present I use their experience to represent the past. In one way, however, the contemporary immigration is not at all like theirs. Today, large numbers of immigrants arrive with relatively extensive education—at, or even well above, the norm for the native-born American workforce. They therefore take jobs open to more educated workers. Many immigrants today also come with some economic resources and can set up a business quite soon after arrival. Such educationally and economically advantaged immigrants raise intriguing and subtle issues about absorption into the American mainstream. Nevertheless, these are not the issues crucial to the American narrative of immigration and upward mobility. The question about whether the present will be like the past involves instead families that start out at the bottom. This is not a question we can answer by focusing on Iranian businessmen, PhDs from India or Taiwan, or even nurses from the Philippines or electricians from Jamaica.

However, while the immigrants coming in at the bottom of the economy are no longer as dominant in the immigration flow as in the past, the proportion that do start there is still high, and their absolute numbers are huge. Following Alejandro Portes and Rubén Rumbaut (1996), I refer to these immigrants as labor migrants, as opposed to professional or entrepreneurial migrants. By far the largest single group of contemporary immigrants, in terms of national origin, are from Mexico, and the great majority of Mexican immigrants move into low-wage jobs. The question explored here, then, is whether the Mexican immigrants of today and their American-born children are following the paths of the Italians and Poles of a century ago, or whether too much in American economic life has changed, changed in ways that make the climb more treacherous.

A pessimistic answer is articulated in the influential segmented assimilation theory that deals especially with the second generation (Portes and Zhou 1993). Alejandro Portes and his colleagues have warned that the children of today's low-skill immigrants may not be able to advance in the way that was possible during the 1910 to 1960 period, for several reasons. First, the nature of the economy has changed, especially in the decline of manufacturing jobs. Today far fewer American jobs require minimal education but still offer advancement over the unskilled work of immigrant arrivals. Second, an extended education, necessary for today's better jobs, is out of the reach of immigrant families that enter at the bottom. Third, labor migrants of today and their children are nonwhite, and American society is a long way from ignoring race. Finally, an alienated, inner-city, nonwhite youth culture will appeal to these new lower-class second-generation youth who encounter blocked mobility and reinforce the problem (Portes and Zhou 1993; Portes and Rumbaut 1996, 2001b; Gans 1992). Indeed, part of the power of the segmented assimilation theory is that it not only asks whether the labor migrants of today will be like their European predecessors, but also suggests that perhaps the descendants of today's labor migrants may come to resemble instead today's inner-city black poor. Put differently, the theory implicitly asks which historical analogy is appropriate for today: the upward mobility of European labor-migrant groups or (notwithstanding vast differences in their social history) the blocked progress of African Americans.

I and my colleague Roger Waldinger have questioned the segmented assimilation hypothesis. We noted, first, that low-skill work is not as scarce as claimed; second, that educational attainment may be adequate for notable upward mobility; third, that race divisions are famously social constructions and were constructed to work against the immigrants of the 1890 to 1914 period; and, fourth, that concerns about youth culture are not new to today's inner-city minorities, and in any case such a cultural outcome depends on the first three concerns for its force (Perlmann and Waldinger

1996, 1997; Waldinger and Perlmann 1998).[1] I summarize these arguments not to reopen an old debate but to provide some background on the way the intellectual issues took shape, certainly for me and I believe for many other social scientists as well (Alba and Nee 2003). The theory helped focus attention on the past-present comparisons in a certain way. Indeed, one way I respond to the stimulus of this theory is to structure this book around not merely a comparison of immigrants and their children past and present, but also the comparison of the contemporary Mexican second generation and contemporary native blacks. In chapters 3 and 4, I devote the first part of the chapter to comparing the contemporary Mexican second generation with the European second generation of the past, and the second part to comparing the contemporary Mexican second generation with native blacks.

Another important stimulus to my exploration was a long review of past and present trends in immigration by Christopher Jencks in the *New York Review of Books*. Especially intriguing was the way Jencks drew on work by economist George Borjas to offer a clear measure by which to compare SCE immigrant well-being in 1910 and Mexican immigrant well-being today, and to conclude that the Mexican situation today is much the worse. I argue in chapter 2 that this comparison was based on data which, although tested as fully as possible at the time, must be sharply revised in the light of subsequent work by economic historians. Nevertheless, both the issues that Jencks and Borjas raised and the methods they used have strongly influenced this book.

The book takes up four themes, in successive chapters. The first concerns population history. At first, I specify which national-origin groups can most sensibly be compared to Mexicans today. However, as soon as I tried to determine not only which national-origin groups to include but also from what years, I realized that some questions have received remarkably little attention, given a century of historical study of modern immigration. Just when did most SCE second-generation members emerge on the scene? And, in any case, just who do we mean to include when we conceptualize the second generation? For example, I explore how the particular history of the SCE immigration—in particular its short span and rapid end through restriction—shaped factors such as the pool of potential spouses for immigrants. And as a consequence of the choice of spouses, surprisingly large (and rapidly shifting) proportions of second-generation members had one parent who had been born in the United States or had arrived as a young child. The chapter also takes up the same themes for the Mexican immigration; but almost everything about the Mexican immigration's very long span makes the timing and composition of the contemporary second generation very different from those of the older SCE immigration. These themes are important in themselves and I think they will be new to readers. Furthermore, these explorations turn out to be essential for specifying groups of immigrants and their children that can be meaningfully compared across many decades.

Chapter 2 explores the economic level of the labor-migrant immigrants, then and now. My work draws from the toolbox and the research of economists and economic historians; but I offer reasons early on why those who are not economists should pay attention. Claudia Goldin, Robert Margo, and Lawrence Katz have offered a new historical narrative concerning great swings in American wage inequality over the course of the twentieth century; and this narrative suggests ways to rework the historical comparisons of immigrant well-being. I conclude that the immigrant situation in 1910 was far less advantaged compared to today's than Jencks believed. But placing immigrant well-being, both then and now, within the context of the swings in inequality makes it clear that any single-year comparisons of past and present will be of limited value; the context was changing rapidly within the course of one adult's work life, both then and now. And these shifting realities are now working against the Mexicans.

The third chapter examines the schooling of the American-born generations. I try to offer meaningful comparisons of second-generation educational attainments across a century in which the length of a typical education was greatly extended. Whatever the educational lags of the European immigrants of the past, and of their children, today's Mexican second generation appears to be lagging somewhat further behind native whites than did the relevant immigrants of the past. Quite apart from such comparisons, I also stress the alarming high school dropout rates among the Mexican second generation today. The segmented assimilation hypothesis suggests that such a school pattern would emerge as part of a wider dysfunctional youth subculture of the inner city minorities; in the second half of the chapter I therefore set the high Mexican-second-generation dropout pattern in the context of the prevalence of other risk factors among Mexicans and native blacks–for example, factors related to family and work patterns.

Chapter 4 turns to second-generation economic well-being. Given less-complete educational catch-up than past second-generation members, the Mexican second generation today also experiences less-complete economic catch-up. But there is more involved because American wage inequality is considerably greater today and puts a higher premium on education. In this context, I emphasize particularly the policy implication of the Mexican secondary school dropout rates. Finally, some of the relative wage gap between Mexicans and native whites today is not explained by schooling differences. Once more, the comparisons with blacks today is important. I stress the need to compare not only the full-time workers, male and female, in both groups but also all families in each group before reaching conclusions.

By far the best source of information on these issues remains the decennial census of the United States. The Census Bureau has released giant public use samples—samples that include between 1 percent and 6 percent of the American population—from the decennial enumerations of 1960 through 2000, and teams of historical researchers have constructed comparable samples from the manuscript schedules of the earlier enumerations. Also, during the past decade, the Minnesota Population Center at the University of Minnesota developed the IPUMS datasets, the integrated public use microdata samples, which have made the census samples far easier to use than they originally were, saving countless hours of research time and effort (Ruggles et al. 2005).[2] Far from having been exhausted, then, historical records a century old have quite recently emerged in new forms that permits entirely different modes of analysis than were possible even a decade ago. For our purposes, the old censuses of 1910, 1920, and 1940 through 1970 will be especially valuable for information about immigrants of 1890 through 1914 and about their children (the dataset for 1930 is still being constructed).[3]

Census 2000 is the most valuable for information about the contemporary immigration and about today's second-generation young adults. However, the older censuses, whatever their limitations, have one great advantage over recent censuses for the study of immigration: the earlier censuses all asked respondents for their parents' birthplaces. The censuses of 1980 through 2000 dropped the relevant questions. Why this change from the old format was introduced is a long and sad story; the result, however, is clear: at a time when American second generations are numbering in the tens of millions, and when their social characteristics are a matter of lively and well-deserved interest, we have lost the ability to identify them in an irreplaceable source.[4]

Fortunately, there are two ways to work around this great gap in the evidence. The familiar solution is to turn to another federal sample of the population, the Current Population Survey (CPS). Every person sampled in the CPS is now asked for parental birthplace information.[5] By exploiting the CPS, researchers are able to obtain tens of thousands of sampled households every year and by stringing several years' datasets together, the sample grows in size. For this study, I have exploited the CPS datasets from 1998 to 2001.[6] Nevertheless, while the CPS is huge by standards of a private survey, it is tiny by comparison to the public-use samples that the Census Bureau draws from the decennial census.[7]

I first explored the contemporary issues with the CPS datasets; but in the end I reanalyzed all of it using Census 2000. For the work in chapters 3 and 4, I identified a proxy group very much like the "true" second generation. This proxy group was born in Mexico, but was brought to the United States at a very early age—before their third birthday.[8] I call attention to this proxy measure at the outset because I think it can be useful to others who study contemporary ethnicity. For this study, it provided a way to mine the gigantic but otherwise inaccessible resources of the 2000 census.

CHAPTER ONE

Toward a Population History: A Basis for Comparisons

NO ONE WILL claim that ignoring historical context is a virtue, yet discussions of immigration tend to ignore how it has shaped the characteristics of immigrant and ethnic generations. Here I begin with the past and stress three themes. The first is the rationale for the comparison of the Mexicans of today with the SCE immigrants of the past and why Jewish immigrants should be excluded from the comparison. The second concerns timing, when SCE immigrants and second-generation members were most prevalent. Perhaps because the census public-use samples are recent creations, or perhaps because the topic falls at the boundary of history, sociology, economics and demography, generalizations about the "timing" of the second generation are usually woefully vague as to both dates and magnitudes. The third concerns an important aspect of American ethnic history that has somehow remained virtually unexplored: the problematic complexity hidden behind the term second generation.

Throughout I stress the distinction between unmixed and mixed second-generation children—between the American-born children of two immigrants and of one immigrant and one American-born parent. These two groups are often referred to in the census and elsewhere as "native-born of [a specific] foreign parentage" and "native-born of mixed parentage." While the distinction is well known, it is typically treated in research as a complicating distraction, generally by including both groups in discussions of the second generation. By contrast, I place this distinction at the center of the analysis here, and argue that the process of immigrant absorption and ethnic assimilation can hardly make sense in any other way.

IMMIGRATION AND THE SECOND GENERATION THEN

Which groups to study? Why should we focus on immigrant and ethnic groups at all when our concern is with socioeconomic advancement? Why not instead focus on immigrants coming in at the bottom of the American class structure from all groups? First, because our historical information about specific national groups is much better than our evidence of class origins. The census tells us the place of birth and occupation of an immigrant, but not his or her former occupation. So, too, it tells us the parental birthplaces and occupation of a second-generation member, but not the occupations of his or her parents.

Moreover, it is ultimately simplistic to argue that studying all those who came in at the bottom, without regard to their ethnic origins, will adequately illuminate the outcomes. Their specific reasons for emigration and conditions of immigration differed by national origin. Individuals settled together, created communal institutions, and shared subcultures that were defined by national origins. Finally, the host society's patterns of reception were often shaped by the national and ethnic parameter, not merely by economic conditions in the American labor market. The host of discussions in the immigration literature about networks, niches, modes of incorporation, historical context and the like all bear witness to the intellectual poverty of ignoring context. A crucial part of that context is national origin. The point is not to privilege ethnicity over class; it is rather to ignore neither; but doing so implies that I do not study national origins merely as a way to identify class origins.

Within the ethnic context, I want to study the European peoples whose members were especially likely to enter the American economy on the lowest rungs of the ladder. Why, however, limit the historical focus to European groups? In particular, why not study the Asians and Mexicans of the early twentieth century? The answer lies in the specific conditions of these groups that make them a poor parallel to the low-skilled immigrants of today. Asian immigration was sharply restricted by American immigration law or government pressure on the sending country—the former against the Chinese after 1882 and the latter against the Japanese after 1907. Because of this, the earlier Asian immigration never reached a level remotely comparable to that of the southern, central, and eastern European immigration. The Mexican-origin population remained small before 1910 for other reasons, but even afterward Mexican immigration too was far smaller than the SCE.

There is also a more important reason than numbers for excluding the early-twentieth-century Asians and Mexicans from the comparison to the present. During most of the century after 1850, the Chinese (and in the later part of the period, the Japanese) were subjected to such virulent racial discrimination that their experience of socioeconomic opportunity simply cannot be meaningfully compared to that of the southern, central, and eastern Europeans. The same generalization largely applies as well to the Mexicans of that period. To argue that we should study these early groups nonetheless because they are important today would amount to a reification of race, a claim that "the social construction of race" has essentially not changed for the Chinese or the Mexicans since the 1850s.

Thus we begin with the southern, central, and eastern Europeans. The new IPUMS datasets would permit us to make countless national distinctions among them. Thus place of birth and mother tongue codes in the IPUMS run to more than a hundred for Europeans. Moreover, country boundaries have changed dramatically, especially after the collapse of the multinational empires with World War I. But we need not endlessly differentiate among the groups. First, if we did, we would not have adequately sized samples for analysis—even if we had the time and energy to undertake such study. So choices about aggregation are necessary for various practical reasons. More important, we are by no means interested in all the fine distinctions that the IPUMS categories would permit. Rather, we want to address questions about the nature and pace of socioeconomic progress among the second generations of the past to develop benchmarks by which to assess contemporary second generation patterns. We may certainly find, for example, that the specifics of this story of socioeconomic advance would differ a bit among Estonians, Latvians, and Lithuanians, but are willing to risk losing those subtleties in the interest of the big picture. Generalizations will help us contrast past and present in enlightening ways. But what of the difference between the Baltic peoples and the Finns? Or between all these peoples and Slovaks (from farther south and farther west), or between all these and Serbs (from still father south), or between all these and the Greeks—who dwelt no farther apart from Serbs than the Baltic groups do from each other? Then, too, were Serbs and Greeks more different from each other than northern and southern Italian immigrants were? For well over a quarter of a century, for example, the commissioner of immigration in the United States dutifully recorded northern and southern Italian immigrants as members of two different "races or peoples," just as each was distinguished from Serbs and from Greeks in those reports. Obviously, we need some sense of historical conditions and a few theoretical guidelines if we are to sift and aggregate meaningfully. Sample size and scholarly energy will affect our choices, but they are far from determinative with data so rich.

In the end, I found the story to be about the same whether I treated the relevant groups together or separately; whenever I did try to study the individual groups—especially by concentrating on Italians, Poles, and other Slavs, I found that my generalizations held across the groups and my discussion pointlessly lengthened.[1] Still, readers should understand which groups I included as subjects for study and how I identified them. Table 1.1 shows the SCE groups in the context of the total immigration; for the analyses of timing and generation composition in this chapter, I focus on the entire SCE. But for the analysis of socioeconomic well-being in the three later chapters, I exclude Jewish immigrants from the SCE for reasons I will explain. In those chapters I therefore concentrate on SCEN—southern, central and eastern Europeans, non-Jews.

It is not always possible to classify individuals unambiguously in terms of the classification scheme shown in table 1.1. In particular, the groups from central and eastern Europe are not always distinguishable from each other because the distinctions require not only data on place of birth but also on mother tongue. Nevertheless, even when the data do not permit the full realization of this classification, I try to approximate it.[2] The relevant information comes from two quite different sources, the decennial census (especially in the IPUMS datasets that allow us to study immigrants and the second generation at the individual level) and the annual reports of the commissioner of immigration and naturalization, which provide aggregate data on immigrant arrivals. Both the census and the commissioner's annual reports provide country of birth, but beginning in 1899 the commissioner also reported the race or people to which each immigrant belonged. Whatever ethnological understandings and racialized thinking intellectual historians can find behind this classification, it has proven invaluable to social historians. The race or people classification scheme makes it possible to distinguish among the peoples of Europe's pre-war multinational empires—Austro-Hungary, Germany, Russia, and Turkey. Thus we can determine how many of the people coming from the Russian Empire were Poles, how many were Jews, and how many were Balts. We can also determine that only tiny proportions were ethnically Russian. The same race or people classification scheme also shows that well over a dozen numerically significant peoples were arriving from the Austro-Hungarian empire.[3]

The race or people classification was not used in the federal census. Instead, the censuses of that era routinely recorded country of birth for immigrants and parents' birthplaces for the native-born. However, beginning in 1910, several decennial censuses also recorded information on mother tongue, which can serve as a proxy for race or people, allowing us to identify different peoples who immigrated from the multinational empires and, with less precision, to distinguish among their children as well. Indeed, it was precisely to make these sorts of distinctions, while avoiding the race or people terminology, that the American census adopted the mother tongue

Table 1.1   Overview of Immigration to United States, 1899–1924

	Immigration		
		Percentage for Subtotals	
Group (by Race or People)	Number (000s) a	All b	Net of Return Migration (Estimate) c
SCE groups			
SCEN (SCE, non-Jews)	9074	52	44
Central and eastern European			
Polish	1483		
All other central and eastern European	2795		
Southern European			
Italian	3821		
All other southern Europeans	975		
Jews from central and eastern Europe (Hebrews)	1838	11	14
Non-SCE groups	6379	37	42
German, Northwestern Europe, Canada			
German	1317		
British	984		
Irish	809		
Scandinavian	956		
Canada (Anglo and French)	825		
All other	364		
All other: immigrants not from Europe or Canada			
Mexican	447		
All other	677		
Total	17291	100	100

Source: Archdeacon (1983), table V-3 (see also Ferenczi 1929, tables 13 and 19).
Note: The United States Commissioner of Immigration reported immigrant arrivals by "race or people" beginning in 1899. The following races or peoples are included in the SCEN subcategory "all other central and eastern Europe": Russian, Slovak, Croatian/Slovenian, Magyar, Ruthenian, Lithuanian, Finnish, Bohemian/Moravian, Rumanian, Dalmatian/Bosnian/Herzogovinian, and Bulgarian/Serbian/Montenegrin; the SCEN subcategory "all other southern Europe" includes: Greek, Armenian, Portuguese, Spanish, and Turkish. Hebrews included Jews from any country, but the overwhelming majority in this period were born in central or eastern Europe. See Perlmann (2001) for more detail by immigrant group. The total net of return migration (000s) is estimated at 12309 (or 71 percent of total immigration), of which net SCEN immigration is estimated at 5379. Archdeacon's estimate for totals net of return migration is: (col. c) = (col a) × (1 − r/v) where r = average annual return migration 1908 to 1924 (years for which the data are available) and v = the average annual immigration (1899 to 1924).

question (Perlmann 2004). This historical context helps explain why the 1910 and 1920 censuses asked also about the mother tongue of immigrant parents of the native-born: the parental mother tongue question helped establish the race or people of the second generation. After 1920, however, the mother tongue question was asked intermittently, and only in reference to the respondent, not to his or her parents. And even the data on the respondent become problematic in later years, because the children of immigrants often reported English as their mother tongue—not Yiddish, Polish, or Italian, for example. As a result, our ability to distinguish among the American children of various immigrant peoples from the same country of origin in the 1940 through 1970 censuses is distinctly more limited than in the 1910 and 1920 censuses. In classifying second-generation members, then, we are often limited to the parental birthplace criterion.[4]

SCE VERSUS SCEN: EXCLUDING THE JEWS   I use Stanley Lieberson's designation of southern, central, and eastern Europeans as SCE groups (Lieberson 1980). And for the analysis here, which deals with factors of timing and generational status, I focus on the SCE aggregate. However, the cross-time comparisons of past versus present well-being in later chapters are much clearer when SCE is limited to the SCEN. The rationale for this decision is based on a simple empirical point: the Jewish immigrants were more likely to be employed as skilled workers or to be self-employed, eventually in commerce, than immigrants in the other SCE groups, and they were more rapidly upwardly mobile from their starting positions as well (Kuznets 1975; Lieberson 1980; Perlmann 1988). Consequently, including them in the group compared to Mexicans in our time will not give a true picture of how the labor-migrant immigrants of the earlier period fared, but rather will bias the economic record of that experience upwards. Reasons for the differences in Jewish immigrant advancement have to do with their premigration situation. In terms of minority status and religion, and especially in their economic position, the Jews of central and eastern Europe were indeed "a people apart." They were much more likely to have been tradesmen and artisans, and much less likely to have been farmers or farm laborers, than the other emigrating peoples of the region. So, too, the Jews were much more likely to have had experience of towns and cities, and of related experiences, such as literacy. Whatever other differences may have mattered to their future in the west, these differences surely did. All this might be ignored if the Jews had been a small immigrant group. However, they were in fact the second-largest SCE group, comprising nearly one quarter of the SCE immigration, net of return migration.[5] Consequently, if we ignore the differences between the Jews and others, we will indeed distort the experience we record for others from central and eastern Europe. The mother-tongue question, which identifies the Yiddish-mother-tongue population, is our best, albeit imperfect, guide for the reasons already ex-plained.[6] However, scholars have often used an alternative strategy: identify-ing the "Russian-born" as Jews in these censuses, and I too must rely on it for the censuses of 1940 through 1970.[7] The upshot of this is that I exclude from the SCE group of interest those people who reported Yiddish mother tongue and, in those censuses, also people who reported a Russian-born parent. By contrast, all other children of SCE immigrants are much less likely to have been Jewish: this we know from the reports of the commis-sioner of immigration, who cross-tabulated answers to the race or people and country of birth questions.[8]

Excluding Most Germans   Germans had always comprised an impor-tant immigrant presence in America, and I therefore excluded them from the SCEN groups, whose distinctiveness rests in part precisely on their new-ness as immigrants after 1890. Many Poles also came from the German empire; in the 1910 and 1920 censuses they are probably captured by the mother-tongue question; in later censuses, we must rely on the expectation that such immigrants and their children identified their place of origin as Poland or their mother tongue as Polish. On the other hand, by no means all Germans lived in the German empire. When mother tongue information is available, I classify individuals of German mother tongue as German and exclude them from the SCE classification, regardless of country of origin—with one exception. The Germans from Russia had lived in the Russian lands for several centuries, and while not assimilated into the Russian world, they also were not in close touch with Germans in the German or Austro-Hungarian empires; among imperfect choices, I opted to place the Russian-born German-mother-tongue immigrants with "all other central and eastern European immigrants."

SCE Birth Cohorts Selected from IPUMS Datasets   I have selected young second-generation members from each IPUMS dataset—in most cases children younger than ten in the census year. For the years from 1891 to 1940, when most of the relevant second-generation children of the great immigration members were born, I present five-year birth cohorts; during other years, ten-year birth cohorts.[9] The estimates in turn allow us to determine, for example, when the largest cohorts were born, or reached school-leaving age.[10]

THE TIMING OF IMMIGRATION WAVES: IMPACT ON SECOND GENERATIONS

Whether a person is an immigrant or the American-born child of immi-grants is a fundamental social distinction, but other distinctions in the history of an immigrant group matter greatly too. Particularly important are whether the immigrant arrived early or late in an immigration wave and among few or many compatriots; these distinctions matter not merely for the early experience of the individual immigrant but across generations.

THE FLOW OF IMMIGRATION

Table 1.1 is culled from the reports of immigration by race or people, and because that classification was introduced in 1899, the figures go back only that far. Nevertheless, it is the most illuminating summary we have of the contours of the great immigrations of the 1890 to 1920 period. Several details might be added. While a mere 6 percent of all immigrants came from the third world, the SCE groups contributed 63 percent of the total. And three peoples—Poles, Jews, and Italians—accounted for fully 42 percent of all immigrants. Most of the other SCE groups were from the east, not the south, of Europe—16 percent as against 6 percent. Finally, the older immigrant groups of that time continued to be important in the immigration flows, comprising 31 percent of the total—immigrants from northwest Europe and Canada contributing 23 percent of all immigrants, and those from Germany contributing 8 percent (Perlmann 2001b).

The last column of the table summarizes the impressive efforts of Thomas Archdeacon (1983) to gauge the demographic impact of return migration. There were vast differences in remigration rates among immigrant groups in the period, from well below 10 percent to over 80 percent. A group with a high propensity to remigrate contributed fewer permanent immigrants per 100 arrivals than a group with a low propensity to remigrate. The same consideration also affects the second generation—an immigrant group with a high remigration rate produced fewer second-generation members per 100 arrivals than a group with a lower remigration rate (assuming comparable fertility rates). Our measure of return migration, and hence of permanent immigration, is admittedly imperfect—the ratio of departures to arrivals by country of origin—but certainly does show great differences by groups. Remigration was especially important for the Italians, by far the largest immigrant group of the period. They comprised 22 percent of all arrivals but 17 percent of permanent immigrants. By contrast, very few Jews remigrated and thus comprised 11 percent of all arrivals and 14 percent of permanent immigrants. The northwest Europeans and Germans also had lower-than-average remigration rates, comprising 31 percent of the arrivals, but 35 percent of the permanent immigrants (Perlmann 2001b, Archdeacon 1983).

The SCE wave is often dated as being from 1891 to 1920, or from 1881 to 1920. Figures 1.1 and 1.2 show that it comprised well below 10 percent of all arrivals in the years before 1890. Nevertheless, the absolute numbers

Figure 1.1   Percentage SCE of All Immigrants

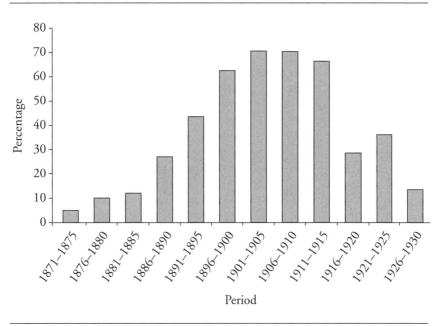

Source: Carter et al. (1997).

involved were such that even during the 1870s more than 300,000 immigrants from SCE countries had come to the United States and by the end of the 1880s nearly two million had. Furthermore, although remigration was also common, SCE immigrant communities were clearly forming during the 1880s. Still, the most striking point about the SCE immigration is the short period during which the great majority of that immigration occurred—67 percent of SCE immigrants arrived between 1901 and 1915.

After the outbreak of World War I, the immigration period we have in mind was, in a real sense, over. Only one tenth of the total SCE immigration of 1871 to 1930 occurred after 1915. After 1914, there was not one year in which SCE immigration flows reached the level of SCE arrivals counted in every year between 1910 and 1914 (figure 1.3). There is no mystery to this pattern. During the war years, little emigration was possible, and then in the early 1920s, Congress passed severe restrictions on immigration generally and on the SCE immigrants in particular. The pattern, of course, differed slightly among groups; for example, 8 percent of the central and eastern Europeans, and 14 percent of the Italians, arrived after 1915. And, most exceptional, almost a third of the other southern Europeans

Figure 1.2   SCE Immigrants (1871–1930) to Arrive in Each Period

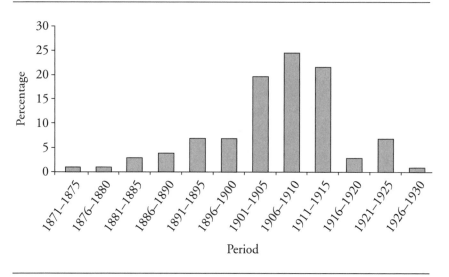

Source: Carter et al. (1997).
Note: For more detail by national origins see Perlmann (2001b, table 5).

Figure 1.3   Post-1914 SCE Immigration in Detail

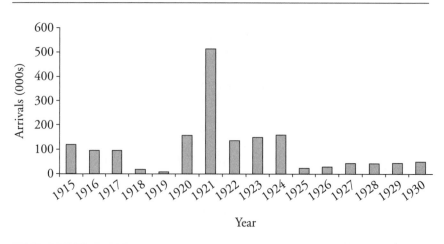

Source: Carter et al. (1997).

arrived after 1915. However, the immigrants from this latter group comprised only a small part of the entire SCE; consequently, their distinctive pattern of late arrival hardly affects generalizations about the SCE as a whole.

The war, followed by immigration restriction, brought down the numbers for all immigrants, but it is easy to see that it affected the SCE groups most of all. Between 1911 and 1915, 67 percent of the immigrants were from SCE groups. Between 1916 and 1920 only 29 percent were from these groups.[11] The SCE proportion rose modestly between 1921 and 1925 and then fell to 14 percent the last half of the 1920s. Consequently, the SCE comprised a majority of all immigrants (a majority of 63 percent to 71 percent) only during the twenty years from 1896 to 1915. We should appreciate, in passing, that any talk about government's inability to control immigrant flows should at a minimum be couched in language that recognizes temporal change and the importance of the special case of the contiguous Mexican border. Government unquestionably choked off immigration from eastern and central Europe after World War I. That flow might have stopped anyway in the Great Depression, and it might not have been able to resume due to war later. Nevertheless, the effect of state action in the early 1920s cannot be seriously questioned.

Although the central period of mass immigration ended in 1914, the period that followed deserves a close look, for reasons that will shortly become clear. Moderately large-scale SCE immigration did resume for the years from 1920 to 1924; during those five years a total of 1.1 million SCE immigrants arrived. This is but moderate immigration, because during each of the years from 1910 to 1914, annual SCE immigration fluctuated between 562,000 and 894,000. Also, a peculiarity of the SCE immigration from 1920 through 1924 is that nearly half the arrivals came in a single year, 1921; in no other year after 1914 did immigration from SCE groups reach a third of the 1921 level (figure 1.3). When we consider the second generation then, we will have to be aware of this pattern, because the children of later arrivals differed from those of earlier in important ways. First, however, it is important to have a general sense of the timing of the second-generation birth cohorts.

BIRTH OF THE SECOND-GENERATION COHORTS

Between eleven and twelve million SCE second-generation members were born in the century after 1870. They comprise, in turn, about a third of all second-generation Americans born during the same period; of the rest, six million had German parents, thirteen million had northwest European or Canadian parents, and all others accounted for less than three million. Earlier I noted that the SCE immigration was compressed into a narrow range of years, 1900 to 1914; the SCE second generation reflects this compression, albeit in muted form (figure 1.4). Very few of the entire century's SCE second-generation members were born before 1890—1 percent in the 1870s and 3 percent more in the 1880s. Likewise, only 11 percent were born in the last three decades (from 1941 to 1970) of the century under consideration (from 1871 to 1970). Thus 85 percent of the SCE second generation was born during the half-century between 1890 and 1940. Of these, only 10 percent were born between 1931 and 1940, which means that 75 percent were born during the forty years from 1891 to 1930. Indeed, fully 40 percent were born during the fifteen years from 1911 to 1925, an echo, we might say, of the fifteen years of the mass immigration between 1900 and 1914.

And just as the SCE comprised majorities (from 63 to 71 percent) of the immigrants over the twenty years from 1896 to 1915, their children comprised somewhat smaller majorities (from 52 to 61 percent) of the second generations born between 1911 and 1935. The timing of family formation may have varied somewhat across groups, making it hard to find very tight parallels in the relative size of the SCE group at the height of their prevalence in first and second generations. Nevertheless, we might have

Figure 1.4   SCE Second-Generation Birth Cohorts

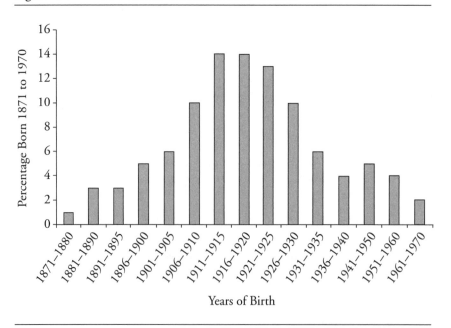

Years of Birth

Source: IPUMS datasets for 1880, 1900 through 1920, and 1940 through 1970 censuses.

expected that the SCE majority would be larger in the second generation, because the typical SCE immigrant family probably had more children than the typical non-SCE immigrant family, who came mostly from more modernized, lower-fertility countries—Germany, northwest Europe, and Canada. Remigration rates in the first generation no doubt account for why the second-generation SCE majorities were not greater than the first-generation SCE majorities. Also, if the gender ratio was more imbalanced in SCE groups, and out-marriage fairly rare among them, then fewer SCE families would have been formed per 100 immigrant arrivals, and fewer children therefore born. There is some evidence that these factors indeed explain the Italian demographic outcomes, for example (Perlmann 2000).

Another reason why the SCE groups comprised fewer of the second generation than we might have expected has to do with another feature of intermarriage. When in-marriage is high, fewer families are formed. For example, if 100 group members in-marry, fifty couples are formed. By contrast, if 100 group members out-marry, they become part of 100 couples. Of course the group members then comprise only half of all partners in these 100 couples. This consideration is relevant to the SCE and non-SCE immigrants. For much of the period under review, the SCE immigrants were nearly all marrying their compatriots, but the same was not true of the Germans, Irish, British, and Scandinavians, who predominated in the non-SCE immigration. These often intermarried with the native-born; often, no doubt, the native-born spouse was of the same ethnic origin as the non-SCE immigrant, or from a similar background—for example, when an English immigrant married a native-born person of part English and part Scandinavian or German descent. My earlier description of SCE second-generation prevalence included both the children of two immigrant parents and the children of one immigrant and one American-born parent, the unmixed and mixed second generation respectively. By contrast, the SCE groups comprised a higher proportion, 65 to 74 percent, of the unmixed second generation during the same period.[12] Later in the century, especially after 1925, the proportion of SCE second-generation members born with mixed parentage rose quickly, from 20 percent in the 1921 to 1925 cohort to 57 percent in the 1936 to 1940 cohort. With this observation we come to the changing composition of the later second-generation cohorts, a product of the late years of the immigration itself, to which we must now devote more careful attention.

THE CHANGING COMPOSITION OF LATER SCE SECOND-GENERATION COHORTS

The changing character of immigrants at the end of an immigration wave deserves more attention than it has received; in the case of the SCE, the effects are great because a huge immigration was cut off very quickly. Increasingly after about 1925, high proportions of SCE second-generation children were born to immigrant parents who were highly atypical of the mainstream SCE immigration. Three factors distinguished that later group.

TIME OF ARRIVAL   Consider the SCE immigrants who arrived after 1914, and especially those who arrived after 1924. Their late departure from Europe, in the face of American restriction, suggests that they may have come from somewhat different social circumstances than the earlier arrivals. They surely faced a somewhat different process of incorporation into American society, because they were few in number where their predecessors had arrived with many more like themselves. They were also likely to profit from the connections of those predecessors. With these considerations in mind, the immigrants who arrived between 1919 and 1922 appear as an in-between case. They were surely more like the prewar immigrants, than like those who arrived in the late twenties or in the thirties; but they still were arriving at a distinctive, somewhat atypical, moment.

CHILD IMMIGRANTS   The SCE immigration was dominated by young working men yet included many children as well. We can follow the implications in the case of the Italians. Nearly a million immigrants arrived from Italy in the five years preceding 1914, and about 15 percent of them were children younger than ten—some 150,000 child arrivals. This group reached the ages of twenty-five to thirty-four between 1925 and 1940. By contrast, in the last half of the 1920s, Italian immigrant arrivals numbered about 85,000 and during the entire decade of the 1930s only another 70,000 arrived. During the 1930s, then, a majority of the Italian-born who reached the age range of twenty-five to thirty-four apparently were not recent young-adult arrivals. Rather, the majority were probably Italian-born people who had arrived in the United States as young children between 1909 and 1914 (the "1.5 generation" of those years) and were reaching adulthood in the 1930s. These people had spent much of their childhood or youth in the United States, not in Italy; and they reached adulthood in distinct times, long after mass immigration had ended.[13]

MARRIAGE WITH NONIMMIGRANTS   Immigrants arriving late in the process of immigration are more likely to marry the native born than those who came before. First, by definition, with the flow of immigration much lighter than before, these arrivals will find that more members of the opposite sex in their age range living in America are not immigrants. Also, those arriving at the tail end of an immigrant wave will be less unfamiliar to other members of the host society than their predecessors from the same country. Finally, more children of earlier immigrants from the same country of origin should be available as potential spouses than were early in the immigration period.[14]

These three factors, then, distinguished the parents of the later second-generation SCE cohorts: time of arrival, child immigrants, and marriage with nonimmigrants. We can gauge just how much the parents of those later second-generation cohorts differed by examining crucial birth cohorts drawn from the 1940 census IPUMS dataset: 1921 to 1925, 1926 to 1930, 1931 to 1935 and 1936 to 1940. First, notice the sharp decline in the size of the cohorts (figure 1.4). Those of 1921 to 1925 and 1926 to 1930 are among the largest second-generation birth cohorts; the next two are very much smaller, reflecting the timing of the immigration. However, even that of 1936 to 1940 includes more than 400,000 members, meaning that social scientists will always find enough sample members from the last cohorts—but such sample members are nonetheless atypical. Next notice the sharp rise in the percentage of mixed parentage among the second generation members across the cohorts, especially those born after 1925 (figure 1.5). And, finally, consider the composition of SCE second-generation birth cohorts in terms of all three parental characteristics discussed: parents who arrived after 1925, arrived as children, or married a native-born individual

Figure 1.5   SCE Second Generation with Native-Born Parent

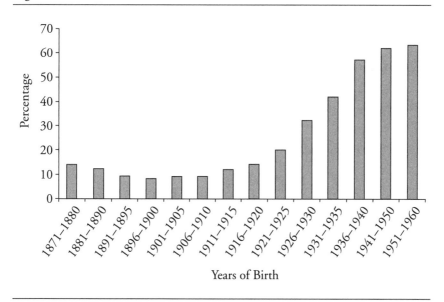

Source: IPUMS datasets for 1880, 1900 through 1920, and 1940 through 1970 censuses.
Note: For more ethnic detail see Perlmann (2001b, table 6).

(figure 1.6). Even in the huge and mainstream cohorts of 1911 to 1920, 20 to 23 percent had a parent who had arrived as a child or had married a native-born American. Thereafter, however, the relevant proportion with these characteristics (or, in later cohorts, who had a parent that arrived after 1924), rises quickly: to 36 percent, 53 percent, 65 percent and 81 percent in succeeding cohorts. Should we choose to focus only on conditions of arrival—on immigrants who arrived as children or arrived after 1924—we find that they comprised 14 to 15 percent in the 1910s, 23 percent and 36 percent in the two birth cohorts of the 1920s, and 48 percent and 64 percent in the two birth cohorts of the 1930s (including many NBMP in figure 1.6).

Such compositional differences in turn influenced the behavior of the cohort members. To appreciate the point, consider table 1.2, which presents the mean educational attainments of the SCE second generation, for

Figure 1.6   "Atypical" Among All SCE Second Generation Born
             1911–1940

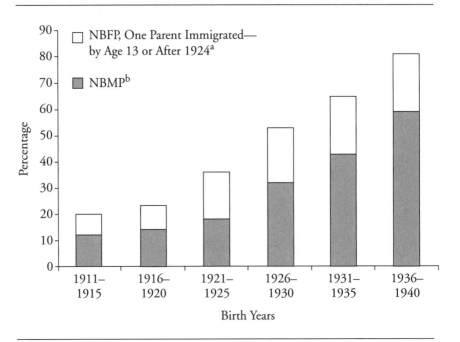

Source: IPUMS datasets for 1880, 1900 through 1920, and 1940 through 1970 censuses.
Note: For details of estimation, see Perlmann (2001b, tables 8 and 9).
[a]NBFP: native born of foreign parentage (both parents are foreign born).
[b]NBMP: native born of mixed parentage (one foreign- and one native-born parent).

Table 1.2   Educational Attainment for Selected Second-Generation
             SCE Groups

Group	Cohort	Percentage of Second Generation			Mean Grades of Education	
		NBFP	NBMP	Total	NBFP	NBMP
Men						
SCE	1916–1925	81	19	100	11.14	11.57
	1926–1935	63	37	100	12.03	12.32
Italians	1916–1925	82	18	100	10.64	11.12
	1926–1935	64	36	100	11.37	11.79
Poles	1916–1925	84	16	100	10.75	10.99
	1926–1935	67	33	100	11.94	12.11
Other C + E	1916–1925	79	21	100	11.31	11.85
Europe	1926–1935	61	39	100	12.24	12.64
Women						
SCE	1916–1925	81	19	100	10.63	11.24
	1926–1935	65	35	100	11.52	11.76
Italians	1916–1925	81	19	100	10.18	10.80
	1926–1935	66	34	100	11.06	11.45
Poles	1916–1925	83	17	100	10.31	10.69
	1926–1935	67	33	100	11.51	11.70
Other C + E	1916–1925	79	21	100	10.84	11.64
Europe	1926–1935	62	38	100	11.76	11.93

Source: IPUMS dataset, 1960 census.
Note: NBFP: native born of foreign parentage (that is, two foreign-born parents).
NBMP: native born of mixed parentage (that is, one foreign-born parent).

the group as a whole, and separately for Italians, Poles, and other central and eastern Europeans. The table shows the attainments of two birth cohorts, 1916 to 1925 and 1926 to 1935; the attainments of all groups were higher in the later birth cohort. But it is also true that in every case the attainments of the second generation of mixed parentage were higher than the attainments of those of foreign parentage. And the percentage of the mixed parentage was greater in every case in the later cohort. Thus, when one examines the educational attainment for any group's entire second generation, the rise in educational attainment across time is partly due to the changing proportion of the two types of second-generation members, not to a rise in the mean educational level of each subgroup.[15]

The implications for past-present comparisons are crucial. If one asks whether the present-day cohorts resemble the children of the so-called last great wave of immigration, the questioner does not have in mind SCE cohorts in which 80 percent of the members have a U.S-born parent, a parent who arrived in the United States as a child or a parent who arrived after the last great wave of immigration had in fact ended. In order to avoid such misleading comparisons it is usually simplest to exclude the cohorts born after a certain year—for example after 1925. However, the chief point is not to urge an arbitrary cut-off date but to urge sensitivity to the implications of changing cohort composition. This issue will also arise in connection with the contemporary immigration, albeit in different ways because the factors of timing are so different in the contemporary immigration.

THE SCE SECOND GENERATION'S EXPERIENCE OF TWENTIETH-CENTURY SOCIAL HISTORY   Generalizing about generational experience requires sensitivity not only to generational standing—second mixed or second unmixed for example—but also to the historical time that the individuals passed through. In the case of the larger SCE second-generation cohorts the historical conditions were changing as quickly and dramatically as they ever did in modern American history. For the sake of simplicity here, I concentrate on those born between 1891 and 1925, which includes nearly nine million souls. The oldest were thirty-five years old when the youngest were born, on the eve of the Great Depression. The oldest may have fought in World War I, the youngest were too young to serve in World War II (see table 1.3). More than half, those born after about 1915, probably spent at least part of the depression in school; those born before 1920, about two out of three, spent at least part of that period either in or trying to be in the labor force. And probably about 80 percent would have been younger than forty at Pearl Harbor, or older than eighteen when Japan surrendered; such people, or at least the men, might have served in the military. A similar proportion passed through some part of the years of postwar growth, from 1945 to 1970, in their twenties or thirties.

It was both these great events and the changing composition of the cohorts that shaped second-generation experiences. Consider, for example, SCE second-generation mother tongue. The later cohorts, born after 1960, were much more likely to report English as the mother tongue than those born before 1916. This change is no doubt due in some measure to a process that would have operated in any decade of the past two centuries in the United States—a certain fraction of the parents resident in the new land for many decades would have switched to English, and therefore raised their children on English. And some of the change has been sensibly ascribed to the larger historical features of the period just described—to the changes in work and residence that accompanied the Great Depression, the New Deal, and World War II (Alba 1985, 1988). Yet also operating was the increasing prevalence of "atypical" second-generation members. These

Table 1.3 Ages of SCE Second-Generation Cohorts

Cohort	1891–1895	1896–1900	1901–1905	1906–1910	1911–1915	1916–1920	1921–1925	1926–1930	Total
Number in SCE (000s)	400	527	720	1117	1582	1658	1536	1183	8723
Proportion of all cohorts	5	6	8	13	18	19	18	14	100
Age at									
Start of Great Depression (circa 1930)	35 to 39	30 to 34	25 to 29	20 to 24	15 to 19	10 to 14	5 to 9	0 to 4	0 to 39
America enters World War II (1941)	46 to 50	41 to 45	36 to 40	31 to 35	26 to 30	21 to 25	16 to 20	11 to 15	11 to 50
End of World War II (1945)	50 to 54	45 to 49	40 to 44	35 to 39	30 to 34	25 to 29	20 to 24	15 to 19	15 to 54
Near end of the postwar growth period (1970)	75 to 79	70 to 74	65 to 69	60 to 64	55 to 59	50 to 54	45 to 49	40 to 45	40 to 79

Source: IPUMS datasets, 1910 through 1920, 1940 through 1970 censuses.

were more likely to hear English as the language common to both parents, and the offspring of an immigrant who had arrived as a child was more likely to have had a parent who knew English well, indeed perhaps better than the ancestral language.

MEXICAN IMMIGRATION AND THE SECOND GENERATION TODAY

We can construct systematic comparisons between immigrant and second generations then and now, but it is well to appreciate that we are able to construct them despite vast differences in the histories of the SCEN and Mexicans in American history. Also, it would be foolhardy to study the results of those comparisons without appreciating the historical differences involved.

HISTORICAL BACKGROUND

Much of the western United States was part of Mexico before the mid-nineteenth century, and it is a truism that some Mexican-origin Americans are not descended from immigrants, but from people who lived in areas that became American through treaty or wartime conquest. On the other hand, it is worth appreciating that the numbers of people living in those lands at the time were few and that they were concentrated in New Mexico and southern Colorado, long the most isolated part of the southwest, and the most Spanish. Some 60,000 Mexican residents were living there around 1850. But in the rest of the Southwestern states, the numbers were astonishingly low—perhaps 4,000 in Texas in 1821, when American immigrants began to predominate, and 7,000 in California at the time of the conquest, and far fewer in Arizona.

There was relatively little permanent immigration from Mexico to the United States during the nineteenth century, although cross-border movements were not fully formalized either. Most of the history of Mexican American demography, then, despite the nineteenth century conquest of territory, actually takes place in the twentieth century. Still, it is hard to be sure just how many of the Mexican-origin population today are descended from the nineteenth century, especially given that relevant census inquiries about distant ethnic origins—the Hispanic-origin question and the ancestry question—are subjective. We cannot be sure how many descendants of Mexicans are so assimilated into the mainstream that they no longer declare those origins. From one estimate, it seems possible that from 20 to 25 percent of the Mexican-origin population of 1990 was of pre-twentieth century origin. In any case, there was already some movement because the

1900 census listed about 100,000 Mexican-born individuals, too many to have survived from pre-conquest days.[16]

The modern immigration, however, began after the construction of north-south railway lines starting in the late nineteenth century, and then increased greatly during the violence of the revolutionary decade, from 1910 to 1920. From 1901 to 1909 some 50,000 immigrants were recorded, and during the fateful second decade, nearly 220,000. After these beginnings made immigration more familiar by establishing communities and patterns of settlement, and in the context of increasing demand for immigrant labor in the southwest, the number of immigrants doubled again during the 1920s. However, the depression decade not only brought a cessation of new arrivals, it also saw the forced deportation of close to half a million Mexicans from the United States—including some with American citizenship. Consequently, despite the arrival of 730,000 immigrants in the three decades after 1900—fully 680,000 of these arriving during the twenty years from 1910 to 1929—by 1940 the U.S. census recorded only 377,000 Mexican-born individuals. If we ignore for the moment the pre-1900 arrivals, the first modern second generation of Mexican Americans was coming into the world in the 1920s, 1930s, and 1940s. The first modern third generation came about thirty years later, beginning in the 1950s.[17]

The post-depression history of the Mexican immigration is bound up with the contract-labor system, the Bracero Program, that began during World War II, but continued and expanded greatly after the war, providing experience with temporary work in the United States for some five million individuals over two decades. Legal permanent immigration was far smaller, but by the 1950s it had climbed back up to 300,000. After the Bracero Program was terminated in 1964, and no remotely comparable legal opportunities emerged to replace it, large numbers of undocumented sojourns replaced the program; Massey, Durand, and Malone estimate that in the two decades following the termination of the program, twenty-eight million undocumented Mexicans arrived in the United States for stays of various duration, but 23.4 million also departed during these years, "a de facto guest worker program" (2002, 45). Since the end of the 1980s, the border enforcement has made it more likely that migrants who have succeeded in crossing the border will remain. And the Immigration Reform and Control Act (IRCA) of 1986 provided an amnesty for some two million of them by 1994. In addition, without the IRCA amnesties, the number of legal immigrants from Mexico has hovered between 450,000 and 700,000 in the decades between 1961 and 1990, and at about a million during the 1990s. In sum, more than for immigrations in the past, and perhaps more for Mexicans than for other immigrants today, lurches in American immigration policy have an impact on the fate of immigrant families—legal conditions for Mexican immigration changed several times between 1930 and

1965, and again after 1986. Were they to change yet again in the next decade, no careful observer would be astonished. Table 1.4 shows the size of the Mexican-born population since the census of 1900.

The history of Mexican migrant movements could not be more different from the history of the SCEN immigrations. The SCEN came during a narrow band of years, and the border authorities registered their arrival with reasonable accuracy; the Mexican American population draws in some relatively small part from pre-conquest ancestors, and then from a migration that has been growing since 1910, with only a few breaks other than the Great Depression years. Moreover, many early Mexican immigrants crossed a relatively informal border and since 1965 great numbers have come as undocumented migrants, with many of them eventually returning to Mexico. Thus the figures on decennial documented immigration must be seen in a much wider context for the Mexicans than for the SCEN, and the number of Mexican-born living in the United States at any given census year includes, as it does for the SCEN, a large number who would remigrate.

The generational composition of the American-born population of Mexican origin is difficult to specify because of this long and partly undocumented historical movement. Fortunately, we need not disentangle all these origins; for our purposes—mostly to compare the contemporary Mexican second generation to the contemporary Mexican third or later generation—the information in table 1.5 will provide enough background. In the 2000 census, 62 percent of all Mexican-origin individuals had been born in the United States (panel 1). Given the huge recent immigrations, this propor-

Table 1.4   Mexican-Born Population

Year	Population (000s)
1900	103
1910	222
1920	486
1930	617
1940	377
1950	454
1960	576
1970	759
1980	2199
1990	4298
2000	8771

Source: Bean and Stevens (2003, 54).

Table 1.5   Generational Standing of Mexican-Origin Population in 2000

| | Percentage Each Age Group | | |
Generational Standing	All Ages	25–34	55–64
1) *All persons of Mexican origin*			
U.S. born	38	39	49
Mexican born	62	61	51
Total	100	100	100
2) *U.S.-born persons of Mexican origin*			
Two parents born in Mexico		22	15
One parent born in Mexico		16	21
Both parents born in United States		62	64
One to four grandparents born in Mexico		*32*	
No grandparents born in Mexico		*30*	
Total		100	100

Source: IPUMS dataset, 2000 census (for panel 1); CPS 1998–2001 and CPS, October 1979 (for italicized cells in panel 2).
Note: The 1979 CPS data on birthplace, parental birthplaces and ancestry was used as follows. 1. To identify children, four to thirteen years of age, native born of native parentage (NBNP), with a parent reporting Mexican ancestry. 2. To determine the proportion of this group with a Mexican-born grandparent (from the survey data on the children's parents, which includes their own parents' birthplaces). The proportion in number 2 was applied to the respondents twenty-five to thirty-four years of age, NBNP, reporting Mexican origin in the 1998 to 2001 CPS datasets.

tion is no surprise. And, given the likelihood that immigrants will be young, it is no surprise either to see that the proportion Mexican-born is somewhat smaller among older individuals.

The table also tells us something about the more distant origins of the U.S.-born who claimed Mexican origin, and here the results are less familiar (panel 2). Both younger and older adults show roughly the same proportions in the second generation and in the third-or-later generations—a solid majority, just over three fifths are in the third or later generational group. And most intriguing, we can further divide the younger cohort of third-or-later generation adults into third-generation members and fourth-or-later-generation members. The information comes from a Current Population Survey (CPS) from 1979, when this young-adult cohort were still children living with their own parents (Hicks 1997). That CPS reports the birthplace, parental birthplaces, and ancestry of those parents. Since the information on those parents extends back three generations, the information on their children extends back four generations. Just about half of the third and later generation members were in fact fourth generation or later. Because the group in question was born between 1966 and 1975, their grandparents were probably born roughly between 1906 and 1915—and in the United States. Given the importance of immigration after 1900 and especially after 1910, it is probable that many of these people were in fact fourth generation rather than fifth or later generation, but on this point we have no additional evidence.

CONTEMPORARY IMMIGRATION

Three features of the contemporary Mexican immigration are especially noteworthy for our purposes: their numerical dominance among all immigrants, their socioeconomic position, and the prevalence of a mixed second generation among their American-born children.

NUMERICAL DOMINANCE   The Mexicans comprise a far greater proportion of the total contemporary immigration than any single group did during the last great wave of immigration. Table 1.1 showed that the Italians, the largest immigrant group of 1899 to 1924, comprised 22 percent of all arrivals and probably about 17 percent of permanent immigrants. By contrast, in the 2000 census, 32 percent of the immigrants who had arrived since 1965 hailed from Mexico (table 1.6). One has to reach further back in American history, to the mid-nineteenth-century Irish and German immigrations, for single groups that dominated the immigration stream of their time as heavily, or even more heavily, than the Mexicans dominate the immigration of our own time. Also, the situation early in the twenty-first century is unique in that Mexicans alone dominate the numbers; no other country of origin today provides even a quarter as many immigrants. By contrast, in the early twentieth century, the Jewish and the Polish immigrations were each nearly half as large as the Italian (see table 1.1).

The Mexican primacy is, if anything, even stronger in the contemporary second generation, given fertility patterns. Thirty-four percent of all second-generation children born since 1965 have Mexican parents, and 39 percent of those born since 1995 do (table 1.6).[18] The steady rise in the size of the new second-generation cohorts—totaling some 16.5 million individuals—and the steady rise in the Mexicans among them is captured in figure 1.7. One implication of that figure is that the second generation that has come of age remains special and still only an imperfect indicator of how those who follow them in ten or twenty years will fare, if only because the numbers and composition of the group will change sharply in years to come. For us, the rapidly increasing size of the Mexican second generation is especially important. The cohort born from 1996 to 2000 is 5.7 times larger than

Table 1.6   Immigrants and Second Generation in 2000

Place of Origin	Immigrants Arrived Since 1968, Born 1936 to 1985 Percentage	Second Generation, Born 1966 to 2000 Percentage
Mexico	32	34
Caribbean	9	8
Central America	7	6
South America	6	5
China	4	3
Philippines	5	3
Other Asia	17	14
Europe	12	19
Canada	2	3
Other	4	5
Total	100	100

Source: IPUMS datasets, 1980 to 2000 census.
Note: Second generation, U.S.-born children living with an immigrant parent. Origins of 1991 to 2000 birth cohort: Mexican, 39 percent; European 13 percent.

that born between 1966 and 1970; the comparable increase for all other groups is 2.4. In fact, a result of this great growth is that in the youngest of these birth cohorts, the total number with Mexican origins—of whatever generation—actually exceeds the number identified as non-Hispanic black—making the Mexicans alone (as opposed to all Hispanics) the largest American group counted as a minority for that birth cohort.[19]

SOCIOECONOMIC CONDITION NEAR THE BOTTOM   The Mexican Americans are near the bottom of all immigrant groups in terms of well-being. The economic situation of the Mexican immigrants and their children, however, is by no means as unique as the magnitude of that immigration. Several other major groups, notably those from the Caribbean or Central America, are not so very different in educational background or in earnings. Nevertheless, it is the combination of a giant immigration, a long common border and the economic position near, if not always at, the bottom that uniquely characterizes the Mexicans.

A convenient way to highlight their economic situation is to focus on immigrant parents of American-born children born since 1966, a particularly important group for our purposes, which I can briefly summarize (not shown in tables). The Mexican parents had lower levels of educational attainment than their Asian, European, or African counterparts; and among

Figure 1.7   Second-Generation Birth Cohorts, 1966–2000

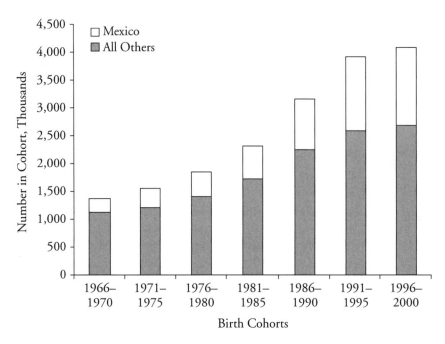

Source: IPUMS datasets for 1980 to 2000 censuses.
Note: Based on 5 percent samples of 1980 to 1990 and 6 percent sample of 2000 census.
Includes all U.S.-born children living with an immigrant parent. Three earliest cohorts were
drawn from 1980 census, fourth cohort from 1990 census, and the three most recent cohorts
from 2000 census.

the groups from the Americas (whom I classified as Mexican, Cuban, other
Caribbean, Central American, South American), the Mexican educational
attainments were also lowest, if only slightly lower than Central American.
Only about one in twenty of Mexican-immigrant parents were college graduates, and only about half were high school graduates. Still, high school
graduation has become more common over time, climbing from 35 percent
for parents of the earliest-born second generation to 55 percent for parents
of the most-recent-born.

The Mexican families are also at the bottom in terms of total family
income—well below the average for Asian or for European and Canadian
immigrant families, and somewhat below that for Central and South
Americans. The income comparisons among immigrants from the Americas
are made more complex because they are greatly affected by whether a family

has two parents present in the household. For example, in recent years the percentage of second-generation children being raised in one-parent households hovered around 50 percent for the Puerto Ricans, 40 percent for the Caribbeans, 30 percent for the Central Americans and 20 percent for the Mexicans; it was about 10 percent for Europeans and Canadians, and for Asians. At least among the two-parent families, where 80 percent of the Mexican Americans are being raised, the Mexican family incomes are lower than in any of the other groups mentioned. When all families are compared ignoring family structure, Mexicans, Central Americans and other Caribbeans have about the same total family incomes. Interestingly, Puerto Rican families, though not formally immigrants, are the worst off. The Cubans and South Americans are better off than the other Latin-American groups.

UNMIXED AND MIXED SECOND GENERATIONS: PREVALENCE   The history of contemporary immigration waves is so different from the history of the SCEN waves that we hardly expect to find unchanged patterns of evolving parental intermarriage and second-generation mixed parentage today. What is similar is simply that the prevalence of intermarriage and second-generation mixed parentage is heavily determined by the historical context of immigration from different parts of the world. And because that historical context today differs for the major groups of contemporary immigrants, so does the prevalence of mixed parentage among contemporary second-generation groups. A graduate student may well be more likely to interact with the American-born than a day laborer; Americans stationed in Vietnam or Germany may return with a spouse met abroad; Canadians and western Europeans may decide on immigration to the United States only if they have already decided to marry an American. So, too, immigrant groups in which the sex ratio is sharply unbalanced will be more likely to seek a spouse from outside the group. And especially important for consideration of the Mexican case, a long history of earlier immigration from the same country of origin creates an ethnic subculture from which American-born spouses are especially likely to be found; the same is true for Chinese immigrants of our time and, of course, for European immigrants. Yet at the same time there is a countervailing force of great importance in the size of the contemporary immigration: specifically, as the contemporary immigration from any country progresses, a pool of potential immigrant spouses grows, compared to the size of the pool of potential second- or later-generation spouses. And finally, there has been much speculation about the similarity of origins across national borders, especially among the Hispanic groups. Just how many of the mixed second generation involve the offspring of such panethnic unions? Although recent censuses do not provide information on parental birthplaces, it is available for children living with both their parents.

These many influences operate in contradictory directions, some tending to raise and others to lower the prevalence of mixed parentage in the second generation. The result is a complex pattern that varies across group and within group across time. Among the Mexican second generation born since the mid-1960s, the proportion with two foreign-born parents has risen steadily from 48 percent to 74 percent between 1966 to 1970 and 1996 to 2000 (figure 1.8).

In the other families, with an American-born parent, marriages tend to be mixed only in terms of generation, not ethnicity: the large majority of these American-born parents themselves claimed Mexican ancestry. Note too that panethnicity is of trivial significance for the Mexican marriage pat-

Figure 1.8   Second-Generation Children with Two Foreign-Born Parents, Selected Groups

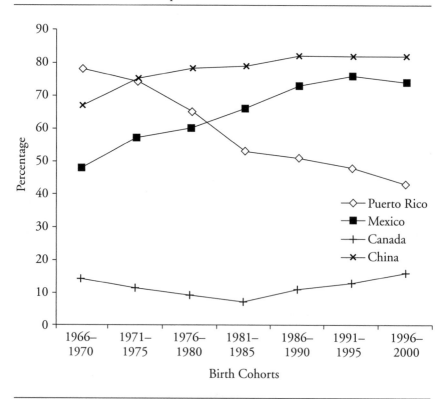

Source: IPUMS datasets for 1980 to 2000 censuses.
Note: On censuses from which each cohort was drawn see note to figure 1.7.

terns (table 1.7). It may be stronger for smaller immigrant groups or perhaps among Mexicans outside the southwest or among later-generation
Mexicans in the United States; but among Mexican immigrants nationally
it plays little role in spousal selection.

With this context in mind, the falling rate of mixed parentage in the
Mexican American second generation between the 1966 to 1970 period
and the 1996 to 2000 period makes sense. The early prevalence of the
mixed origins is probably explained by the long history of immigration
that created second-, third-, and later-generation communities of Mexican
Americans from among whom new arrivals from Mexico might choose a
spouse. By contrast, by 2000 the number of recent arrivals was much larger
relative to the later-generation members than it had been in 1970, making
the choice of a spouse from among the immigrant group more likely than
earlier. These factors seem to have produced a similar, if more muted, pattern among the Chinese, while declining numbers of arrivals in the most
recent years seem to have created a reverse pattern among the Puerto Ricans
(figure 1.8). A radically different pattern can be seen in the smaller-scale
and culturally less distinct Canadian immigration: among the second generation the mixed component never comprised less than 84 percent of the
group.

Table 1.7   Origins of Native-Born Children with a Mexican Parent
             (Two-Parent Families Only)

Other Parent	Percentage						
	1966–1970	1971–1975	1976–1980	1981–1985	1986–1990	1991–1995	1996–2000
U.S. born							
No Hispanic ancestry	11	9	10	9	8	7	7
Hispanic (but not Mexican) ancestry	2	2	2	3	3	3	3
Mexican ancestry	39	32	28	22	16	14	16
Subtotal:	52	43	40	34	27	24	26
Foreign born							
Other country	3	4	4	4	3	3	3
Mexico	45	53	56	62	70	73	71
All origins	100	100	100	100	100	100	100

Source: IPUMS datasets, 1980 to 2000 censuses.

In our later analysis of the Mexican American second generation, we will be especially concerned with those people who were born to post-1965 immigrants and who have already reached adulthood; among that group, the proportion with mixed origins was especially high. Nevertheless, my theoretical interest is in the progress of the unmixed Mexican and SCEN second generations—the American-born children of two immigrant parents. And I will try to focus on that subgroup to the extent that data will permit. But it is illuminating to understand how the history of immigration—operating differently on the SCEN then and the Mexicans now—has created in both periods a second generation in some cohorts that include considerably higher numbers of mixed-origin children than in others.[20]

CHAPTER TWO

IMMIGRANT WAGES THEN AND NOW

I CONCENTRATE on the SCEN then and on the Mexicans now because these immigrant groups arrived in great numbers as low-skill workers in two periods of American history. Portes and Rumbaut (1996) have helpfully called these immigrants labor migrants as distinct from human capital migrants; the latter can trade on their advanced education and professional skills. Human capital migrants have been much more prevalent in the contemporary immigration than during the 1890 to 1914 immigration, but such migrants are a very small proportion among Mexicans now, as they were among the SCEN then. The question is just how much similarity in economic standing these groups shared, separated as they are by nearly a century, and alternatively how great a difference in experiences the phrase "came in as low-skill workers" hides.

I compare the two immigrant groups to native whites. For the contemporary period, native whites were further restricted to those who did not claim Mexican origins; for brevity's sake, I use the term native whites in both periods. Similarly, when I refer to blacks, the reference is always to native-born blacks, and in the contemporary period to native-born blacks who did not claim Mexican origins.[1]

And to simplify, as well as for comparisons to other studies, I focus only on men.[2] For the SCEN, we have detailed occupational data as well as year of arrival and age in 1910 and 1920. We can also gain a reasonably clear view of what they were doing at the end of their work lives. The later censuses of 1940 and 1950 unfortunately did not report year of arrival, but there was relatively little immigration after 1915 and almost none after

1925. We can therefore be quite confident that the large majority of SCEN older adult workers found in the 1940 or 1950 census had arrived before 1915, and virtually all of them before 1925. We also know how old they had been in 1910 and 1920, and that they had had many years during which they could have chosen to remigrate; those remaining in 1940 were nearly all permanent immigrants. The most relevant birth cohorts, of 1876 to 1885 and 1886 to 1895, would have been between fifteen and thirty-four in 1910, between twenty-five and forty-four in 1920, and between forty-five and sixty-four in 1940.

OCCUPATIONS, 1910 TO 2000

Table 2.1 shows the broad similarity of SCEN and Mexican jobs compared to those of native whites in each period in terms of broad occupational strata. A useful summary is the proportion of each group in low-skilled work—including the semi-skilled, service, farm laborer, and other laborer. In 1910, some 37 percent of the young native white men and 77 percent of the SCEN were in these low-skill strata; in both 1970 and 2000, about 29 to 30 percent of the native whites and 64 to 65 percent of the Mexicans were. By the twilight of their work lives, all three groups were modestly less likely to have been in low-skilled work than at the outset, but the contrast between native white on the one hand and SCEN and Mexican on the other is nearly as striking: 29 percent versus 58 percent for the 1940 cohort and 26 percent versus 60 percent for the 2000 cohort.

To be properly understood, these cross-time ethnic comparisons must be placed in the context of the general move of American workers out of agriculture. Almost a third of the native whites in the 1910 through 1940 period worked in agriculture. By the end of the twentieth century, the fraction had shrunk to minimal levels (2 percent). At the same time, the shift out of agriculture was not of much consequence for the SCEN who had come to work in American industry: only 5 percent of the 1910 SCEN were in agriculture. By contrast, in the contemporary period, while Mexican laborers were still very important to the remaining agricultural sector, farm labor nevertheless accounted for only 12 percent of the young Mexican labor force in 1970, and only 6 percent in 2000.

Consequently, comparisons among nonagricultural workers are also useful (table 2.1a). There were relatively few professionals in either group, but there were still far more among the native whites than among the immigrants; and the same ethnic imbalance characterized all white-collar work, which comprised 37 percent of the native whites and 9 percent of the SCEN not employed in agriculture. Similarly, 24 percent of the native whites and 14 percent of the SCEN immigrants were skilled workers. These were the so-called good jobs of the period, together comprising 61 percent of

Table 2.1   Occupations over a Century: Native Whites and Immigrants

A. SCEN and Native Whites: Men in 1910 and 1940

| | 25 to 34 in 1910 | | 25 to 34 in 1910 | | 35 to 44 in 1920 | | 55 to 64 in 1940 | |
| | | | NW | SCEN Excl. Farming Strata | | | | |
Strata	NW	SCEN			NW	SCEN	NW	SCEN
Professional	4	1	7	1	5	0	6	2
Farmer	21	2			25	5	24	7
Managers, officials, and proprietors	8	5	12	6	11	9	13	11
Clerical and sales	12	2	18	2	11	3	11	4
Skilled	16	13	24	14	19	20	18	18
Semiskilled	15	28	21	29	12	26	10	23
Service	3	4	5	5	3	5	6	9
Farm laborer	11	3			4	2	4	2
Other unskilled	9	41	13	44	8	27	10	24
Total	100	100	100	100	100	100	100	100
Subtotal: low skill	37	77	39	78	27	60	29	58

B. Mexicans and Native Whites: Men in 1970 and 2000

| | 25 to 34 in 1970 | | 55 to 64 in 2000 | | 25 to 34 in 2000 | |
| | | | NW | Mexicans in U.S., 30 Years and Older | | |
Strata	NW	Mexicans			NW	Mexicans
Professional	20	5	22	5	22	3
Farmer	2	0	2	1	1	1
Managers, officials, and proprietors	10	3	17	6	13	4
Clerical and sales	14	6	15	6	14	6
Skilled	25	21	19	21	21	23
Semiskilled	19	33	14	25	14	24
Service	5	9	7	14	9	15
Farm laborer	1	12	0	8	0	6
Other unskilled	5	12	4	13	6	19
Total	100	100	100	100	100	100
Subtotal: low skill	30	65	26	60	29	64

Source: IPUMS datasets 1910, 1920, 1940, 1970, and 2000 censuses.

native whites and 23 percent of the SCEN who held nonagricultural jobs.

Another transformation of the occupational distribution during the course of the century is the striking growth of professional work. Still, it is important to remember, in the context of so much contemporary discussion about the native-white Americans holding jobs that require college degrees, that even in 2000 only 22 percent of the young native-white American men were working as professionals. On the other hand, this figure is more than five times the comparable 1910 proportion.

Because SCEN immigration increased so rapidly between 1900 and 1910, and then fell off sharply after 1914, the composition of the group, in terms of date of arrival and propensity to remigrate, depends heavily on the year. In 1910, very high proportions of the young SCEN adult immigrants had arrived during the preceding ten years, and especially during the preceding five. By contrast, in 1920, many had arrived five to ten years earlier, but relatively few had arrived within the preceding five. Moreover, by 1920, many of the 1900 through 1910 arrivals had already returned to Europe. These patterns make it hard to judge immigrant progress in the early years. By 1920, fewer of the 1900 to 1910 arrivals were working as unskilled laborers; but we don't know how much of that change was due to upward mobility since 1910 and how much to the departure of unskilled laborers.

In the end, we want to ask whether Mexicans entering the labor force today are doing so in worse economic circumstances than SCEN immigrants did ninety years ago. However, no simple answer leaps out from this review of broad occupational strata. When they started out, the SCEN immigrants were at least as concentrated as the Mexicans of today in low-skill work, and at least as over-concentrated there relative to native whites—and this is also true if we restrict attention to those not working in agriculture. On the other hand, was the concentration in low-skill work as great a disadvantage in 1910 as it is today—judged in terms of wage differentials from the mean native-white worker for example, or judged in terms of the difficulty of moving up to something better, whether for oneself or for one's children? Moreover, how are we to evaluate the relative standing of farmers, so prevalent among the native whites in 1910? What was their economic standing, and how important was it to their children that urban schools, for example, were generally not within their reach? At the other end of the spectrum, how are we to assess the fact that today the professionals are nearly as prevalent as the farmers were then, and that a far higher proportion of native whites than Mexicans are enjoying these good jobs? One response is to argue that such questions show that no single answer can meaningfully address the relative levels of well-being of immigrants then and now; and, similarly, that the impact of these differences in starting points has been too much altered by time to permit us to generalize about the contexts within which second generations then and now grow up. But there may be a valid alternative to dismissing comparisons of then and now.

SHARPENING THE COMPARISON: THE ETHNIC WAGE RATIO

An alternative strategy is to shift the focus from occupations and occupational strata to wages. Our interest in the occupational situation, after all, is mostly as a measure of economic well-being, and insofar as we seek a measure of economic well-being, the preferable focus is directly on wages. Furthermore, occupational strata involve at best a vertical ranking of broad occupational groups; the wage involves a continuous scale, indicating how far apart individuals stand in relation to a single metric. Consequently, the advantage of the professionals, or the disadvantage of the low-skill workers, is expressed in terms of that single scale. Moreover, by considering the ratio of wages in the SCEN or Mexican immigrant group to those in the native white group at the same period, and across comparable age groups, we have a basis for comparisons in terms of some useful social standard, especially relevant to assimilation, and not an absolute wage figure whose meaning would have to be teased from a social and economic context.

Of course, the wage scale represents only one aspect of social realities separated by ninety years of transformation. Generally speaking, there are good reasons to be skeptical about precise measures of past versus present conditions; and the immigrant-native wage ratio is a case in point. We determine the mean wage for immigrants and for natives, and then calculate the ratio of the means—all this for immigrants and natives at two or more times, decades apart. We can also compare ethnic wage ratios across ethnic generations—showing how the immigrants had fared relative to native whites, and then how, a generation later, the children of immigrants were faring relative to the children of native whites. But the average wage is a single number extracted from the full texture of economic histories—not to speak of history generally—and the ratio of two averages is even more abstracted from social reality. Past and present differ in so many respects that comparisons along a single dimension of measurement is likely to leave anyone with a sense of history feeling misled. We are often far better off comparing in a looser way. Thus we are stimulated by some feature of the present to explore the past in a new way. For example, the segmented assimilation argument speculates that the decline of manufacturing has been a significant factor in the difficulties that the second generation will face today compared to what their predecessors faced. This formulation might lead us to explore more carefully just how and how much the immigrants of the 1910 era, and especially their children in the decades after, relied on manufacturing work, without necessitating quite so abstracted and precise a comparison of two periods, each reduced to a single number.

Nevertheless, I think there are reasons to think very carefully about the evidence related to immigrant wages then and now, and good reasons for a summary in terms of wage ratios. The first is simply that precise comparisons are in fact unavoidable; if one thinks that immigrants are more disadvantaged compared to native whites today than they were in 1910, an implicit comparison has been made, and it is far better to examine it explicitly than to discuss the comparison relying only on implicit measurement.

The second reason is that the ethnic wage ratio serves as a measure of relative well-being. Thus the question about the changing place of the professionals in the occupational distribution reduces to another about the wage of professionals relative to the wage of others then and now. So, too, the wage ratio helps operationalize theoretical formulations about how contemporary immigration is distinct. For example, a reasonable interpretation of the segmented assimilation theory predicts that we should find that the second generation today is faring less well, compared to the children of the native born, than in the past. The theory suggests various explanations, such as the decline of manufacturing jobs over time and the high barriers that stand in the way of people struggling to leave poverty through a college education. However, before getting to explanations for the phenomenon, we will want to know what evidence indicates that the phenomenon itself—the decline in the relative position of the second generation over time—has been observed. The ethnic wage ratios can be the measure by which to confirm or refute the prediction of decline. Also, for the explanation of contemporary first-generation difficulties to lie in the decline of manufacturing, the ethnic wage ratio for the first generation must be lower than in the past, and its decline across time or region must have some connection with the fate of manufacturing. Moreover, in focusing on the ethnic wage ratios, we raise a further question: if the decline of manufacturing jobs is not reflected in ethnic earnings ratios, how exactly did such a decline matter? Similarly, if the ethnic wage ratio is deemed an inadequate way to capture second-generation decline, why is it inadequate? What would be a better way to operationalize the theory?

Indeed, one way into the use of the ethnic wage ratio is to review the relationship between the formulations of several recent social scientists on the questions of past and present relative positions. I have already discussed the perspective of Alejandro Portes and his colleagues (Portes and Zhou 1993; Portes and Rumbaut 1996), who developed the segmented assimilation argument; but it is worth stressing the extent to which this theory begins with the economy. America needs far fewer strong backs and untrained minds than it did when the Italians and the Slavs were arriving a century ago. Moreover, the children of these poor immigrants will not have the economic supports for a college education, and without that education they will face a life of unrewarding jobs. According to Portes and his colleagues, these considerations, all fundamentally economic, are supplemented by another critical difference: the new immigrants are typically nonwhite and will face discrimination that the Slavs and Italians of the past did not encounter. In the context of these realities, an inner-city dysfunctional minority youth culture will seem to these second-generation members the most authentic portrayal of their situation and of their options; they will lose the will to break out of their situation. And without that will, whatever chance there is for such an escape from poverty will be lost. But despite these additional themes of racial discrimination and related cultural dynamics of inner-city youth culture, the view of the changing economic position of the first generation is essential to the segmented assimilation perspective.

This feature of the theory ties concerns about segmented assimilation to the economist George Borjas and others who deal with immigrant prospects. Borjas has written extensively on all aspects of the economics of immigration, and much of his writing concerns change over time; so I should first emphasize that I do not refer here to one well-known and important strand of Borjas's work, namely his and Barry Chiswick's writings on whether immigrants today will catch up to the native born (with the same formal education) over the course of a lifetime. Borjas (1999) argues that this catchup has become increasingly unlikely across recent decades, in part because of shifting self-selection of immigrants and above all because some countries of origin (notably Mexico) have been sending higher proportions of all immigrants than was formerly the case. However, this trend within our own time—or even since 1940, when the relevant data became available—ultimately tells us nothing relevant to the comparison of the post-1965 and pre-1920 immigrations. Shifts in the likelihood that immigrants reach parity with natives may well have occurred during the years from 1880 to 1920 as well, and for similar reasons: declining self-selection and shifts in the importance of specific countries of origin. The shifts within an immigration era, however, cannot resolve comparisons about catchup between two eras—cannot tell us when the likelihood of catchup in our own time will have declined below what the likelihood of catchup had been, for example, in 1910. Moreover, this line of research also can be set aside for an even simpler reason: our understanding of the distant past never specified that immigrants caught up to comparably educated natives within the course of one lifetime (Thernstrom 1973; Lieberson 1980; Perlmann 1988); the question for us is rather whether the economic assimilation of a labor-migrant immigrant group over several generations takes longer in our own time than it did for the immigrants of 1880 to 1920 and their descendants.

Borjas (1994) has conducted other research that is more directly relevant to these questions. Specifically, he noted the considerable differences across

1910 immigrant groups that existed in literacy rates and job skills (as measured by wages); he then explored how fully the original ranking of the
groups (in education and wages) continued to characterize their children
and grandchildren. Borjas was not using his evidence to determine when
the descendants of immigrants would cease to differ from native whites.
For reasons having to do with his wider intellectual agenda, the question
he posed in this context concerned differences among immigrants. For example, it is possible that some degree of difference might survive among
the descendants of thirty-two immigrant groups even after these groups
of descendants had equaled or exceeded the levels of other native whites.
Nevertheless, because Borjas stressed that it took a long time—more than
two generations—for the initial differences among immigrant groups to
disappear, it followed that those immigrant groups that started at the bottom of the ladder also took a long time to catch up to the descendants of
the native born.

Also, Borjas (1994) was far less interested in any specific group than he
was in finding an average rate of transmission of ethnic ranking covering
all immigrant groups across generations. Thus he offered a single generalization to cover the experience of the thirty-two immigrant groups on which
he had collected data: about half the strength of the immigrant rankings
could be traced into the second generation, and roughly half of the remaining strength of the rankings could in turn be traced into the third generation.[3] Borjas went on to offer some intriguing arguments about how this
transmission occurs. "Ethnic capital" (shared advantages derived from being
a member of a given group) helped the groups that had started out ahead
even when controls were imposed, for example, for the specific educational
level attained by individuals in each group. These features of his argument
are actually intriguingly close to discussions in the sociological literature
about the differing "social capital" of immigrant groups, and their conse-
quent differences in so-called modes of incorporation. Nevertheless, these
formulations are also less important to our present purposes. For us, the
key point is that in the course of building his argument, Borjas generated
evidence on the condition of each of the thirty-two immigrant groups in
1910, 1940, and 1980—data on literacy rates (that were familiar to historians of immigration) and estimates of the average wage in each ethnic group
(that were novel).

Christopher Jencks drew on this part of Borjas's research but redirected
the use of Borjas's historical data, especially the new estimates of immigrant
wage levels, to highlight a single simple feature inherent in them: a measure
of native versus immigrant well-being then and now (Borjas 1994). Writing
in the *New York Review of Books,* Jencks teased from the Borjas study an
ethnic wage ratio for immigrants compared to native whites in 1910, and
juxtaposed it with another found in contemporary data. Jencks also focused

his attention on groups in much the same way I have outlined earlier. He focused especially on immigrants from southern, central, and eastern Europe (SCE immigrants) of about 1910 and Mexicans starting out today. Jencks argued that one reason

assimilation . . . proceeded quickly in the past was because the economic gap between immigrants and natives was far smaller than today's folklore suggests. Most immigrants were poor, but so were most natives. Northern Europeans held most of America's best professional and managerial jobs, but they also held most of the worst agricultural jobs. George Borjas has found that southern and eastern European immigrants typically earned about 88 percent of what American-born whites did in 1910. Even Italians, the most disadvantaged major immigrant group, earned 83 percent. (Jencks 2001, Part I, 59–60)

By contrast, "Mexican-born men in the United States earn less than half what non-Latino whites earn." A footnote adds: "Mexican-born males who worked full-time throughout 1999 earned an average of $23,200. Non-Latino whites averaged $50,000" (Jencks 2001, Part I, 60–61). That is, a ratio of .46.

Thus, 88 percent then, 46 percent now. The form in which Jencks captured the comparison, and the specific way he linked it to the Borjas research, is both conceptually and empirically very suggestive. Nevertheless, additional conceptual and empirical considerations should make it clear that these magnitudes cannot be taken as a summary of the situation.

THE CONTEXT OF AMERICAN WAGE INEQUALITY

A crucial characteristic of American wages during the twentieth century is the great swings in the degree of wage inequality; and like all other workers, immigrants and their children prospered or suffered setbacks within the context of these swings.

SWINGS IN WAGE INEQUALITY   The gap between the best and worst paid workers went through two periods of contraction in the first half of the century, then expanded again during its last three decades. The recent changes are often mentioned in connection with contemporary income inequality, but the earlier changes are much less known, and indeed have only been highlighted in research of the past decade by several economic historians. Only in the light of these swings in wage inequality can we make sense of the ethnic wage ratios that capture the relative wage condition of ethnic groups at one or another moment in time.

We can think of workers in a queue, lining up for the best-paid jobs they can get, and we can express each worker's position in terms of the percentile position he or she holds in the queue. The ratio of the wages of workers at the 90th percentile to the wages of workers at the 10th percentile has been used as a convenient measure of the change in wage inequality over time. In recent papers, economists Claudia Goldin, Lawrence Katz, and Robert Margo have shown that two great compressions sharply reduced wage inequality during the first half of the century (especially Goldin and Margo 1992; Goldin and Katz 2001; Katz and Autor 1999). The earlier of these two compressions occurred between 1890 and the 1920s, and mostly between 1910 and 1920; the second compression occurred between 1940 and 1950. Finally, Goldin and Katz also conclude that whatever the fluctuations in wage inequality during the roaring twenties and the Great Depression, by 1940 the wage structure was about as unequal as it had been in the 1920s, after the first great compression. Inequality in the wage structure rose slowly during the 1950s and 1960s, but by 1970 was still much less than it had been in 1940, before the second great compression (Goldin and Margo 1992; Goldin and Katz 2001; Katz and Autor 1999). Between 1970 and 2000, however, the wage structure again became much less equal—so that today the ratio of wages at the 90th and 10th percentiles is roughly the same as it was in 1940, if still improved over what it had been in 1910 (figure 2.1).[4]

These swings in the level of wage inequality should not be thought of as some new, mysterious feature of twentieth-century life; on the contrary, familiar great themes of American economic and social history determined the evolving wage structure—whatever uncertainties may exist about exactly how much weight should be given to each source of change in any given decade. As high school and later college education became more widespread, special wage premiums for educated workers fell. As unions became stronger, wages of many lower-skilled workers rose. As immigration rose and fell, and rose again in recent years, the supply of cheap labor also shifted. The compressions were especially concentrated around the decades of World War I and World War II, periods of "inflation, tight labor markets, strong demand for manual workers, rising union strength and substantial government intervention in the labor market" (Goldin and Katz 2001, 69). Whereas various shocks of war on the economy disappeared soon after peace was restored, the wage compressions held for decades, not least because they came about when the long-term process of educational expansion (which eroded the premiums to educated labor) was well underway. By contrast, the decompression of wages since about 1970 has involved increasing premiums to educated labor. Economists are still uncertain about the

Figure 2.1   Wage Inequality, 1940 to 1995

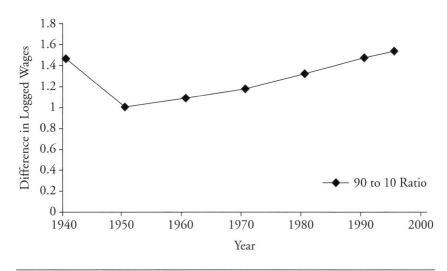

Source: Katz and Autor (1999).
Note: Inequality is measured here by the ratio of wages for workers at the 90th to the 10th percentile of wage workers (full-time adult male nonagricultural workers included).

weight to place on each source of the contemporary rise in wage inequality, but those sources do seem to be related to the greater productivity of more educated workers, at least partly in turn because more educated workers can manipulate technology more fully. At the same time, the declining relative wages to low-skilled work reflects downward wage pressure from globalization—the competition of foreign production at lower wage scales. Probably contributing as well are the decline of union power and the rise in numbers of low-skilled immigrant workers.[5]

Finally, it is helpful to bear in mind that the great swings in American wage inequality are related to the changes in real wages over time, but in complex ways. Generally speaking, workers in later decades of the twentieth century earned more than those in earlier decades, even after adjusting for inflation (Goldin 2000); but the rapidity of the rise in real wages within each portion of the wage hierarchy is what determines the degree of wage inequality at any one time. Wage compressions reflect the fact that the big transformations before 1970 meant that wages were increasing during those transformations more rapidly in the lower than in the upper part of the wage hierarchy. Recent increases in wage inequality mean that real wages are increasing less rapidly, or are declining, in the lower part of the hierarchy.

The great swings in wage inequality affect both the level and the inter-pretation of the ethnic wage ratio. When the inequality is lower for all workers, the ethnic wage ratio will be lower as well. On the other hand, the lower ethnic wage ratio will not necessarily imply that the changed relative position in dollar value of wages also reflects a changed position of immigrants in terms the ranking of all workers. Consider a curve that repre-sents the distribution of all wages (a normal curve can serve as an approxi-mation). When the wage structure is relatively equal, for example in 1950, the curve is narrow in the sense that the 90th and 10th percentiles are separated by a relatively low difference in dollar terms. By contrast, when wages are relatively more unequal—in 1910 or in 2000—the curve is wide in the sense that the 90th and 10th percentiles are separated by a relatively great difference in dollar terms. Yet the proportion of all workers that sepa-rates those at the 10th percentile from those at the ninetieth percentile has not changed. The same observations, in less extreme form, will be true for workers less far apart in wages—for example at the 75th and 25th percen-tiles of all wage workers, or at the 60th and 30th percentiles. And the same will be true of the relative standing of two ethnic groups.

Moreover, the ethnic wage ratios capture a snapshot from a moment in time and not the direction in which trends are moving. Thus ethnic wage ratios could have been about equal in 1940 and 1970, but in 1940 wages were heading toward less inequality and in 1970 towards more inequality; the implications affect not only the immigrant workers but the conditions in which the second generation grows up. Thus, we may measure the ethnic wage ratio in 1940 and 1970 with great precision, and we may then be able to say that the immigrant group was relatively better in the one or the other year; but unless we attend to the dizzying swings of wage inequality we will not get far in interpreting those ethnic wage ratios.

IMPLICATIONS FOR SCEN–NW WAGE RATIO MEASUREMENTS BEFORE 1940   The census did not report wages prior to 1940; it is therefore nec-essary to estimate wages before 1940 indirectly, by using the information on worker occupations reported in those earlier censuses. I use the same general logic as George Borjas and Christopher Jencks; I construct a scale that provides an estimate of the mean wage for all Americans in an occupa-tion in 1910 and apply that mean to every worker in that occupation found in the 1910 census dataset. Then I compute the mean occupational wage for all workers in a given ethnic group, and finally calculate the ratio of the mean occupational wage for two ethnic groups.

I believe, however, that there is a serious flaw in the particular scale Borjas used for determining the mean wage for each occupation in 1910. I therefore not only use a different scale, I also introduce several other refine-ments. These changes in technique radically depress the estimates of the

1910 ethnic wage ratio from that which Jencks derived from Borjas's study. The devil may be in the details of these changes, yet I suspect they will interest only economists and a few other readers. Those details are isolated in the appendix. Here I mention only the logic behind the methods.

The particular scale Borjas used had been created by two other social scientists, Samuel Preston and Michael Haines (1991), from early twentieth-century surveys of workers that listed occupations and wages in particular locales. At the time Borjas conducted his analysis, there was no way to test the adequacy of the Preston-Haines occupational wage scale; but more recent work by Claudia Goldin and Lawrence Katz (2001) on the swings in wage inequality prior to 1940 does permit such a test. The Goldin-Katz research leads to a prediction that an adequate scale should reveal a greater level of wage inequality in 1910 than in 1940. I show that, to the contrary, the Preston-Haines scale does not display such an outcome. However, the same expectations derived from Goldin and Katz suggest a new way of creating an occupational wage scale for 1910—the desired scale should display wage inequalities as much greater than 1940 wage inequalities as 1940 wage inequalities are greater than 1950 wage inequalities. Then, following Borjas, I apply this new occupational wage to each worker in the 1910 census. Similarly, a wage scale for 1920 should have a structure comparable in levels of inequality to that of 1940, and I applied that scale to the workers in the 1920 census. This procedure yields a new estimate of the mean wage level for the SCEN workers and for the native whites—based on the concept of the occupational wage.

Thus far, the new estimates ignore possible ethnic wage differences among workers within occupations. Obviously, for workers generally, there was considerable wage variation within occupations; the big question is how systematically wages varied by ethnicity within occupations. I show that wages almost certainly did differ by ethnic group because both wages and ethnicity were associated with geographic location and with educational attainment. And I provide a basis for estimating how much of the ethnic difference in wages related to geographic location and educational attainment are being missed by the occupational wage. Accordingly I adjust the ethnic wage ratio derived from the occupational wage so that the adjusted ratio also takes into account ethnic differences in wages within occupation that were associated with geographic location and education attainment. I conclude that the ethnic wage ratio for SCEN immigrants and native whites in 1910 was no higher than the low .6 range. As with any comparisons based on estimates across long periods, large changes should be taken seriously, and small differences should not be overinterpreted.[6]

ETHNIC WAGE RATIOS, 1940 TO 2000   We are on much surer footing when we consider the wage evidence from 1940 and after, when the federal census routinely reports it for each worker. Also in 1940 the census replaced the literacy question with one about the highest grade of schooling in which respondents had enrolled (Ruggles et al. 2004). These twin changes allow us not only to measure the ethnic wage ratio more accurately; we can also explore how much of the inequality in the ethnic wage ratio was due to the longer schooling that the native whites had received.

The individual-level IPUMS datasets created from the 1940 and 1950 censuses allow us to capture SCEN wellbeing at the end of their work lives. The older of the two relevant decennial cohorts, born between 1876 and 1885, can only be observed in the 1940 census because this cohort was already between fifty-five and sixty-four that year, and had passed beyond the prime work ages by the time of the next enumeration. The next cohort, born between 1886 and 1895, can be observed at forty-five to fifty-four years of age in 1940 and at between fifty-five and sixty-four in 1950. Evidence on Mexican well-being in our own time focuses on 1970 and 2000. The young immigrants of 1970 were at the end of their work lives in 2000 and their second-generation children were young adults, whom we will study in later chapters.

IMMIGRANT WAGE RATIOS

Figure 2.2 shows estimates for 1910 and 1920 ethnic wage ratios—that is, the mean SCEN wage as a proportion of the mean native-white wage, for each ten-year birth cohort. Because of the estimations required to derive the ratios, the figure shows minimum and maximum estimates for each ratio. In 1910 the SCEN averaged 50 percent to 60 percent of the native white mean wage, except in the youngest adult cohort, in which wage differences generally tend to be more muted. In 1920, after some compression of the wage structure (and with a higher proportion of the SCEN immigrants being resident in the United States for a number of years), the wage ratios were about 10 percentage points higher. In 1940 they were very similar to 1920 levels, although possibly a few percentage points higher (at least compared to the minimum estimates for 1920). By 1950 the ethnic wage ratios had risen considerably, so that the SCEN were then averaging 85 percent of the native-white mean wage.

These shifts fit the narrative of swings in wage inequality quite well, and they suggest that after a long residence in the United States the relative skill levels of the SCEN probably were not changing much relative to the skill levels of the native whites; changes in the relative wages of the two groups in later life therefore was probably much related to the changes in wage inequalities affecting the whole labor force. Consider in particular the greatest decennial change, between 1940 and 1950. The workers we are tracking had already reached age forty-five at the start of this period; changes in

Figure 2.2   Ethnic Wage Ratios, Estimated and Observed 1910 to 2000

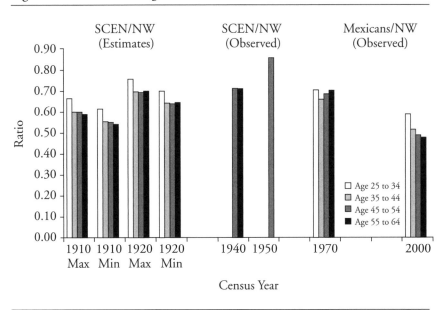

Source: IPUMS datasets for 1910 to 1920, 1940 to 1970, and 2000 censuses.
Note: See appendix for a description of the 1910 and 1920 estimates. Ratios for 1910 to 1970 include all SCEN male immigrants without regard to length of residence in the United States. See discussion in text (and see table A.3 for 1920). Ratios for 2000 include all Mexican male immigrants without regard to length of residence in the United States. Restricting the eldest cohort to men who had arrived in the United States by 1970 increases the ratio from .47 to .54.

relative skill-levels and years of experience are unlikely past that age. Because the SCEN immigration had been much diminished since 1915 and was almost nonexistent since 1925, the great majority of these SCEN workers had been in the United States for at least twenty-five years. Whatever mastery of the new environment they would achieve, they probably had done by 1940. Reasons for changes in relative wage levels between 1940 and 1950 must lie elsewhere.

Could these reasons be found in lingering effects of the Great Depression in the 1940 evidence? At first sight, it might seem so: the SCEN were more concentrated in factory jobs and if wages in these jobs rebounded more slowly than in higher-skill jobs, the 1940 to 1950 rise in the ethnic wage ratio might simply reflect that slower rebound.[7] But stimulated by just such concerns, Goldin and her colleagues intensively explored the possibility that the wage structure reflected in the 1940 census was a product of Great Depression conditions. They unequivocally reject that suggestion. The 1940 to 1950 compression is novel, not a return to pre-depression conditions (a point discussed further in "Other Features of the Ethnic-Wage-Ratio Estimation Process" in the appendix). And so most or all of the 1940 to 1950 shift observed in the ethnic wage ratio from .69 to .85 is probably part of this larger transformation of American wages. In sum, the ethnic wage ratios involving the SCEN immigrants began at extremely low levels in 1910, but rose sharply over four decades, probably by 25 percentage points in all; much of this gain was experienced by the same workers, and much of it was related to the two compressions in the wage structure.

The experience of the Mexican immigrants with the swings in wage inequality has been almost the reverse of that for the SCEN. The Mexicans of 1970 did not start out as far below the native whites as the SCEN had in 1910. In terms of relative well-being, the 1970 Mexicans were probably comparable to the 1920 SCEN—notwithstanding (we should note in passing) that many of the Mexicans but virtually none of the SCEN arrived as undocumented workers and that that status certainly takes a toll on wage prospects. However, the decades after 1970 saw the consistent growth of wage inequality. By 2000 the disparity was worse in all age cohorts than it had been in 1970.[8] The young adult cohort in 1970 had begun by earning 70 percent of the native white wage, and by 2000 men in the same birth cohort, now nearing the end of their work lives, were earning only 47 percent. The more relevant figure for our purposes, however, pertains to the subset of those older male Mexican workers in 2000 who had arrived in the United States by 1970. This is the group most representative of the fathers of the second generation, and they were earning 54 percent of the native white wage (not shown in figure 2.2). Finally, the young Mexican men just starting out in 2000, those immigrants born between 1966 and 1975, were earning 58 percent of the native white wage. This last figure is likely to drop somewhat in coming years as wage inequality opens up at older ages. Today, then, the Mexican level of relative well-being is comparable to, or slightly worse than, the minimum estimate for the relative well-being of the 1910 SCEN, the lowest point measured for that group.

The difference in the economic well-being of immigrants in 1910 and 2000, then, is small, although probably already, or soon to be, modestly worse in our era. The inadequacy of the wage data and the massive changes in the social and political contexts across nine decades are such that we may reasonably argue that these differences swamp the social significance of any current differences between 1910 and 2000 wage ratios. And this is an important conclusion, because the force of Jencks's (2001) presentation was precisely that for all the problems of measurement and changes in sociopolitical context, differences as massive as .88 to .46 could not be ignored, and indeed suggested the need for policy interventions—particularly in immigration policy. Interventions in immigration policy, as Massey, Durand, and Malone (2002) have forcefully argued, might well be wise; but not because of a supposed radical change in the relative wage status of labor migrants in 1910 and 2000.

On the other hand, while such a summary deals with the two moments in time that have been compared, most explicitly by Jencks (2001) and implicitly in Borjas's (1994) work, this summary is based on snapshots that isolate two moments in time. Greater attention to the swings in American wage inequality situate these two snapshots within the history of SCEN and Mexican experience over time, and that perspective shows improvement over time for the SCEN—with the nontrivial exception of the Great Depression decade—and deterioration over time for the Mexicans. An extreme contrast resulting from these temporal changes can be seen in the comparison of the oldest working SCEN and Mexican cohorts in 1950 and 2000 (see figure 2.2). The relevant SCEN cohort (born between 1886 and 1895) started out in 1920, earning about the same proportion of what native whites earned as did young Mexicans who started out in 1970. However, three decades later, when these cohort members were all between fifty-five and sixty-four years old, the mean wage of the SCEN group had climbed to 85 percent of the native-white mean wage; this was in 1950, at the high-point of wage equality. By contrast, the mean wage of the Mexican birth cohort, limited here to those who had lived in the United States since 1970, had slipped to 54 percent of the native-white mean wage; this was in 2000, after wage equality had declined sharply for three decades. In sum, by the end of their work lives, these two birth cohorts did differ by nearly as much as Jencks believed that the immigrant workers of 1910 and 2000 had differed. Of course, through most of the century, the contrast was not as extreme as for the oldest SCEN workers in 1950 and the oldest Mexican workers in 2000. Nevertheless, this comparison shows how important the dynamic perspective is to these comparisons. To repeat, if the general slide in the relative standing of low-skilled workers in the American economy continues decade after decade, it is hard to see how this slide will not extend the length of time, and ultimately the number of generations, required for the descendants of present-day immigrants to reach wage parity with the descendants of present-day native whites.

THE ROLE OF EDUCATION   The relatively low-skilled immigrants were low skilled partly because they lacked formal education (summarized in figure 3.1, in the next chapter). In the 1876 to 1895 birth cohorts, for example, native-white men averaged about eight years of schooling and SCEN immigrant men about five years; the native white cohorts born six to nine decades later average about twelve to fourteen years, and the Mexican immigrants of those later decades about eight to nine years. We will look more closely at the ethnic educational comparisons later, but for the moment are most interested in the effect of these great educational differences upon first-generation well-being.

Before 1940, only information on literacy can capture ethnic differences in formal education. However, the literacy measure only isolates those with the lowest formal schooling from the rest. Not surprisingly, literacy is moderately associated with the occupational wage (see appendix table A.2). Beginning in 1940, we can explore how ethnic differences across the whole range of educational attainments affect ethnic wages. Specifically, in regression analysis I control for years of education as well as for high school graduation, some college study, and college graduation.[9] The educational controls explained much of the ethnic wage inequality in each of the six cohorts we have been tracking; in every case, for example, the net impact of education exceeds the entire impact of geographic location on ethnic wage differences.

More illuminating is the fact that educational differentials help to explain the slide in relative wages for the Mexican cohort that entered the U. S. labor force around 1970. With education controlled, the Mexican cohort that entered the workforce in 1970 earned 84 to 85 percent of what the native whites were earning both at the start of their career and thirty years later. The drop in their standing over thirty years that we observed earlier—the slide from 70 percent to 54 percent of native white wages—is now seen to be explicable as the changing rewards to schooling. Moreover, the residual ethnic wage ratio of between .84 and .85 places them quite close to the SCEN situation in 1940: with their schooling taken into account, the 1876 to 1885 and 1886 to 1895 SCEN cohorts were respectively earning 86 percent and 82 percent of the native-white mean wage.[10]

The contemporary young cohort (twenty-five to thirty-four years of age in 2000) appears, for reasons we cannot explain, to suffer a modest additional handicap—earning some 78 percent of native white wages even after educational controls are imposed. Still, education does explain a considerable part of the ethnic inequality in this cohort too, raising the ethnic wage ratio from 58 percent to 78 percent. Thus, while we cannot fully explain all the differences in the wage-earning experience of these immigrant groups across a century by invoking the differences in formal schooling between them, we can explain a great deal.

The Role of Undocumented Status   One factor working against Mexican immigrant wages since at least the mid-1960s is that many have been undocumented workers—making it harder for them to obtain better-paying jobs and harder to demand improvements in working conditions (Massey, Durand, and Malone 2002). This status is one unambiguous difference between them and the SCEN.

The census and CPS datasets do not permit us to disentangle the impact of undocumented status from other problems the Mexicans face in the changing American wage structure. For one thing, we cannot distinguish the undocumented from other non-citizens, such as legal residents who hold green cards. Moreover, even if we choose to ignore this important distinction, we cannot meaningfully compare citizens and non-citizens in order to observe the economic value of citizenship. There is an element of self-selection involved in obtaining citizenship, involving initiative and attitudes that may well be relevant for economic success too. We will have to simply recall that some part of any Mexican wage handicap relative to native whites may be due to the disadvantages of undocumented status that many face. At the same time, this factor probably cannot explain the decline in the relative well-being of the Mexican cohort between 1970 and 2000, since it typified the individuals even at the start of that period. And indeed by its end some may have escaped undocumented status under the amnesty terms of the 1986 IRCA law, or by marrying a citizen (Massey, Durand, and Malone 2002).

IMMIGRANT WAGES AS SECOND-GENERATION ORIGINS

In terms of the long-run, the relative well-being of SCEN or Mexican immigrants compared to native whites is a measure of the family background from which the second generation emerges. It serves as a measure of how much economic support the immigrant family can provide its second-generation offspring. In order to restate our findings about immigrants in terms of the second generation, we need first to establish what years deserve most attention—recognizing that any choice of years is freezing a moving picture into a snapshot. A useful approach is to "freeze" the story at the points when successive second-generation cohorts reach fifteen, an age when critical choices about schooling and direction begin to be made.[11] Assuming that thirty is the fathers' average age when the second generation was born, the immigrant generation was about forty-five when the second generation was fifteen. And with these guidelines we can target the most relevant census years and age groups for this analysis, as shown in table 2.2.

The table focuses attention on second-generation birth cohorts who reached age fifteen in the decades centered on 1915, 1925, and 1935 for the SCEN and in 1985 for the Mexicans. Constructed in this way, comparisons catch the SCEN and Mexican immigrant families well into the periods in which the SCEN's condition improved and the Mexican's worsened. Consequently, the conclusion is that the Mexican relative launching position for the second generation is somewhat worse than was that of the SCEN. Nevertheless, with the exception of the youngest SCEN cohort,

Table 2.2   Ethnic Wage Ratios for Immigrants When Second Generation at Age Fifteen

Second Generation Birth Cohorts a	Second Generation at Age Fifteen b	Wage Ratios for Years in b		Wage Ratios (from Figure 2.2) e	Midpoint Estimates f
		Census Years c	Men of Age d		
1896–1905	1911–1920	1910	35–54	0.58⎱	0.63
		1920	35–54	0.67⎰	
1906–1915	1921–1930	1920	35–44	0.67⎱	0.69
		1940	55–64	0.71⎰	
1916–1925	1931–1940	1920	25–34	0.73⎱	0.72
		1940	45–54	0.71⎰	
1966–1975	1981–1990	1980	35–54	0.61⎱	0.60
		1990	35–54	0.59⎰	

Source: IPUMS datasets for 1910 to 1920, 1940 to 2000 censuses.
Note: Column e: ethnic wage ratios are means of ratios shown in figure 2.2—for most cells, a mean for 2 or 3 decennial age cohorts. Also, ratios from 1910 and 1920 are means of minimum and maximum estimates given in figure 2.2. Ratios for the 1980 and 1990 Mexicans in column e do not derive from figure 2.2; they were calculated here for Mexican men who had arrived by 1970.

these differences are fairly modest: only 3 to 9 percentage points separate the relevant SCEN and Mexican ratios (column f). Moreover, the youngest of the three relevant SCEN cohorts all reached age fifteen during the decade of the Great Depression, the impact of which is hard to factor in to this perspective based on wage ratios at specific times. Indeed, the depression also catches the middle SCEN cohort at ages fifteen through twenty-four.

Finally, the postwar expansion of the economy, and the relative gains of those in the lower half of the wage distribution during those years, probably came too late to effect the first-generation context in which the children of the next generation grew up. However, the two younger cohorts of the next generation were young enough to have enjoyed the effects of that expansion directly when they were adults themselves, having been between twenty-five and forty-four in 1950. Just as the perspective on the economic situation of families of origin does not capture the disadvantages of passing through a decade of depression, it does not capture the advantages of the postwar growth.

I concluded earlier that the contrast between the relative economic situation of young immigrants in 1910 and in 1970 does not show much if any advantage to immigrants in either period. The reformulated comparison, made at the time the next generation was about fifteen years old, shows a modest, but hardly drastic, advantage for the SCEN. This is the proper summary, I think for the second-generation of today on which we have data: those who were between twenty-five and thirty-four in 2000 and their parents, who were in the same age range in 1970. Yet the caveat mentioned before applies here too: if wage inequality continues to increase, the families of new Mexican immigrants arriving in 2000 will face a still-steeper climb than those who arrived in 1970.

MEETING THE COSTS OF AN EXTENDED EDUCATION FOR THE SECOND GENERATION   Part of our concern is that the children of Mexicans today face a job market in which an extended education, and most obviously graduation from a four-year college, is required for real success. How can that education be financed by labor-migrant parents? And if it cannot be obtained, how will the second generation escape poverty? And how can the hurdles facing present-day immigrants be compared to those of the past, when college enrollment was far less important? But several considerations reduce the pessimism implied by these questions. College graduation is not the only criterion for a helpful education; educational attainment is a continuum, in which every level involves economic returns greater than those at the next-lower level (at least between early high school and early graduate school, as discussed at length in chapter 4). Indeed, it is worth recalling that among today's native-white young adults, fewer than one-third graduate from a four-year college (as may be seen in table 3.3 and appendix table A.10). Lower-level attainments matter, and they can be obtained without incurring heavy tuition costs. American public education is free through high school, and a large part of the problem of second-generation Mexican schooling, as we shall see, concerns high school dropouts. Moreover, public community colleges are within geographic reach of much of the second-generation population, and their direct costs are on average much lower than four-year colleges and universities. Thus, large and remunerative upgrades in Mexican second-generation attainment would not involve education costs particularly greater than those the SCEN faced in its time.

True, the longest-educated third or quarter of the population were not college graduates in the days of the SCEN. And the economic payoffs resulting from being in the longest-educated third are greater today, although this should not be assumed; we return to that topic in the last chapter. So it is possible that both the costs and benefits of entering that highly educated circle may be greater today. Still, this formulation also suggests the possibility that today's greater benefits might be enough to pay off the greater costs. In any case, there is a more fundamental point about the past and present costs of educating the second generation that needs to be appreciated.

Expressed in constant dollars (dollars adjusted for cost of living) wages have grown dramatically over much of the twentieth century. Figure 2.3 shows the mean wage in constant dollars of the immigrant male cohorts we have been examining throughout the chapter. The SCEN improved their lot considerably over the life span, while the Mexicans' mean wage (in constant dollars) has fallen notably since 1970. This recent decline is not, of course, limited to Mexicans or even to low-skill workers, but is part of the deterioration affecting most groups below the top fifth of the income distribution. However, for us the crucial point is that, notwithstanding this important recent decline, the actual level of wages even in 2000 is far higher than it was in the early days of the twentieth century. Indeed, the real wage of the young Mexican immigrants of 2000 stands at about *three times* that of the young SCEN immigrants of 1910.

There is nothing numerically incompatible about this result and the gloomier assessments derived from the ethnic wage ratio: the native whites have also greatly improved their wages in constant dollars during the cen-

Figure 2.3   Real Wages of Immigrant Male Cohorts: SCEN and Mexican

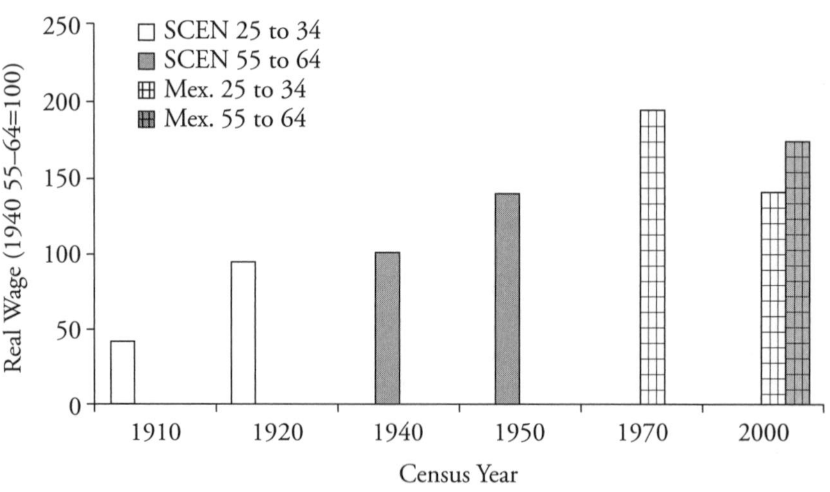

Source: IPUMS datasets for 1910 and 1920, 1940 to 1970, and 2000 censuses and U.S. Bureau of Labor Statistics (2005).

tury. For most purposes related to questions of economic assimilation and upward mobility, the ethnic wage ratio (the comparison to native whites in two periods) is our relevant measure. That measure, of course, implies that native whites can more easily fund their children's extended education than can Mexican immigrants. But we are also interested in whether the new educational job requirements and costs mean that the children of Mexican immigrants are blocked from the upward-mobility launching pad in some absolute sense that was not true in the past. To address this question, the appropriate comparison is between real costs of schooling and real wages then and now.

I cannot work out the result of all the factors here (another is the forgone earnings of late adolescents remaining in school). Moreover, to repeat, the change in real wages across the twentieth century does not erase the news that the ethnic wage ratio has worsened and will probably continue to worsen in the future. But it does mean a difference in living conditions for today's compared to yesterday's labor migrants—even if poverty is conceived of mostly in relative, not absolute, terms (relative to others in the same society). And one such difference in living standards that should be considered in further work is the costs and benefits of children's education. In the meantime, today's costs of college graduation cannot in itself prove that the second generation's educational ticket out of poverty is harder to come by than it was in the past.

CHAPTER THREE

SECOND-GENERATION SCHOOLING

LOW LEVELS of formal schooling among SCEN and Mexican immigrants, compared to that of the native whites of their times, account for much of their wage handicap. Would education pave the way for their children to escape from the bottom? This question directs our attention to second-generation schooling by focusing, first of the SCEN and then of the contemporary Mexican second generations—in each case relative to the children of native whites.

MISLEADING ANALYSES

However, before turning to these comparisons, I argue that two approaches to contemporary educational trends produce misleading findings. Both approaches have become widespread, the first in governmental reports on schooling and the second among social scientists.

HISPANIC EDUCATIONAL ATTAINMENT

Everything we know about the shifts from immigrant to second-generation status should suggest how misleading it is to speak of Hispanic or Mexican educational attainment in the United States today without taking account of the dramatic differences between immigrant and native Hispanics or Mexicans. Evidence of dramatic changes between immigrant and second-generation educational attainments is easy to come by. For example, in

IPUMS 2000 we can observe that only 56 percent of Mexican-origin men born between 1966 and 1975 completed high school—some 30 percentage points less than native black men in the same age group. However, more than three-fifths of these young Mexican-origin males are immigrants who came to this country with most or all of their education already behind them; and of these immigrant men only 40 percent had completed high school. Among the rest, 79 percent completed high school—about twice the immigrant rate. To say that 56 percent rather than 79 percent of a group are high school dropouts is to assign an extra one person in four to the social category at risk.

Is the point—that immigrants need to be distinguished from the native born in studying educational patterns—too obvious to be worth discussing? Before concluding, consider first that the U.S. Department of Education presents "race and ethnicity" data on educational attainment for those of Hispanic origin only in the way criticized here, that is, without distinguishing the native born from the foreign born.[1] In essence, such a presentation ignores huge generational differences in favor of treating people of a given origin group as one. This presentation probably arises out of an effort to present evidence on blacks and Hispanics in the same way: we do not attend to generational status of American blacks, why do so for Hispanics? But, of course, the overwhelming majority of blacks trace their American origins back countless generations, and nothing would be gained by trying to distinguish among late-generation descendants—whereas a majority of American Hispanics are now first generation or young second generation.[2]

A future generation may well look back on the figures that the Department of Education publishes today in the way that we look back today on the crude figures found in early twentieth-century government reports that described European groups primarily in terms of the race or people to which they belonged, and privileged that classification over other explanatory factors, such as generational status or class origin when explaining school attainments of that era (Hourwich 1912; Handlin 1957; Gerstle 2001; Perlmann 2001a).

A more subtle point about educational attainment and generational standing involves distinctions among the Americans born of Mexican origin. This latter grouping is itself made up of generational groups that differ in educational attainments—second, third, and later generational groups, the last including all those who have claimed Mexican origin, however many generations back their roots in Mexico may lie. We really want to know mostly about the children of immigrants, especially the children of immigrants born in the United States. The decennial census does not help to encourage the proper distinctions either, because it no longer asks respondents to report their parents' birthplaces. At least, however, the census does distinguish between the immigrants and the native born.

TODAY'S THIRD AND LATER GENERATIONS

Distinguishing people by recent generational standing, especially by immigrant versus second generation, matters. It is also crucial to set different generations within historical context. Consider comparisons of second- versus third- and later-generation progress—in educational or economic attainment, and in the same year and age group. Table 3.1 presents an example. Often the attainments of the third and later generations do not look much different from those of the second, at least when compared to the difference between the second and the immigrant generations (all in the same year and age group). These figures are then used to predict the future well-being of a third-generation group as yet unborn, or at any rate quite young: the children of today's second generation. The assumption is that this future third generation's attainment will be roughly identical to that of today's third generation. And the conclusion is that, somehow, progress will stall in the second generation: that future third generation will not much outdistance its parents, just as today's do not much outdistance today's second generation. Thus, for example, in the young-adult cohort today, Mexican immigrant men average 9.35 years of schooling, the second generation 12.47 years, and the third and later generation 12.52 years. Patterns for women are very similar (see table 3.1, younger age cohort). Second-generation educational attainment exceeded immigrant educational attainment by more than three years, while third or later hardly exceeded second-generation at all.

There are three features of this sort of analysis that deserve comment. First, in contemporary America, it is no doubt true that the second generation generally outruns the first by much more than the third outruns the second—at least in the educational attainment of labor migrants, as opposed to immigrant professionals, for example. The labor migrants come with educational attainments roughly typical of their social position in the country of origin. Their American-schooled children tend to differ from the American norm by far less—notwithstanding ethnic differences in second-generational schooling that may be relatively large compared to American-born groups. There is nothing unique to contemporary immigrants, or to nonwhite labor migrants, in this pattern, and the pattern suggests the rapid degree of second-generation catch-up, not some sort of glass ceiling thereafter.

Second, we cannot assume that the attainments of the future third generation will be like those of present third and later generation. What is more revealing, surely, is to compare the historical shift from the preceding second-generation to the contemporary third generation. That shift may be something of a predictor of the shift from the present second to the future third generation attainments. The point can be appreciated by considering the

Table 3.1   Educational Attainment Among Selected Cohorts Circa 2000

	Years of Schooling Completed (Group Means)	
Selected Origin Groups	Cohort Born 1936 to 1945	Cohort Born 1966 to 1975
Men		
Mexican		
Immigrants	7.21	9.35
Second generation	11.10	12.47
Third+ generation	10.55	12.52
Others		
NWNP	13.37	13.65
NBlkNP	11.73	12.78
All in cohort	13.04	13.19
Women		
Mexican		
Immigrants	6.43	9.63
Second generation	10.41	12.68
Third+ generation	10.57	12.52
Others		
NWNP	12.91	13.84
NBlkNP	12.09	12.97
All in cohort	12.53	13.42

Rearranging the crucial figures for greater conceptual clarity (men only)

Preceding Generation (Born 1936 to 1945)		Produces	Current Generation	
Immigrant	7.21	→	Second generation	12.47
Second generation	11.10 ⎫	→	Third or later generation	12.52
Third and later generation	10.55 ⎭			

Source: 1998 to 2001 CPS datasets.

Note: Immigrant = Mexican-born; second generation = U.S.-born, to a Mexican-born parent; third+ generation = U.S.-born to two U.S.-born parents, Mexican origin reported; NWNP = native white of native parentage, no Mexican origins; NBlkNP = native black of native parentage, no Mexican origins; All in birth cohort: includes also groups not shown. The standard deviation for years of education: older men 3.51, older women 3.07; younger men 2.77, younger women 2.68.

graphic display at the bottom of table 3.1. The appropriate conclusion one might hazard about the future should be drawn from the attainments linked by the arrows. The inappropriate conclusion would be to focus only on the current cohort, and link the current second-generation outcomes to the current later generation outcomes.[3] The appropriate comparison suggests an improvement of at least 1.42 years of schooling (from the range of 10.55 to 11.10 to 12.52); the inappropriate comparison suggests an improvement of .05 years of schooling (from 12.47 to 12.52). In other words, by focusing on the current generation only, we ignore the difference in family origins from which the present generation sprang compared to the family origins from which the next generation will come—specifically the differences in parental education. Yet if there is a staple finding in the sociology of education it is that parental schooling is positively correlated with children's.[4]

Third, a more general formulation of the second observation is that when we juxtapose second and third and later generations of people in the same birth cohort, we are juxtaposing people whose family histories intersect the broader history of the Mexican American people in very different ways. Earlier arrivals—the grandparents and great-grandparents of today's third and later generation Mexican Americans—grew up under radically different conditions in the United States and in Mexico than exist today. And in particular, the history of Mexican American standing in the Southwest, where the group was until recently so highly concentrated, shares elements of social, legal, and educational discrimination with the history of blacks in the South. These conditions simply do not exist any longer, whatever else one may care to argue about the state of group relations today. To ignore all this is to ignore the intersection of generational standing and historical development: the Mexican second generation born between 1921 and 1930 grew up in very different conditions than the Mexican second generation born between 1971 and 1980.[5]

SCHOOLING THEN AND NOW

In the early decades of the twentieth century, while huge numbers of second-generation Italians and Poles were growing up in the North, much smaller but still significant numbers of second-generation Mexicans were growing up in the Southwest. Their Mexican-immigrant parents had arrived with less education than the SCEN immigrants (figure 3.1 shows the pattern for men; it was similar for women). Children's school attainments reflect those of their parents; so we might expect to find that there was some difference in schooling between the second-generation SCEN and Mexicans as well.

However, the ethnic educational differences that we do find are far too large to be explained as a residue of educational differences among the im-

Figure 3.1   Men's Education: Immigrants Versus Natives

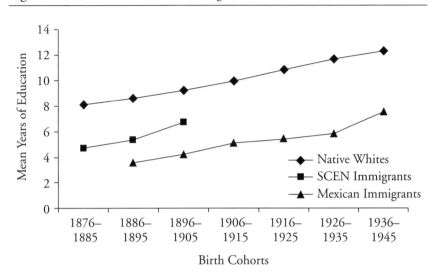

Source: IPUMS datasets for 1940 to 1970.
Note: Data on attainment are unavailable before 1940, and for some cohorts much larger samples are available from 1960 to 1970 than from 1940 to 1950. So education data for the birth cohorts 1876 to 1885, 1886 to 1905, 1906 to 1925, and 1926 to 1945 were drawn when respondents were respectively fifty-five to sixty-four, forty-five to sixty-four, twenty-five to forty-four and twenty-five to thirty-four years of age. This selection method introduces a source of distortion because responses about eduational attainment tend to rise modestly with age.

migrant parents (figure 3.2, again shown for men and similar for women). The educational attainment of the second-generation SCEN appears very similar indeed to the educational attainment of the children of native whites; and in fact, by the 1930s, when the 1916 to 1925 birth cohort was reaching high school, the SCEN second generation erased the educational gap between themselves and the native whites of native parentage (NWNP). By contrast, that era's Mexican second generation continued to lag far behind other groups in schooling. A small part of this difference between the SCEN and the Mexicans of the early twentieth century is due to the difference between educational standards in northern urban areas and southwestern rural areas, especially for the families of agricultural workers.[6] But most of the deficit in Mexican schooling must be explained in other terms. Whatever the animosity towards the SCEN children by the natives of the Northeast, discrimination against Mexicans in the Southwest was incomparably more institutionalized, and hence systematic. Indeed, as I have already

Figure 3.2   Men's Education: Second Generation Versus Natives

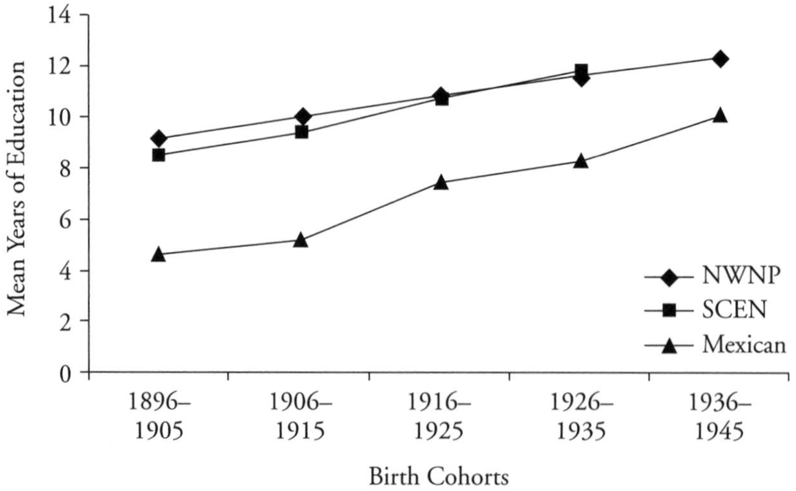

Source: IPUMS datasets for 1940 to 1970.

stressed, Mexican American schooling in that era and region should not be thought of in the context of schooling for immigrants in the North, but in the context of schooling for blacks in the South (Grebler, Moore, and Guzman 1970, 155–8; Cortes 1980, 709; Olneck and Lazerson 1980, 313–14).

We are sure to find that Mexican American educational attainment today is far closer to that of other Americans than it was in 1930. But this conclusion will take us only so far; for if the starting point is a Mexican educational handicap similar to the one Southern blacks carried in 1930, it will hardly suffice to say that there has been improvement since then. If our question is whether the Mexican second generation of today is joining the mainstream, we need a more meaningful measure of educational progress. And that measure is to compare educational attainments among today's young second-generation Mexican American adults to those of their earlier SCEN counterparts—in each case relative to native-white groups.

In other words, we now turn the method we have just used to compare the relative well-being of immigrant fathers to the education of the next generation. Earlier we compared immigrants to native whites. Here we would ideally compare the children of immigrants to those of native whites. We can do so for the earlier period, when the SCEN second generation are compared to the children of native whites, the native whites of native parentage (NWNP). However, because the 2000 census does not include information on parental birthplace, we are limited to comparing the children of Mexican immigrants to all native whites. CPS data, which does include this information, confirms that this compromise in defining the native-white comparison group for 2000 makes virtually no difference to results. However, the absence of parental birthplace information poses a larger challenge, to which we now turn.

A PROXY FOR THE TRUE SECOND GENERATION: THE 1.53 GROUP

Because the 2000 census does not provide parental birthplace information, we cannot identify the second generation.[7] For this reason, many researchers have relied instead on the Current Population Survey (CPS), another federal survey which does include the parental birthplace questions. But the CPS has its own disadvantages, of which size is key. CPS datasets from five years of surveys (1998 to 2001) include fewer than two hundred Mexican American wage-earning men, twenty-five to thirty-four years of age. While I have worked extensively with the CPS data in connection with this study, virtually all of the evidence on the contemporary Mexican Americans that I present in the text rests instead on a novel research strategy: I identify and study a proxy group for the true second generation, namely those people born in Mexico and brought to the United States before their third birthday.

My strategy here is similar to another one used in numerous studies: reliance on the 1.5 generation, those brought to the United States before their twelfth birthday. However, my much more stringent selection criterion makes a great difference. Those arriving when they are younger than three will have virtually no memories of Mexican life and indeed have developed most language skills after immigrating to the United States. By contrast, the criterion of the twelfth birthday, used in work on the 1.5 generation, creates a far more heterogeneous group (Rumbaut 1999, n5; Oropesa and Landale 1997). Those brought to a new country between the ages of six and twelve can be expected to have faced the special problems of school adjustment—which restricts the value of studying that group. To distinguish this new research strategy from the older method, I have dubbed the proxy group the 1.53 group (although the group is similar to another that Rumbaut has suggested: those arriving before the age of five; Rumbaut 1999, n.5). Because the sample in the 2000 census includes fully 6 percent of all Americans, the 1.53 group is some ten times as large as the true second generation found in the CPS dataset and therefore permits much richer analysis. The method I propose here is made possible by a small change in the 2000 census. For the first time since 1920, the question asked of immigrants as to when they arrived in the United States requires an exact answer for year of arrival.

Just how good a proxy for the unmixed second generation is the 1.53 group? The families of the true second-generation group will have, on average, lived longer in the United States. Thus when a given child is fifteen years old, the parents of the 1.53 group member have been in the United States for twelve to fifteen years (from the time the child was younger than three), and the parents of the true second generation have been in the United States for at least fifteen (from a time before the child was born).[8] Both types of families would have long since surmounted the early challenges of arrival in a new country; but socioeconomic differences related to length of residence might remain. Moreover, there is a more subtle reason why the parents of the 1.53 group might differ from those of the true second generation. The fact of having come with a child may indicate something distinct about these parents. For example, they may have been more likely to have married in Mexico and hence may be older, or at least more settled as a family. So too, the families of the 1.53 group may have been more likely to maintain a pattern of back-and-forth movement between the United States and Mexico. The appendix exploits the data available to investigate the adequacy of the proxy. The 2000 census permits a comparison of the families in which the true second generation and members of the 1.53 group are growing up. The parents from these two types of families do not differ appreciably in educational attainment. Generally, however, the families of the true second generation are somewhat better off economically than the families of the 1.53 group members, as longer residence would lead us to expect. Fewer of the second generation are therefore below the poverty line, more own their own home, and total family incomes are on average 11 percent higher. Most important for us is how much the moderately better economic situation of the parents affects the children. Whereas we would expect intergenerational transmission to favor the true second generation, the magnitudes of the differences and the imperfect nature of the transmission would also lead us to expect relatively small differences in the next generation's standing. And that is more or less what we do find—when we make some basic comparisons between adults of the 1.53 group in the census and adults of the true second generation in the CPS.

The census 1.53 group typically seem to have received modestly less schooling than the CPS true second generation, perhaps .3 to .5 of a year's worth (see appendix). On the other hand, the 1.53 group and the true second generation are remarkably alike in early career outcomes (percent in the full-time labor force and mean earnings), particularly among the men. The modestly greater educational differences, then, do not appear to have translated into strong earnings differences in early careers. On the whole, so long as we take into account the likelihood that true second-generation educational outcomes are modestly better than those in the 1.53 group, we can gain a great deal by the strategy of exploiting the 1.53 group to learn about the second generation.

Citizenship   The true second-generation members have one clear advantage over the proxy group: they are citizens by birth. This difference cannot be an overwhelming advantage, however. If it were, the 1.53 group would be a much poorer proxy than it turns out to be. Nevertheless, just as clearly, citizenship must be of some advantage to the true second generation. Still, it does not follow that we should limit our proxy group to 1.53 group members who have attained citizenship—because a certain self-selection is involved in arranging for citizenship. This may involve personality factors, such as taking initiative and savvy in dealing with the American bureaucracy or aspects of social origin, such as having parents whose mastery of English was well above the average for Mexican immigrants. There is ample evidence even in the census data that self-selection is involved in acquisition of citizenship (see appendix). So, while those born with citizenship profit from it, focusing on those who made successful efforts to acquire citizenship does not refine our proxy but distorts it.

SCEN Then, Mexicans Now

To recapitulate, the early twentieth-century patterns of Mexican American education in the Southwest show a group much more disadvantaged in education than the SCEN in the North, especially in the second generation; and the narrative record tells us that this story is wrapped up in institutional discrimination and in the obvious social structural differences between urban industrial and rural agricultural wage workers. The implication of these findings is that it will not be very illuminating to compare Mexican American progress today to that in the first half of the twentieth century. The group was so constrained then that progress will signify little if our concern is with full equality. For this reason, the better-formulated comparison is between Mexican second-generation educational attainment today and SCEN in the past. Our proxy for the contemporary second-generation Mexicans is the 1.53 group in the census of 2000.

Measuring Ethnic Educational Differences Across Historical Periods   As in chapter 2, the ethnic differences are best presented after being adjusted for region, metro status, and individual year of age within the birth cohort. We also need some way to take into account shifts in the mean and distribution of years of schooling over time. In the case of wages, we took account of shifting means by comparing ratios of mean wages and discussed the significance of a shifting wage structure. Turning our attention to educational attainment, we could again rely on the ratio of mean ethnic attainments—in this case, mean grades of schooling completed. However, in studies of schooling such a ratio would be quite unfamiliar, and for good reason—given the narrower distribution of years of schooling than of dollars of earnings, as well as the income advantages of an additional year of college compared to an additional year of high school. Instead, I rely here on the standardized difference in mean grades of schooling completed. First, the differences between the second generation and the native-white group are computed, in terms of mean grades of education completed, after controlling for region, metro status, and age. The ethnic difference in means is then divided by the standard deviation of grades of schooling completed for the entire birth cohort.

We can pause a moment to return to the contrast we first explored, between Mexicans then and now (figures 3.3 and 3.4). The Mexican second

Figure 3.3   First- to Second-Generation Catch-Up: SCEN and Mexican Men

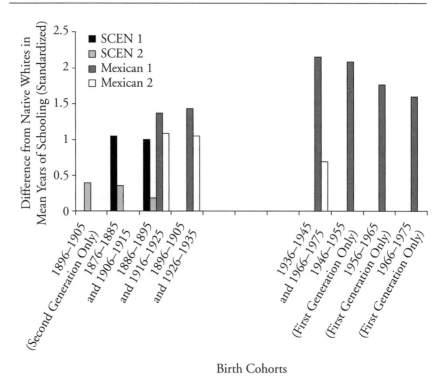

Source: IPUMS datasets for 1940 to 1970, and 2000 censuses.
Note: See note to figure 3.4.

Figure 3.4   First- to Second-Generation Catch-Up: SCEN and Mexican Women

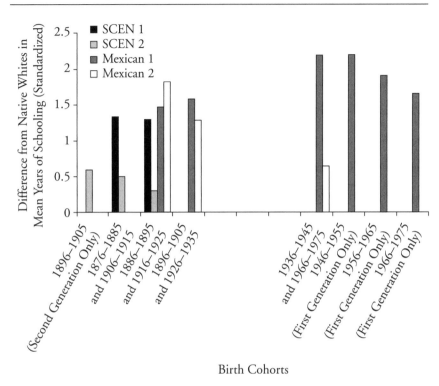

Source: IPUMS datasets for 1940 to 1970, and 2000 censuses.

Notes: Birth cohorts shown together are thirty years apart, approximating first and second generations. Standardized ethnic difference in educational attainment: grade of schooling attained was regressed on ethnic dummy variables, age (continuous var.), region, and metro status. Coefficient on ethnic dummy variable for SCEN (or Mexican) is ethnic difference in mean education. The coefficient was then divided by the standard deviation for grades of schooling completed in the male or female birth cohort. The 1936 to 1945 Mexican cohort: see note to figure 3.1 on censuses used for each cohort. However, for figures 3.3 and 3.4, the data for the 1936 to 1945 birth cohort were drawn from the 2000 (rather than 1970) census—so that all the evidence on recent Mexican cohorts comes from Census 2000. Based on the 1970 data, the 1936 to 1945 Mexican immigrant columns (male and female) would be about half a standard deviation lower than shown above, but still well above the earlier SCEN immigrant levels. (On discontinuities in education data across recent censuses, see also appendix and Mare 1995.) Also for comparability with later Mexican cohorts, the 1936 to 1945 immigrant cohort was not limited to Mexicans resident in the United States since 1970 because most parents of the second-generation members probably were. Imposing that limitation would reduce the standardized difference to 1.91 and 1.85 for men and women respectively.

generation today is able to close much more of the educational attainment gap than past Mexican second generations. Indeed, in one of the early cohorts, the Mexican women actually lost ground across the two generations relative to the native whites.

The more meaningful comparison for today's Mexicans is therefore to yesterday's SCEN. That comparison is conditioned by the situation of the parents; the Mexican immigrant men lag 2.15 standard deviations behind the native whites in years of schooling, whereas their SCEN counterparts lagged only one standard deviation behind. The younger Mexican immigrants in 2000 appear to differ from native whites of the same age by notably less, but the gap remaining even in the youngest cohort is still greater than any the SCEN experienced, about 50 percent larger for men.

Second-generation comparisons are best made separately for men and women. For second-generation Mexican men today, the gap between them and native whites is greater than it was for the SCEN second generation then—.69 standard deviations of years of education compared to between .39 and .18 standard deviations across three cohorts of SCEN men. For women, in the two earlier SCEN cohorts, we do find a situation roughly comparable to that of today's Mexicans—an ethnic gap of .59 to .50 standard deviations for the SCEN against .64 for the Mexicans today (see figures 3.3 and 3.4).

In terms of second-generation success in overcoming first-generation educational deficits, the picture is mixed. We have complete data for both generations on only two SCEN birth cohorts. In relative terms, the earlier SCEN second-generation cohort and the current Mexican 1.53 group fared about the same. Those SCEN second-generation men narrowed the education gap from 1.04 to .35 standard deviations, and the Mexican 1.53 group narrowed it from 2.15 to .69. Among women, the ethnic comparison is similar, and slightly more favorable to the Mexicans. However, the next SCEN birth cohort was notably more successful in wiping out the gap, reducing it from .99 standard deviations in the first generation to .18 in the second. Thus the Mexican relative experience may be within the range of at least some of the SCEN cohorts in terms of educational catch-up within a generation, but it is the absolute educational difference from native whites that will matter for second-generation wages—and that gap is clearly larger for the Mexicans than it was for most SCEN cohorts, especially among men.

Parental educational levels help explain children's, of course, but much of the literature on second-generation schooling revolves instead around the low level of economic well-being of the Mexican or SCEN immigrant families as a source for second-generation educational deficits. Can the economic standings of the first generation adequately explain the next generation's educational outcome? In chapter 2, I stressed that the economic well-being in the relevant immigrant cohorts of 1910 and 1970 differed far less than had been supposed; nevertheless, they did differ, particularly by the time the next generation was into adolescence. The question now is whether the SCEN and Mexican immigrant wage situation differed enough to account for the extent to which their children's relative educational positions differ.

A clear-cut conclusion is not possible; but the magnitudes do point toward a greater educational handicap today, even after the fathers' economic handicap has been taken into account. Table 2.2 showed the SCEN and Mexican fathers' wages as a percentage of native-white wages when their sons were about fifteen; we can also express the fathers' wages in terms of a standardized difference—the difference in the logged mean wage in each ethnic group divided by the standard deviation of logged wages (table 3.2). That recasting of the ethnic wage differences, along with the ethnic educational differences measured earlier, gives us both first-generation wage and second-generation education expressed as standardized differences from native-white levels. The most useful comparison is between the middle SCEN cohort and the Mexican cohort, for several reasons. The youngest SCEN cohort enjoyed a far lower educational handicap than the other cohorts. We can speculate about why this was so, but the point is that any similarity between the SCEN and Mexican educational situations must be sought in the two earlier SCEN cohorts.[9] These two differ little in the extent of their educational handicap, but by focusing on the middle cohort we avoid some complications regarding wages before 1940.[10]

The upshot is that in our most useful comparison, an SCEN wage handicap of .55 is associated with an SCEN next-generation educational handicap of .35 standard deviations, or an increase of .35/.55 = .64 of a standard deviation in educational handicap for each standard deviation increase in fathers' wage handicap. We can apply this association to the Mexican wage handicap of .78 (midpoint of .76 and .80 for earlier and later years)—assuming, of course, that the association between fathers' wage handicap and sons' schooling is linear. The Mexican wage handicap is .23 standard deviations larger than the SCEN wage handicap (.78 − .55 = .23). So we would expect by the same association of first- and second-generation handicaps found among the SCEN, that the Mexican second-generation educational handicap would be about .23 x .64 higher than the SCEN educational handicap, or a predicted Mexican educational handicap of .50 standard deviations of education (.35 + .23 × .64). In fact, we find .69 standard deviations; put differently, instead of a predicted increment of .15 over the SCEN handicap, we observe one of .34. Thus, more than the fathers' wages seem to be operating in creating the differences between the relatively greater educational handicaps of Mexicans versus SCEN second generations. Or at least this is the tentative conclusion if we can trust such a method and all the estimations—including, besides those mentioned, the difficulties of measuring grades of schooling across changing census defini-

Table 3.2   Immigrant Generation's Wages and Second-Generation Schooling

| | Immigrant Wage Handicap | | | | | | | |
| | Difference from NW in Logged Weekly Wages a | | Standard Deviation of Logged Weekly Wages b | | Immigrants' Wage Handicap in Standard Deviations (Column a/Column b) c | | Next Generation's Handicap, in Educational Attainment Expressed in Standard Deviations | |
Immigrant Birth Cohorts, Observed in Census Years	Earlier Year	Later Year	Earlier Year	Later Year	Earlier Year	Later Year	Cohort	Handicap d
SCEN 1866–1875 in 1910 and 1920	0.54	0.40	0.95	0.73	0.57	0.55	1896–1905	0.39
SCEN 1876–1885 in 1920 and 1940	0.40	0.34	0.67	0.68	0.59	0.50	1906–1915	0.35
SCEN 1886–1895 in 1920 and 1940	0.31	0.34	0.63	0.64	0.49	0.53	1916–1925	0.18
Mexican 1936–1945 in 1980 and 1990	0.50	0.53	0.66	0.67	0.76	0.80	1966–1975	0.69

Source: IPUMS datasets for 1910 to 1920 and 1940 to 2000 censuses.
Notes: Column a: See notes to table 2.2. Ratios there are presented as log point differences here. Column b: Standard deviations for 1910 and 1920 were estimated from the occupational wage for that year modified by the following ratio observed in the 1940 census data: [standard deviation of the individual-level wage]/[standard deviation of the occupational wage]. On occupational wage see appendix.

tions of educational attainment and of estimating true second-generation Mexican educational attainment from the Mexican 1.53 group attainment, as discussed.

We have already seen two possible factors that could explain some of the greater educational handicap of the second-generation Mexicans. One is the undocumented status of many Mexican parents; this status may affect their children's schooling directly, and not merely through the wage level of the fathers. Thus, undocumented parents may feel unsafe contacting their children's teachers. Also, the American-born children of undocumented workers, although citizens themselves, may feel they endanger their parents if they seek economic or other support that could focus the attention of the authorities on their families. A second factor that could be influencing Mexican children's schooling, over and above the father's wage, is the father's educational handicap, which was greater than the SCEN father's educational handicap. And so the news that the Mexican immigrant educational handicap has been declining across recent birth cohorts suggests that the parallel second-generation handicap might also decline moderately across the coming decennial birth cohorts.[11]

Still, the bottom line here is that even if the dynamics creating much or even all of that second-generation handicap today are historically familiar, the result is a moderately greater educational deficit suffered by the Mexican group than by its SCEN counterpart in the past. And, once in the labor force, it will not help the Mexicans that the same processes that created their educational deficit also operated in the past to create somewhat smaller educational handicaps.

A SECOND MEASURE OF ETHNIC EDUCATIONAL DIFFERENCES ACROSS HISTORICAL PERIODS   The measures just discussed, while probably the best way to summarize ethnic differences decades apart, does not give much of a feel for how people were passing through the system. Here instead we highlight the proportion of young people in each group who reach crucial plateaus of educational attainment—high school graduation then and college graduation now. I have focused on birth cohorts in which about the same proportion of the native-white group was reaching this educational plateau in each period—30 percent of the men and 33 percent of the women completing college today, 28 percent and 35 percent respectively completing high school then (table 3.3). Focusing the comparison this way means that the educational plateau had about the same meaning in terms of social selectivity: about a third of the native-white group reached it. The cohorts that meet these criteria are the 1896 to 1905 birth cohort then (our earliest second-generation birth cohort) and the 1966 to 1975 birth cohort now.

Table 3.3   Levels of Schooling: Selected Groups and Cohorts

Then Cohort	Education	Sex	Ethnic Groups	Percentage Graduating	Odds Ratios: SCEN/NWNP	
					Observed	With Controls
1896 to 1905	High school	Men	NWNP	28		
			SCEN second generation	18	0.56	0.43
		Women	NWNP	35		
			SCEN second generation	15	0.33	0.23

Now Cohort	Education	Sex	Ethnic Groups	Percentage Graduating	Odds Ratios: Mexican 1.53/NW	
					Observed	With Controls
1966 to 1975	College	Men	NW	30		
			Mexican 1.53	9	0.23	0.20
		Women	NW	33		
			Mexican 1.53	12	0.28	0.23

Source: IPUMS datasets for 1950 to 1960 and 2000 censuses.
Note: Odds ratios show the odds that an SCEN (or Mexican) second-generation member completed the school level relative to the odds that a person in the native-white comparison group (NWNP then or NW now) did so. The "observed" odds ratio summarizes the percentages at left; for example: $(.09/(1.00-.09)/(.30/(1-.30)) = .23$. The odds ratio "with controls" is the exponentiated logit regression coefficient from a model that includes age (continuous var.), region, and metro status.

In both periods, the second-generation boys and girls lagged far behind the native-white groups. Within that punishing context, the SCEN men were more advantaged than the Mexicans now: 18 percent reaching the educational plateau then, 9 percent now. However, among women the ethnic contrast then was somewhat more extreme than it was among men, whereas today the reverse is true. The result is that, especially with controls imposed, the historical comparison shows a rough equality of condition for the second-generation women then and now (odds ratios for graduation .23 then and now), but a worse situation today for the second generation men (.43 then, .20 now). This finding confirms the comparison of the cohorts' standardized mean attainments presented earlier (from figures 3.3 and 3.4; standardized difference in ethnic means, with controls—women, .50 then .59 now; men, .39 then .69 now).[12]

HIGH SCHOOL DROPOUT AND OTHER YOUNG-ADULT RISKS: MEXICANS AND BLACKS TODAY

We now highlight the serious gaps between Mexican American and native-white educational attainments today, and then explore whether these gaps are best understood as part of a general pattern of socially risky behavior that is associated, especially in the segmented assimilation literature, with a subculture of a poor, disaffected racial minorities in the United States. To make the case that this way of viewing Mexican American schooling does not appear to be correct, I shift the focus from second generations then and now to a comparison of the Mexican American 1.53 group and native blacks—for both educational attainment and for these other socially risky behaviors for young adults. These behaviors include teen pregnancy, single motherhood, low labor-force attachment, male institutionalization, and missing (possibly dead) men. I argue that the rates for these behaviors among native blacks are distinctively high, as are black rates of high school dropout. By contrast, Mexican American rates of high school dropout are alarmingly high, much higher than black rates, but involvement in the other socially risky behaviors mentioned are far less common among Mexican Americans than among blacks. Consequently we do not need an explanation for Mexican American educational patterns that places them in the context of a wider complex of socially risky behaviors, growing out of a disaffected racial minority's perspective on their world. Instead, we need, and can find, other explanatory frameworks. In making this case, my point is not to argue about whether Mexican American young adults will tell interviewers that they encounter racism, or that their life chances are poor—perhaps they do tell interviewers such things. My point is that such interview results would be irrelevant here—either because they do not in fact reflect a culture of disaffection, or because that culture of disaffection does not in fact produce the social behaviors predicted from it.

To set the discussion in as wide a context as possible, I present evidence on several subgroups of Mexican American young adults, defined by generation. I distinguish conceptually among three groups in the 2000 census—immigrant (those who arrived at age 6 or later), the 1.56 group (brought between their third and sixth birthdays, an intermediate group) and the 1.53 group (the proxy for the unmixed true second generation). I also present results for the U.S. born of Mexican origin, a group that includes within it three subgroups of quite different origins: the unmixed (true) second generation, the mixed second generation, and the third or later generation. Unfortunately, these three subgroups cannot be distinguished from each other in the census (see appendix table A.4). We know from the CPS, which does allow us to break out these three groups, that five-eighths of the U.S. born of Mexican origins are in fact in the third or later generation; among the rest, the unmixed second generation are somewhat more prevalent than the mixed second generation (appendix table A.5). For comparison purposes, I also present each measure for native whites and native blacks (who reported no Mexican ancestry).

HIGH SCHOOL DROPOUT RATES

The children of Mexican immigrants drop out of high school at very high rates, and this pattern is very important for later wage earning (figures 3.5 and 3.6). True, I argued earlier that misleading approaches to the evidence were leading to mistaken claims about the Hispanic or Mexican educational gap. However, it does not follow that there are no well-founded grounds for concern. By way of a benchmark consider that 9 percent of native-white young men and close to twice that rate of native black men (16 percent) left school without a high school diploma. For the 1.53 group of Mexican American men, the rate was 33 percent—twice the black rate. The situation is slightly muted among young adult women, but only slightly.

I have actually adjusted downwards the high school dropout rates for all groups observed in the 2000 census, and the adjustment makes the ethnic differences in high school dropout rates smaller than they are in the unadjusted data. The reasons for the adjustment are discussed in detail in the appendix. Briefly, the 2000 census gave respondents two choices relevant to high school completion: first, "completed twelfth grade but did not receive a diploma" and, second, "high school graduate." Comparisons with CPS data suggest that higher proportions of nonwhite ethnic groups than native whites misread the question, inadvertently choosing the first response when the second was correct. By contrast, the CPS was administered by trained interviewers.

Figure 3.5   Educational Attainment in 2000: Men 25 to 34, by Origin

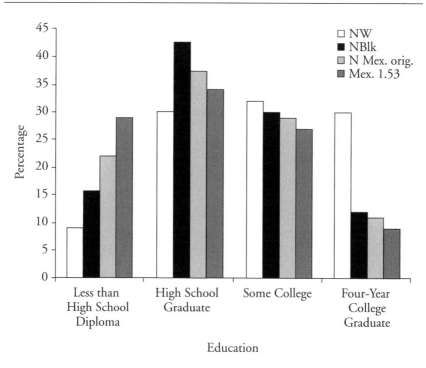

Source: IPUMS datasets for 2000 census and 1998 to 2001 CPS datasets.
Note: See note to figure 3.6.

Also, the true (unmixed) Mexican second generation probably enjoys somewhat higher high school graduation rates (whether adjusted or observed) than the 1.53 group proxy does. Nevertheless, this consideration is but a small source for optimism; the CPS datasets, in which we can identify the true group, shows quite similar dropout rates for the same cohorts (appendix table A.10). Among men, for example, the CPS figures are: native whites 7 percent, native blacks 10 percent and Mexican second generation 23 percent; a reasonable guess is that at least one in four (perhaps 25 percent to 28 percent) of the true Mexican second-generation men in the census sample did not complete high school.[13] The rates for the U.S. born of Mexican origin fall about midway between those for blacks and the Mexican 1.53 group. I discussed the issue of interpreting patterns such as these at the beginning of the chapter and will return to them again later.

The crucial issue for the Mexican 1.53 group, compared to blacks in par-

Figure 3.6   Educational Attainment in 2000: Women 25 to 34, by Origin

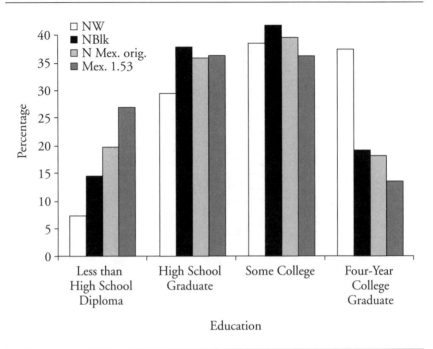

Source: IPUMS datasets for 2000 census and 1998 to 2001 CPS datasets (for adjustment to census data described below).

Note: Based on adjusted educational attainments. Unadjusted figures would reveal higher rates of high school dropout for Mexican 1.53 group. See text and appendix. NW = native white; NBlk = native black; N Mex. orig. = U.S.-born reporting Mexican origin; Mex. 1.53 = Mexican 1.53 group. For group definitions see table A.4.

ticular, concerns high school dropout rates. If we limit attention to the group that receives a high school diploma—the large majority in every group—the Mexicans differ little from the blacks in attainment (figures 3.7 and 3.8). In particular, about equal proportions of Mexican 1.53 group and black male high school graduates go on to graduate from four-year colleges; among women there is but a modest difference. Indeed, the striking difference among high school graduates is not between Mexicans and all others but between Mexicans and blacks on the one hand and native whites on the other.

If more Mexican Americans graduated from high school, some of that additional number would also surely continue through college. However, it is important to remember that most young people today—including nearly two-thirds of native whites—do not complete a four-year college. More-

Figure 3.7　　Educational Attainment of High School Graduates in 2000:
Men 25 to 34, by Origin

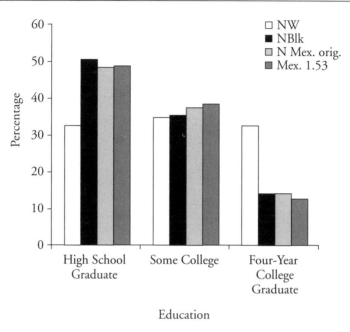

Source: IPUMS datasets for 2000 census and 1998 to 2001 CPS datasets (for adjustment to census data described below).
Note: Based on adjusted educational attainments. Unadjusted figures would reveal higher rates of high school dropout for Mexican 1.53 group. See text and appendix. NW = native white; NBlk = native black; N Mex. orig. = U.S.-born reporting Mexican origin; Mex. 1.53 = Mexican 1.53 group. For group definitions see table A.4.

over, for all the importance of collegiate education, simply completing high school does matter in America. Quite apart from what greater mastery of literacy means for political participation in a republic, and for general mastery over the environment, secondary school completion does matter in the job market, a theme we will take up in the next chapter. Some might argue that the payoffs to high school completion may be important to native whites but not to Mexican Americans. Mexican American dropouts, especially the men, might thus be making choices about the education they need for the job market based on an awareness of discriminatory patterns in hiring or of the jobs most readily available to them through ethnic networks. We will return to this issue at the end of the next chapter, when

Figure 3.8   Educational Attainment of High School Graduates in 2000: Women 25 to 34, by Origin

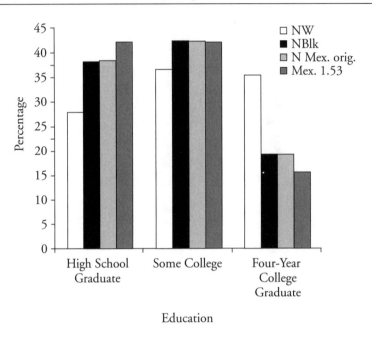

Source and note: See figure 3.6.

discussing income returns to schooling. Suffice it to say here that there is a wide range of jobs for which a high school diploma still helps.

The Polish and Italian men of the earlier second generation also tended to leave school earlier than the sons of the native whites of their time. In this sense, the Mexican Americans of today do resemble those groups. But as we saw earlier, the pattern of early school leaving is more extreme in relative terms today than it was, at least among the men. And even if the pattern of early school leaving were not more extreme, its implications for work today may well be more so than before.

DROPOUT RATES IN CONTEXT

Elevated high school dropout rates are a serious warning sign that upward mobility in future years may well be restricted for the group. For this reason, Mexican American dropout rates should bring to mind the warnings of the segmented assimilation hypothesis: that an important part of the contemporary second generation will assimilate downwards, into an inner-city minority subculture, in which dropouts are prevalent. But this hypothesis assumes that more than schooling is involved; that high dropout rates for high school are one indicator among several of a wider complex of behaviors that reveal what amount to a prevalent cultural pattern driving those behaviors. We therefore focus now on other risky social behavior in a group near the bottom. These social behaviors are more prevalent among blacks than whites, and are especially associated with inner-city black ghettos. The comparison with blacks should not be taken to imply that these behaviors are as prevalent among all blacks as they are among blacks in inner-city ghettos; obviously they are not, and indeed, relatively prevalent does not mean that even a majority of inner-city residents are characterized by most of these behaviors. But because the inner-city black poor are an important minority among American blacks, the risk factors do show up much more commonly in the native-black population as a whole than in the native-white population (Wilson 1987; Jencks 1992; Stier and Tienda 2001). How commonly do they show up among the Mexican Americans?

TEEN PREGNANCY AND SINGLE MOTHERHOOD   Because of the interest in young people of high school graduation age, I concentrate on women between fifteen and nineteen and between twenty and twenty-four in the 2000 census. Throughout American society, the proportion of children born out of wedlock, and the proportion being raised by women without a spouse present, are high by historical standards—high in white America, and far higher in black America. Moreover, these patterns have serious effects on the economic well-being of mothers and children. Such effects may be muted or erased entirely among upper middle-class women, but young women in less-favored circumstances with a child are especially prone to drop out of high school or college, and have a hard time arranging and paying for daycare (which might permit attending school or working). So the prevalence of teen motherhood, and of young adult women raising children alone, is an important measure of potential economic hardship for the women involved as well as for their children.

Teen mothers are relatively rare in all groups; indeed, even among women in their early twenties, a majority in every group are not yet mothers. Still, teen motherhood is more common among blacks than among whites; in relative terms, several times more common, although in actual percentages, only a few points higher (table 3.4). The proportion is higher among Mexican Americans too, but 75 percent of these teen mothers are married, whereas almost none of the black teen mothers are. Among women in their early twenties, 36 percent of blacks and 37 percent of Mexicans in the 1.53

Table 3.4   Young Mothers, Single or With Spouse, in 2000

		Mothers			
Age	Group	No Spouse Present	Spouse Present	Not Mothers	Total
15 to 19	Mexicans				
	Immigrants	3%	9%	88%	100%
	1.56 group	2	3	94	100
	1.53 group	4	4	92	100
	U.S. born	4	3	92	100
	Non-Mexican				
	NW	2	1	97	100
	NBlk	7	0	93	100
20 to 24	Mexicans				
	Immigrants	6%	34%	59%	100%
	1.56 group	9	31	59	100
	1.53 group	12	25	64	100
	U.S. born	15	19	67	100
	Non-Mexican				
	NW	8	14	78	100
	NBlk	29	7	64	100

Source: IPUMS dataset, 2000 census.
Note: See table A.4 for group definitions.

group are raising children; but the odds of raising those children without a spouse present are almost nine times as high among blacks as they are among Mexicans.

LABOR FORCE ATTACHMENT   I classify the men of each group first in terms of whether they are employed full-time; if not, by whether they are in school; and if not, by whether they are working part-time (table 3.5). This classification scheme is crude but it has the advantage of highlighting the full-time workers and those not working (or in school) at all. It reveals that notably more native whites than blacks are full-time workers (54 percent versus 39 percent; see table 3.5); and notably more native blacks than whites are neither in school nor working even part-time (28 percent versus 11 percent). By contrast, the Mexican Americans are more likely to be working full-time than either whites or blacks (63 percent) and the proportion neither at school or work is about the same as among native whites (12 percent). The distinctive Mexican American feature is the low proportion in

Table 3.5   Work Status: Men, 20 to 24, in 2000

| | | | Percentage Not Full-Time | | |
| | | | Not in School | | |
Group	Full-Time	In School	Working Part-Time	Not Working	Total
Mexican					
Immigrants	55	5	23	16	100
1.56 group	53	12	23	12	100
1.53 group	53	17	19	11	100
U.S. born	48	20	21	11	100
Non-Mexican					
NW	48	28	18	6	100
NBlk	32	22	25	21	100

Source: IPUMS dataset, 2000 census.

school; indeed, their higher than native-white full-time employment rate is the result of the school enrollment.

I classified women's work status in the same way as men's, but distinguished mothers among all women without work (table 3.6). Generally, of course, fewer women work full-time than men; the exception is blacks, among whom about the same proportion of each work full-time. This pattern is the flip side of the relatively low proportion of black men working full-time and the relatively low rate of married black women. By contrast, what most distinguishes women in the Mexican 1.53 group, like men, is a notably lower proportion in school.[14]

INSTITUTIONALIZED AND MISSING MEN   Among all groups, some young people are institutionalized, typically not by choice, and most notably in prisons. In every group, the proportion of young men who are institutionalized vastly exceeds that of women; indeed, the percentage of women who are institutionalized rounds to 0 percent in every group except blacks, and to only 1 percent among blacks (table 3.7a). Among young men, typically 1 to 2 percent are institutionalized. However, 8 percent of U.S.-born of Mexican origin and 13 percent of native blacks are in institutions. As usual, because the census does not specify parental birthplace, we cannot isolate the second generation from the third or later generation among the U.S.-born of Mexican origin. Other evidence, however, strongly suggests that

Table 3.6   Work Status: Women, 20 to 24, in 2000

			Percentage			
			Not Full-Time			
				Not in School		
					Not Working	
Group	Full-Time	In School	Working Part-Time	Mother	Other	Total
Mexican						
Immigrants	23	9	21	24	24	100
1.56 group	34	17	23	14	12	100
1.53 group	32	17	26	12	13	100
U.S.-born	34	25	24	9	8	100
Non-Mexican						
NW	36	33	22	5	5	100
NBlk	32	27	25	7	9	100

Source: IPUMS dataset, 2000 census.

the proportion institutionalized in the second generation must be much lower than 8 percent. Specifically, in both the 1.53 and 1.56 groups of Mexican Americans, only 1 percent are institutionalized, a lower rate than among the native whites. It seems most unlikely that the true second generation could have an 8 percent rate while the 1.53 group has a 1 percent rate—such a contrast would be far greater than found on any measure on which I have been able to compare them (see appendix). Clearly the situation involving the 8 percent institutionalized U.S.-born of Mexican origin deserves a closer look with better data. Nevertheless, from the 2000 census we certainly cannot conclude that second-generation Mexican American men are falling prey to the high rates of institutionalization that typify young black men.

Institutionalization removes a certain fraction of men from the productive sector, and reflects earlier harsh social conditions. But in the case of American black men, there is grim data suggesting that yet other men have also been removed, possibly by early death. The male-to-female sex ratio is a good indicator of this phenomenon. Among blacks in the noninstitutionalized population, the ratio stands at .78. Among all blacks in this age range—institutionalized and not institutionalized—the sex ratio still amounts to only .88; in every other group it equals or exceeds 1.00. To put it differently, among black men, only slightly more than three in four are active in

Table 3.7   Institutionalized Population by Origin and Birth
             Cohort, 2000

A. The 1966 to 1975 Birth Cohort, 25 to 34

| | Percentage Institutionalized | | Male to Female Ratio | |
Group	Male	Female	Non-Institutionalized	All
Mexican				
Immigrants	1	0	1.36	1.36
1.56 group	1	0	1.03	1.04
1.53 group	1	0	1.02	1.03
U.S.-born	8	0	0.96	1.04
Non-Mexican				
NW	2	0	0.99	1.01
NBlk	13	1	0.78	0.88

B. Males, 15 to 34

| | | Male to Female Ratio | |
Group	Percentage Institutionalized	Non-Institutionalized	All
Black			
25–34	13	0.78	0.88
20–24	13	0.84	0.95
15–19	5	0.98	1.03
U.S.-born with Mexican ancestry			
25–34	8	0.96	1.04
20–24	5	1.03	1.09
15–19	3	1.04	1.07

Source: IPUMS dataset, 2000 census.

free society, because of institutionalization or other factors. Nothing remotely like this proportion is to be found in the other groups. Table 3.7B shows the development of this pattern across the fifteen to thirty-four age range, and compares it to the vastly more muted patterns among the U.S.-born of Mexican ancestry (whose elevated rate of institutionalization, just discussed, prompts the comparison). It is of course possible that distinctively black male under-enumeration in the census—rather than distinctively black male early death—is creating some or even all of this pattern. One must still appreciate, I think, that such a distinctively large population that could not be found—despite intensive efforts by the Census Bureau, and in contrast to the results reflected in the sex ratios of other racial minority groups—suggests that such black men typically may also be lost to the economic mainstream of the community, even if the worst-case hypothesis is incorrect. This view of the missing men as a social problem is strengthened by our knowledge that half the reduction from an equal sex ratio among young black adults can be accounted for by institutionalization.

Blacks and whites differ on high school completion, young unwed motherhood, male and female labor-force attachment, institutionalization, and sex ratios. In each case the difference is consistent with the presence of an oppositional youth culture prevalent among an inner city racial minority (Portes and Zhou 1993). However, the Mexican 1.53 group is much less involved than blacks in all these socially risky behaviors—except for high school dropout, on which the Mexican 1.53 group is much more at risk than native-born blacks. In a word, the Mexican 1.53 school patterns seem distinctive, unlike those of blacks, and not part of a complex of underclass behaviors.

An important caveat must be registered in connection with the data on the U.S.-born of Mexican origin; this group does exhibit somewhat higher proportions on two of the measures surveyed here, unwed motherhood and male institutionalization. On both measures the rates fall between those of Mexican 1.53 group members and blacks. Still, the proportion of unwed mothers among blacks is twice as high as among this Mexican group, and black mothers are five times as likely to be unmarried as the U.S. born mothers of Mexican origin. So, the most striking figure is the very much higher institutionalized proportion among the U.S.-born of Mexican origin—yet this figure finds no reflection among the 1.53 group. In sum, a quick reading of the patterns among the U.S.-born of Mexican origin might lead us to suppose that at least this Mexican American group shows some similarity to black patterns. But upon closer inspection even this similarity is decidedly limited. Moreover, whatever similarity does exist should also be considered in terms of the observations made at the beginning of this chapter: there are likely to be considerable differences between the behaviors of Mexican Americans descended from families resident in the United

States for generations and the behaviors of the children of the Mexican immigrants who have arrived during the past thirty years or so.

In the light of the material reviewed, the educational behavior of the Mexican 1.53 group can be said to be consistent with an early turn to work for men and perhaps a turn to homemaking for women. Indeed, these patterns seem strikingly reminiscent of earlier second generations, more like the behavior of the Italians or Poles of 1940 than like the patterns of young-adult blacks in 2000. In those earlier SCEN second-generation groups, young men in particular were more likely to leave school before native whites did in the cities of the Northeast and Midwest; and the women were more likely to either stay at home (even when single) or to work than to remain in school as long as native-white women. But whether it is still possible in the American job structure of the twenty-first century to obtain decent economic returns from the school-work-family patterns of 1940 Italians and Poles is another matter.

CHAPTER FOUR

SECOND-GENERATION ECONOMIC OUTCOMES

BY 2000, A contemporary second-generation cohort had been in the labor force long enough for us to assess their early experiences. We begin with the familiar past-present comparisons between the SCEN and Mexicans. Later, we will focus in more depth on the contemporary Mexican second generation through a comparison of their well-being with that of American-born blacks.

WAGES THEN AND NOW

Most of the SCEN immigration occurred between 1900 and 1910, and most of the second generation was thus born in the twentieth century. Nevertheless, an appreciable number of SCEN immigrants had already arrived during the 1890s, producing a sizable SCEN second generation, of nearly 1.5 million, born during the decade from 1896 to 1905 (see table 1.3). We can, therefore, explore the wage experience of SCEN second-generation members born during that decade as well as during the next two. The children born later included so many atypical second generation members that we do better to ignore them here, as I explained in chapter 1.

THE SECOND-GENERATION SCEN   The SCEN second-generation men generally earned 90 to 95 percent of the native white native parentage (NWNP) mean wage, thus radically improving their relative standing over that of the immigrant generation (figure 4.1). Nevertheless, the two earliest SCEN cohorts clearly fared somewhat less well especially in 1940; the eldest cohort was then earning 84 percent of the NWNP mean wage. The middle cohort was then between twenty-five and thirty-four years old, and at that age the full extent of wage inequalities associated with ethnicity are not yet as visible as they are among older workers. When they were ten years older, the middle SCEN cohort members were in fact earning 91 percent of NWNP wages. The somewhat less favorable position of the earlier cohorts does not appear to be due to their fathers' starting positions (see figures 2.2 and 3.3), but partly to the higher educational handicap they faced compared to the youngest cohort, and probably also to their having arrived earlier. They may have had fewer contacts, role models, and information, and may have faced more prejudice. By the end of their work lives, in any case, in the favorable conditions of the 1950 to 1960 period, these cohort differences almost entirely disappeared. The crucial point in all this is that the range of well-being across SCEN second-generation cohorts and census years is rather wide, and should be borne in mind in comparing outcomes then and now. And finally, nearly all of the wage difference between the SCEN second generation and the NWNP is associated with the fact that SCEN

Figure 4.1   Second-Generation Ethnic Wage Ratios, Men 1940 to 2000

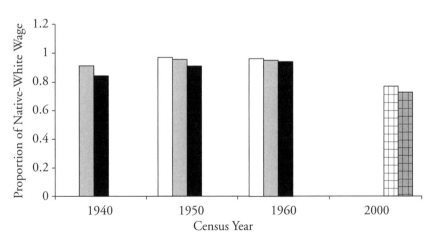

□ SCEN 1916–1925 (25–34 in 1950)   ▨ SCEN 1906–1915 (25–34 in 1940)
■ SCEN 1896–1905 (35–44 in 1940)   ⊞ Mex. 1.53 1966–1975 (25–34 in 2000)
⊞ Mex. 1.53 1956–1965 (35–44 in 2000)

Source: IPUMS dataset for 2000 census.

91

educational attainment was lower than that of the NWNP. With ethnic educational differences taken into account, the wage ratios generally hover around 1.00; only the members of the earliest cohort may have faced a moderate additional handicap, at least during their early careers.

THE MEXICAN SECOND GENERATION TODAY   The picture for the Mexican American 1.53 group is mixed. The most dire prediction one might draw from segmented assimilation theory is not confirmed—that the second generation, blocked in the labor market and vulnerable to a dysfunctional youth culture, could end up earning less than the immigrant generation. Instead, relative to native whites, the 1.53 group earn more than Mexican immigrants of their own age, more than those of their fathers' age, and more than those their own age had earned in 1970 (figures 4.1 and 2.2). Nevertheless, the 1.53 group men still earn on average only 77 percent of what the native whites of non-Mexican origin earn, 73 percent in the next-oldest cohort.[1]

As we have just seen, in its time the SCEN second generation had not lagged that far behind the native-white comparison group. Still, the force of this contrast between then and now is notably muted if we compare the Mexican outcomes today to the well-being of the earliest SCEN second-generation cohort in 1940, when the SCEN cohort earned 84 percent of what the NWNP were earning; at the same age (from thirty-five to forty-four), the contemporary Mexican cohort is earning 73 percent of today's native-white comparison group. To repeat: there is a wide range in SCEN well-being across the three birth cohorts and across several decades of American history. The contrast with the Mexicans today can be as low as the 84 percent vs. 73 percent just mentioned, and as great as 96 percent vs. 73 percent.

THE ROLE OF EDUCATION   Much of the second-generation ethnic wage disparities then and now are explained by education; taking it into account, even the earliest SCEN cohort reaches 93 percent of the native-white wage—and even the Mexican 1.53 cohorts of today reach 86 percent to 90 percent of it (figure 4.2). However, the education handicaps pull the Mexican wage today down more than they did the SCEN wage before—about 13 percentage points today against no more than 7 to 9 points for the 1940 SCEN, and less in 1950 and 1960.

Educational handicaps operate on the ethnic wage disparities in two ways. First, the educational attainment of the second-generation group averages less than that of the native whites, and that of the Mexican 1.53 group is somewhat further behind today's native whites than the SCEN attainment was behind native whites of their time (see figures 3.3 and 3.4). Second, the wage structure rewards educational advantages more handsomely

Figure 4.2   Second-Generation Ethnic Wage Inequality Associated with
Education, Men 1940 to 2000

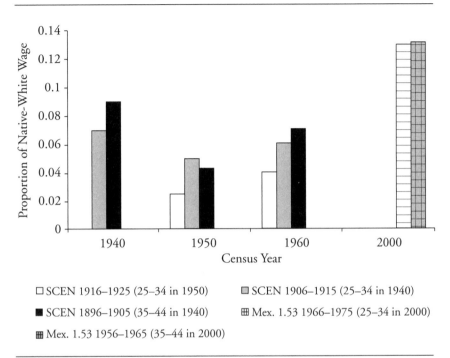

☐ SCEN 1916–1925 (25–34 in 1950)   ▨ SCEN 1906–1915 (25–34 in 1940)

■ SCEN 1896–1905 (35–44 in 1940)   ⊞ Mex. 1.53 1966–1975 (25–34 in 2000)

⊞ Mex. 1.53 1956–1965 (35–44 in 2000)

Source: IPUMS dataset for 2000 census.
Note: Columns show the part of the ethnic wage inequality that is associated with ethnic
differences in education. It is expressed as a proportion of the native-white wage.

today than it did during the decades when the SCEN second generation
were at work. Thus, even the same handicap in educational attainment then
and now would have produced a greater ethnic wage inequality today than
it would have produced in 1950.

Table 4.1 allows us to observe how these two factors, ethnic educational
attainments and the shift in returns to schooling, operated on ethnic wages
in different historical conditions. Specifically, we can observe how each of
the two factors contribute to creating the temporal difference in ethnic
wage ratios for young adult men that we find in comparing 1940 to 2000
and 1950 to 2000. To simplify the presentation, I treat educational attainment more crudely than in most contexts in this study, namely as a single
linear variable, highest grade of schooling completed. The total impact of
this variable upon the ethnic wage inequality, seen in panel A, is 12 log
points in 2000. Another 12.6 log points in the ethnic wage ratio remain

Table 4.1   Educational Attainment, and Returns to Schooling, as Sources of the Ethnic Wage Inequality, Men 25 to 34 in 1940–1950 and 2000

A. Second-Generation Wage Gap Associated with Education

Group	Cohort and Census	Difference in Education (in Standard Deviation Units) (a)	Wage Returns to a Standard Deviation of Education (in Log Points) (b)	Product: a × b: Ethnic-Wage Gap Due to Education (in Log Points) (c)
SCEN	1906–1915 cohort in 1940 (1)	0.38	15.6	5.9
	1916–1925 cohort in 1950 (2)	0.14	9.7	1.4
Mexican 1.53	1966–1975 cohort in 2000 (3)	0.62	19.3	12.0

B. Decomposing the Change in the Ethnic Wage Gap Due to Education

Sources of Change	Change in Ethnic Wage Gap Due to Education (in Log Points) From 1940 to 2000 (a)	From 1950 to 2000 (b)
Second-generation education lag in 2000	3.8	4.6
Returns to education in 2000	1.4	1.4
Factors operating jointly	0.9	4.6
Total	6.1	10.6

Source: IPUMS datasets, 1940, 1950, and 2000 censuses.

Notes: Column a, panel A: Measuring grades of schooling completed in 2000 involves some estimation because higher educational levels were classified by degree, not grade, that year (see appendix and Mare 1995). Standardized differences in mean years of schooling shown here are unadjusted for region or metro status. Column b in panel A: The returns to education are taken from a model in which logged weekly wages were regressed on grades of schooling completed, individual age, region and metro status for full-time workers. Columns a and b in panel B: The decomposition was calculated from panel A as follows (using the change from 1940 to 2000 as an example). Change due to difference in education = (a3 − a1) × b1; due to returns = a1 × (b3 − b1); due to interaction: (a3 − a1) × (b3 − b1).

unexplained even after this education variable has been taken into account; but our focus here is only on the 12-point difference accounted for by education. Earlier in the century, the total impact of schooling on ethnic wage gaps was lower; for the youngest adult group in 1940, the SCEN wage lag due to schooling was only 5.9 log points. For the youngest adult group in 1950, it was a mere 1.4 log points.[2]

Both relevant factors work to put the Mexicans further behind than the SCEN had been in their day. The Mexican 1.53 group is relatively further behind native whites in educational attainment and returns to schooling for all Americans have risen. In 1940, returns to schooling were quite high, about three-quarters what they were in 2000 for the age group. Most of the change between 1940 and 2000 is thus due to the impact of differences in the educational profile of Mexicans now compared to SCEN then. Had the SCEN suffered the Mexican levels of educational disadvantage, their wage gap would have increased by the amounts shown in table 4.1b. By 1950, the next SCEN cohort had improved its educational profile even more; nevertheless, returns to schooling had also fallen very appreciably, so each factor accentuated the difference between 1950 and 2000 compared to the difference between 1940 and 2000. Actually, if the SCEN group starting out in 1950 were instead starting in 2000, they would not suffer much more of a wage gap—despite the higher returns to schooling in the later year—for the simple reason that they had pretty much equaled the native white educational profile (differing by .14 of a standard deviation only). By contrast, the Mexican 1.53 group in 2000 bring their great handicap in educational profile into the labor market in the worse possible context, when the returns to educational advantage are higher than at any point in the period from 1940 to 2000.

One way to summarize is to say that the relative economic handicap of immigrant fathers' starting positions in the economy today compared to the last great wave of immigration is not at all as great as had been thought. But it is somewhat worse, and could have been expected to produce a some-what worsened educational profile in the next generation. That profile, however, may be somewhat worse still than what would have been expected by the fathers' situation. The reason is probably not due mostly to the high cost of a four-year college degree, as explained in chapter 2, or to a dysfunctional youth culture, as explained in chapter 3. Nevertheless, the Mexican second generation does suffer a lower educational profile than the SCEN did. And, finally, that profile comes in a much more unforgiving wage context, when educational differences receive a high return, twice what they received in 1950.

INTERGENERATIONAL MOBILITY, THEN AND NOW   I have argued that, for all the difficulty of estimation, the SCEN in 1910 probably started out at levels roughly comparable to those of the Mexicans today (in both cases, relative to native whites), but that the trajectory of change was more favorable for the SCEN than for the Mexicans, given the swings in wage inequality across the twentieth century (figure 2.2 provided a graphic summary).

Generally, each succeeding SCEN second-generation decennial birth cohort was more favored than its predecessor. We can simplify by distinguishing the two later cohorts from the earliest. When the two later cohorts were about fifteen years of age, the fathers were probably earning about 10 percentage points more, relative to native whites, than was the younger Mexican cohort—that is, 67–71 percent versus 58 percent of native-white wages. The two second-generation SCEN birth cohorts achieved near-parity with native whites, and the Mexican 1.53 group earned only about 75 cents for every dollar that the native whites did. Thus there can be little doubt that the SCEN second-generation cohorts improved on the SCEN immigrant situation during the course of a generation more than the Mexican 1.53 group improved on the Mexican immigrant generation's situation. Some of the difference between second generations then and now derives from the impact of schooling on wages and some is an unexplained (residual) difference in wages.

The progress of the earliest SCEN second-generation birth cohort is more ambiguous. At least in young adulthood they earned a smaller proportion of native-white wages (84 percent in 1940) than their successors did; nevertheless, later in life virtually all of this ethnic disparity disappears. In any case, from all three SCEN cohorts, only the young-adult experience of the earliest resembles the restricted wage assimilation of the Mexican 1.53 cohorts today.

In sum, it seems plausible, based on current evidence, that the Mexican entry into a situation of near-parity may well require a generation more than it did for the SCEN. This difference would be due less to a radical difference in immigrant starting positions in the groups we have studied and more to the punishing direction of American wage inequality over the past thirty years and the more forgiving direction of wage levels earlier in the twentieth century. Fewer low-skill jobs provide a decent wage today. Unless there is a change in wage inequality, we can also expect that the starting points of the immigrants will be an increasingly important source of slower intergenerational economic assimilation.

RESIDUAL ETHNIC WAGE DIFFERENCES IN HISTORICAL PERSPECTIVE
When educational attainment, as well as region, metro status, and age, have been taken into account a residual, unexplained ethnic difference in wages remains. Some of that difference remains unexplained because of the particular sort of data used here. The census does not include information on the family origins of individual adults that would be routinely available in data-

sets constructed for the purpose of studying intergenerational mobility—for example, father's and mother's income and education. Also, we cannot determine whether a Mexican parent was an undocumented worker. This last factor probably operated mainly through parental economic well-being and second-generation educational attainment. But it may still have affected the second generation in other ways, for example, in the quality of academic work at any grade level.

So, surely, some of the residual ethnic difference would disappear if we could add more explanatory factors, more controls. However, in most studies of ethnic or racial differences in schooling, occupation, or income there remains an unexplained residual (Perlmann 1988), and it is a safe bet that we would find such residuals even if we did add half a dozen other control variables. The residual differences are conceptually of considerable importance, and at the same time impossible to interpret with certainty. They are important because they suggest that something other than the factors controlled are operating to determine wages in different ethnic groups. The interpretation of that something is itself a subject of fierce debate—and of course the something need not be the same for different groups or in different times. Nevertheless, two major competing explanations of the residuals often emerge in discussion: differences in levels of discrimination aimed against one or another group, and differences in cultural patterns that might affect the achievement orientations of groups. The segmented assimilation hypothesis is a good example of an explanation that assumes there will be a residual of consequence, and that both these factors are part of the dynamics that explain the magnitude of the predicted residual. But other factors could easily be relevant, too. One important example is differences in the connections and information available across groups—the social capital common to members of each ethnic group. Another important source of residual differences could be measurement error, especially in the characteristics controlled. Educational controls are a likely case in point. Insofar as unmeasured educational characteristics are associated with both ethnicity and wages, they inflate the residual.[3] Despite these uncertainties, there are differences in the strengths of residuals over time and across groups, and at least some of these seem difficult to explain as measurement error.

If at least part of the residual is not due to measurement error, then a second issue concerns the psychological effects of the residual on those enduring it. In the case of blacks in particular, the observed residual wage difference is often assumed to be the result of discrimination, and high historical levels of discrimination in turn are assumed to have had an effect on the outlook and expectations of blacks—effects that in time took on a self-sustaining character, and which may wear off slowly even in the context of declining discrimination. Stanley Lieberson's discussion of feedback loops in *A Piece of the Pie* (1980), and William Julius Wilson's *The Truly*

Disadvantaged (1987) develop arguments of this kind. Such feedback loops are also relevant to the trajectory of the less-fortunate in the segmented assimilation hypothesis. Are the Mexican 1.53 group residuals also of the sort that would lead to feedback loops? The question is important because the residual wage difference experienced by the Mexican 1.53 group is about as large as the entire wage difference associated with ethnic educational differences.

The second-generation SCEN groups generally experienced only small and residual wage differences from native whites and even these declined over time (figure 4.3). The important partial exception is the earliest large SCEN cohort (born between 1896 and 1905), especially in their young adulthood: they faced a residual wage difference amounting to 7 percent of NWNP wages in 1940 and 5 percent in 1950. On the other hand, later in their own careers, even that birth cohort's residual disappeared—and perhaps not only because of the great compression in the wage structure, but

Figure 4.3   Unexplained (Residual) Second-Generation Ethnic Wage Inequality, Men 1940 to 2000

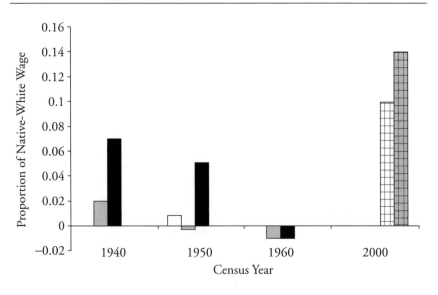

□ SCEN 1916–1925 (25–34 in 1950)   ▨ SCEN 1906–1915 (25–34 in 1940)
■ SCEN 1896–1905 (35–44 in 1940)   ▦ Mex. 1.53 1966–1975 (25–34 in 2000)
▦ Mex. 1.53 1956–1965 (35–44 in 2000)

Source: IPUMS dataset for 2000 census.

also because of declining discrimination toward the SCEN groups in the 1950s and 1960s and after. The SCEN experience was surely not the most extreme case of low residuals; the children of older immigrant groups from northwest Europe may have experienced still lower residuals. Indeed, our rationale for studying the SCEN is that they are the European groups most likely to have encountered conditions especially divergent from those of the native whites. The residual for the Mexican 1.53 group today is worse than the worst observed for the SCEN—10 to 14 percent of the native-white mean wage for the two Mexican 1.53 cohorts in 2000 compared to 7 percent of the native-white mean wage for the oldest SCEN cohort in 1940.

At the other pole of comparisons, the Mexican residual is very much smaller than the historic levels of the black residual (table 4.2). The latter has been so much higher—and indeed so much higher than the residual observed for black men today—as to defy meaningful comparison. As late as 1970, no native black cohort faced a residual wage difference from native whites of less than 20 percent of the latter's mean wage; in the earliest available data, from 1940, the residual amounted to 45 percent. Even for blacks outside the South, there is no comparison between the historical level of the residual for blacks and that of the Mexican 1.53 group today. Indeed, the residual for blacks outside the South is much closer to that for southern blacks than to either of these other groups (note to table 4.2). It is important to emphasize how much lower Mexican residuals today are, compared to black residuals of the past, because the similarity of current Mexican to current black residuals does not resolve the likelihood that Mexican responses in coming decades will parallel black responses. The latter developed over the course of the preceding century in the context of far worse discrimination which the wage residuals for past cohorts surely reflect, whatever their imperfections.

It would be revealing to know something of the historical level of residual income inequality that Mexicans confronted; after all, the descendants of the earlier Mexican second generations, the U.S.-born of Mexican origin, have special bonds to the contemporary second generation. Furthermore, we have several times encountered the question of whether the children of today's second generation will be like today's U.S.-born of Mexican origin. But the evidence is minimal for cohorts born before 1930.[4] Beginning with some evidence on the 1916 to 1925 birth cohort, we have reasonably consistent outcomes, placing most of the residuals—whether for the 1.53 group, the true second generation, or all U.S.-born of Mexican origin—in the range of 10 to 15 percent of native-white wages when education and the other standard controls have been taken into account.[5]

In sum, we cannot situate the recent Mexican cohorts in the long history of Mexican settlement as well as we can situate them in terms of the SCEN and the black experience. From the second, we learn that the Mexican 1.53

Table 4.2   Residuals as Percentages of Native-White Wages

Group and Birth Cohort	Census Year				
	1940	1950	1960	1970	2000
a. Second-generation SCEN					
1896–1905	7	5	−1		
1906–1915	2	0	−1		
1916–1925		1	0		
b1. Native blacks					
1896–1905	45	32	33		
1906–1915	39	29	32	26	
1916–1925		28	31	27	
1926–1935			31	28	
1936–1945				24	15
1946–1955					20
1956–1965					23
1966–1975					17
b2. Native blacks living outside the South					
1896–1905	39	26	26		
1906–1915	34	21	24	19	
1916–1925		20	25	21	
1926–1935			24	22	
1936–1945				18	11
1946–1955					18
1956–1965					23
1966–1975					16
c1. Second-generation Mexicans					
1916–1925		7	10	4	
1926–1935			13	11	
1936–1945			11		
c2. U.S.-born of Mexican origin					
1936–1945					15
1946–1955					16
1956–1965					16
1966–1975					12
c3. Mexican 1.53 group					
1956–1965					14
1966–1975					10

Source: IPUMS datasets for 1940 to 1970 and 2000 censuses.
Note: Based on regression of full-time male workers' wages on region, metro status, age (continuous var.), and education. In 2000, the census comparisons are to non-Mexican native whites. In earlier censuses, comparisons are to native-born children of native whites.

group today suffers a residual difference from native-white income levels that is somewhat larger than the largest SCEN cohorts of the past, somewhat smaller than the contemporary black male residual—for full-time workers—and vastly smaller than the historical black residual. If our only yardstick for what is required to create a powerful feedback loop is the historical black experience, then it seems to me unlikely that the contemporary Mexican residuals, even in a context of heightened ethnic awareness and assertiveness, are severe enough by themselves to produce enough bitterness and despair among enough members of the group to be determinative—that is, to make prevalent strongly negative economic behavior in the foreseeable future. On the other hand, identity, self-consciousness, and cultural patterns generally are not created only by the residuals. To put it more directly, the cumulative effect of the serious educational differences between Mexican 1.53 group members and native whites along with the residual differences, is considerable.

MEXICAN AND BLACK EARNINGS TODAY

Two generalizations about Mexican American geographic concentration emerge from the 2000 census. First, the group is heavily concentrated in the four border states, and, second, this concentration has declined appreciably in recent years. One measure of an important shift in Mexican Americans social patterns is already available to us—the increasing dispersion in Mexican immigrant settlement patterns away from the border.

GEOGRAPHIC CONCENTRATION

A useful comparison is between three groups of Mexican origin—all twenty-five to thirty-four years of age in the 2000 census, and the first two familiar from the preceding analysis.

1. The U.S.-born of Mexican origin: individuals born in the United States who reported Mexican origins (on the ancestry or Hispanic questions). Their families have been in the United States for two or more generations, and 65 percent of them for at least three generations (table 1.4b).

2. The 1.53 group: individuals born in Mexico and brought to the United States before their third birthday (our proxy for the true unmixed second generation). In the young adult birth cohort, members of this group first arrived in the United States twenty-two to thirty-four years before the 2000 census.

3. Mexican immigrants who report coming to the United States at age

eighteen or older. They first arrived in the United States more recently, seven to sixteen years before the census.

The contrast between the residence patterns of the two Mexican-born groups provides a crude but convenient measure of the shifting settlement patterns. At the same time, the location of the U.S.-born of Mexican origin, mostly third and later generation, tells us something of older historical patterns of settlement. Finally, residence patterns of all three Mexican-origin groups can be usefully compared to those of (non-Mexican) native whites.

A majority of all three Mexican subgroups live in the four border states—Texas, New Mexico, Arizona, and California—but the same is true for only 16 percent of the native whites (table 4.3). No residential contrast among the Mexican subgroups will be as stark, of course, as the contrast with the native whites. Still, differences related to time of settlement emerge: 39 percent of the most recent immigrants lived outside the border states, 19 to 25 percent of the other two groups. This trend is probably greatly facilitated by the presence of substantial Spanish-mother-tongue communities in many cities outside the Southwest. Once established, the trend is likely to continue.

Table 4.3   Places of Residence, by Origin: 25 to 34 in 2000

	Selected Mexican-Origin Groups			
Residence	More Recent Immigrants	1.53 Group	U.S.-Born of Mexican Origin	Native Whites
Border states	0.61	0.81	0.75	0.16
All other	0.39	0.19	0.25	0.84
Border states				
Arizona and New Mexico	0.06	0.06	0.08	0.02
Texas, non-metro areas	0.02	0.03	0.12	0.02
Texas, metro areas	0.16	0.17	0.19	0.04
California, non-metro areas	0.01	0.02	0.04	0.01
California, metro areas	0.36	0.53	0.33	0.07
Metro area	0.88	0.89	0.72	0.56
Other	0.12	0.11	0.28	0.44

Source: IPUMS dataset for 2000 census.
Note: "More recent immigrants" are Mexican-born who arrived in the United States at age eighteen or older. For definitions of other groups see appendix table A.4.

The descendants of the oldest arrivals, the U.S.-born of Mexican origin, are the most likely of these groups to be in Arizona or New Mexico, or in the nonmetropolitan areas of Texas and California. The other two groups are much more likely to be in metro areas of those two states; but this concentration is especially true for the 1.53 group: over half are in California metro areas, seven-tenths there or in Texas metro areas. And, finally, as all this suggests, the Mexicans are heavily concentrated in metropolitan areas, notably more so than the native whites for example; this is true even for the U.S.-born of Mexican origin.

Given the very high concentration of our second-generation proxy group in the metropolitan areas of only two states (California and Texas), I have been especially careful in controlling for the effects of residential location. In dealing with the national data I added specific controls for California and Texas metro areas; I have also presented some of the most important evidence separately for California's metro areas. In fact, the elaborated controls for the national data are adequate; the data for the California metro areas raise our confidence in those results but do not fundamentally change the discussion.

MEN'S EARNINGS

I shift the focus of attention here from wages to total earnings. Our present interest is on the well-being of several groups in our own time, and so we are not constrained by the measures of well-being that earlier censuses included or by the nature of earlier research. Total earnings include all wage and salary income, as well as earnings from one's own business or farm, but not government subsidies. On the other hand, a glance at the earnings ratios in subsequent tables will show that they differ only trivially from the wage ratios for the same age group presented earlier. The sample remains restricted as before to those who worked at least forty weeks during the preceding year and thirty-five hours per week. Table 4.4 presents the evidence on the young adult men—members of the 1.53 group and adult immigrants. In addition, the table includes information on the cohort most likely to include the fathers of the 1.53 group men, namely Mexican immigrants born thirty years before that young-adult cohort and who reported arriving in the United States in 1970 or earlier. For the most part, I discuss national figures without controls for residence. Controlling for place of residence in the national data (column c) or limiting the sample to metro areas of California (columns e and f), generally does not change the considerations discussed.

The group of immigrant fathers were earning 57 percent of what native white men of the same age earned, and the younger group of immigrant men an almost identical 60 percent (table 4.4, column b). Against this

Table 4.4   Weekly Full-Time Earnings, in 2000

		Percentage of Native-White Earnings				
		National Sample			California Metro Areas	
			Controls for Age + Place		Controls for Age	
	Earnings (Mean)	No Controls		+Education		+Education
Group	a	b	c	d	e	f
55–64 years old						
Native whites	879					
Mexican immigrants (Resident in U.S. for thirty years or more)	504	0.57	0.51			
25–34 years old						
Native whites	662					
Mexican immigrants	399	0.60	0.57	0.75	0.52	0.73
Mexican 1.53 group	520	0.79	0.75	0.87	0.71	0.87
U.S.-born of Mexican origin	524	0.79	0.77	0.86	0.77	0.90
Native blacks	515	0.78	0.77	0.83	0.75	0.83

Source: IPUMS dataset for 2000 census.
Note: Total earned income regressed on control variables shown: age (individual years; continuous var.), place of residence (region, metro status, Texas, California, Texas metro area, California metro area), education (LT high school, grades 9 to 11, grade 12 [no diploma], high school graduate, some college, college graduate, post-B.A.) ethnicity (as shown + other).

background, the 1.53 group was faring much better, earning 79 percent of what the average native-white did. They had, in other words, made up about half the gap (from 60 percent to 79 percent of native-white earnings) in a generation. Results for the true unmixed second generation in 1998–2001 CPS data (not shown) are virtually identical.

The average young member of the 1.53 group is earning more than the immigrant three decades his senior, $520 compared to $504 per week (column a). To my mind, this evidence indicates considerable advance as the central tendency of the group. In particular, the means suggest that on average group members find mid-level jobs that pay better than those their parents' generation take—even as fewer than one in ten of this 1.53 group completed college.

Clearly Mexican 1.53s are a very long way indeed from parity with native whites; nevertheless, their situation may seem to them like more than standing still, more than facing work that only an immigrant would accept—because an immigrant uses a different frame of reference than a native. Still, these mean dollar figures are very close, implying that there are also a great many young men in the 1.53 group who are earning less than their immigrant fathers are earning. And many young workers may view these outcomes wondering how much they can expect to rise on the basis of their low-manual work. That is, the rough equality with older workers is only good news if the workers now young can expect their own wages to rise appreciably in future decades.

Earnings of the U.S.-born of Mexican origin average almost exactly the same amount as earnings in the Mexican 1.53 group (table 4.4, columns a, b, and c); once again, I don't think this outcome can be taken to be an indication that generational improvement will stop in the second generation. Rather, it is an indication that the earlier second generations were not reaching the levels of well-being that the contemporary second generation is. The children of today's second generation will thus start from a higher point than those of earlier second-generation Mexicans did (see chapter 3).

The more striking evidence that the glass may be half-empty emerges in the comparison with native-born blacks. The Mexican 1.53 group is earning just about the same, on average, as the native-born black population (columns a and b). Moreover, the Mexican 1.53 group members are more concentrated in high-earning areas than native-born blacks, and thus when we control for place of residence the outcomes show a slight shift in favor of the blacks (columns c and d). Making the contemporary comparisons either way, it is hard to avoid thinking about the European second generations of the past, reviewed in the first part of this chapter; their attainments far exceeded those of blacks their own age. Part of the difference, of course is that blacks themselves are faring better today compared to native whites than blacks did from 1940 to 1960. In any case, even ignoring the historical comparison, but taking account of contemporary concern for the black-white divide in American economic well-being, we can hardly be sanguine that a another huge native-born, nonwhite group is earning at the level of native-born blacks.

Nevertheless, this comparison is imperfect, and a wider context tends to favor the Mexican Americans somewhat more. The wider context comes from taking into account the fact that these earnings are calculated for full-time workers only. And the proportion working full-time varies considerably across the groups, as we saw for younger men in chapter 3; here it is enough to note that the main points remain true for the men twenty-five to thirty-four years of age as well. Native whites are most likely to be working full-time (81 percent), followed by the 1.53 group (74 percent) and the U.S.-born of Mexican origin (70 percent); among native-black men the figure is 59 percent. At the other extreme, 6 percent of native-white men, 10 to 12 percent of men in the two Mexican groups, and 20 percent of native-black men reported no earnings at all in census 2000. So while the average black and Mexican 1.53 men who work full-time earn about the same amount, roughly five members of the 1.53 group work full-time for every four native blacks. A fuller analysis must involve women's and family incomes, but at least among the men, broadening the perspective beyond the earnings of full-time workers will clearly reveal meaningful net advantages for the 1.53 group compared to the native blacks.

EDUCATION AND EARNINGS   I controlled for education somewhat differently than I did earlier, exploiting in this context too the advantage of not having to maximize comparability with earlier census data. I included dummy variables for almost every educational level that the census allowed respondents to select. Thus, educational differences found in the census are allowed to explain as much of the variance in earnings as possible: in particular, the analysis assumes no linearity in the association between educational levels and earnings.[6]

About half the difference between the earnings of the Mexican 1.53 group and the native whites is due to the impact of schooling. When schooling is taken into account in the national data, the 1.53 group members earn 87 percent of the native-white mean earnings—compared to 75 percent, when education is ignored (columns a and b). In the California metropolitan areas, the comparable figures are if anything stronger (columns c and d). In both the national and the California comparisons, the role of education differs only slightly for the U.S.-born of Mexican origin; but education does explain about twice as much of the Mexican as it does of the black differences from native whites.

Big payoffs from schooling, we are always told, come from an advanced education—specifically a four-year college degree. But it is important to insist here on the importance of what is happening at the lower branching point, high school graduation. The very high rate at which the Mexican 1.53 group, and especially the men of that group, drop out of high school has serious economic implications. We saw the specific rates in chapter 3; for example, even after making all allowances for problems with the data, 8 percent of native white men failed to complete high school, while 25 percent of the men in the true Mexican second generation failed to do so. At the same time rates of college completion for men in the Mexican 1.53 group who have finished high school are also far lower than the rates of college completion for native whites who have finished high school. In short, for the Mexican 1.53 group, there are two distinct forms of educational vulnerability involved in low college completion: low high-school completion rates and low persistence in school through four more grades by high school completers. By contrast, only the second form of vulnerability has an important impact on white-black educational attainment differences.

How much improvement in Mexican 1.53 earnings might we reasonably expect if either of these levels of vulnerability were eliminated? We have already seen that even if all educational differences between native whites and the Mexican 1.53 group were eliminated, only half of the ethnic earnings gap would disappear—the ethnic earnings ratio rising from 75 percent to 87 percent. But it is still important to explore the impact of the Mexican failure to complete particular levels of schooling at the rates that native whites do. Affecting high school graduation rates implies a different set of societal (and indeed familial) policies than affecting educational persistence among high school graduates. I want to insist upon the point that the vulnerability at the lower level, failure to complete high school, has critical implications. Table 4.5 presents relevant data, addressing the ethnic earnings differences associated with education and estimates of how much of the education-related earnings difference would disappear given various scenarios for change in Mexican 1.53 group educational attainment.[7]

In scenario 1 of table 4.5, each group reaches the native-white education profile and thus would gain the entire dollar amount that they currently lose due to educational differences from native whites. The proportions shown are 1.00 for all three groups. The other two scenarios explore how much of this gap is related to high school and college completion rates. The assumption in scenario 2 is that college enrollment rates for high school graduates in each group would rise to the current native-white rate. In this case, the Mexican group would gain 35 percent of the entire amount that the group loses as a result of educational differences from native whites.

In scenario 3, the assumption is that high school graduation rates for each group would rise to the current rate for native whites. The three variants of scenario 3 model three different possibilities for the later educational attainment of the new high school graduates added by this scenario to the current graduates in each group. The first variant, the most pessimistic, envisions that none of the new high school graduates would go on to postsecondary schooling. The most optimistic variant, scenario 3c, envisions that all the new high school graduates will match the college attainments of the current high school graduates in their own ethnic group. Notice that this scenario 3c still assumes that these new high school graduates will be far less likely to finish college than native-white high school graduates; in this sense, our most optimistic scenario envisions far less than perfect equality of educational behavior. Finally, the intermediate scenario, 3b, is that half of the new high school graduates in each ethnic group would receive no further schooling, and the other half would match the college educational levels of the current high school graduates in their own ethnic group.

Table 4.5   Modeling Improvements in Earnings by Origin, Men 25 to 34

Advantages in earnings gained expressed as a proportion of the entire earnings gap related to education when each group is compared to native whites

Mexican 1.53 group	U.S.-born of Mexican origin	Native black

Scenario 1. Each group reaches native-white educational attainments.

1.00	1.00	1.00

Scenario 2. Percentage graduating from high school unchanged, but high school graduates progress to higher diplomas at native-white rates.

0.35	0.55	0.80

Scenarios 3a–3c. Men in each group complete high school at the native-white rate.

Scenario 3a. None of the new high school graduates progress to higher diplomas.

0.27	0.18	0.08

Scenario 3b. Half of the new high school graduates progress to higher diplomas at the rates prevalent in their group today.

0.37	0.26	0.12

Scenario 3c. All of the new high school graduates progress to higher diplomas at the rates prevalent in their group today.

0.48	0.33	0.16

Source: IPUMS dataset for 2000 census.
Note: Scenario 1 shows the total amount of education-related earnings ethnic men would gain if all educational differences from native whites were erased. It is the dollar value predicted by the regression results summarized in table 4.4, column d less column c. The other scenarios express, as proportions of this total, the amount the men in each origin group would gain from erasing specific (more limited) educational differences from native whites.

Under the most pessimistic variant, scenario 3a, 27 percent of the total dollar amount related to the ethnic difference in education would be recouped. Thus wiping out the Mexican high school dropout problem would raise earnings only modestly less than sending all current high school graduates through college at native-white rates (scenario 2, which erased 35 percent of the total gap). In the two more optimistic scenarios, with some or all new high school graduates reaping still more economic rewards from having attended college, the gain from wiping out the Mexican high school dropout problem exceeds the gain from scenario #2, in which all current

Mexican high school graduates proceed through college at the native-white rate—slightly in scenario 3b and substantially in scenario 3c.

In sum, the claim that steps on the ladder of upward mobility cannot be found for group members who do not complete college seems futuristic at best; above all, the claim should not divert us from noting the need for radical improvement in Mexican high school graduation rates today. The point is not that graduating from high school is nearly as rewarding as graduating from college; of course college graduation produces the far greater payoff. And of course too I am not arguing against efforts to boost the rate of Mexican American college attendance. The point is rather that despite the much higher returns to college compared to high school completion, the lower—but not negligible—returns to high school graduation matter for the individual. Moreover there are a great many Mexican 1.53 group members who are not passing the lower branch point. Consequently, when our perspective shifts from the individual to his ethnic group, the results of changes at the lower branch point can be as great or greater for this group than a radical change at the higher branch point.

Note also that outcomes are very different for the U.S.-born of Mexican origin and native blacks: for these groups, the economic problem tied to the ethnic educational differentials lies less at the lower levels of educational attainment and more in college completion. Even under the assumptions of scenario 3c, these other groups would gain far less than they would from scenario 2.

Many Mexican American young men may believe that their later job prospects will not be much served by finishing high school. At least two considerations might lead to such thinking. They may believe that whatever is true in the mainstream, the sectors of the economy in which they will find their best jobs, as a result of ethnic contacts or discrimination for example, do not reward a high school diploma very highly. Such suggestions amount to a hypothesis that the returns to a high school degree for Mexican Americans will be lower than for other groups. But the hypothesis is not borne out by the experience of the Mexican 1.53 group in the 2000 census; higher-order interaction terms for ethnicity, schooling, and earnings are not statistically significant. A particularly vivid demonstration can be found in the metro areas of California; I regressed earnings on specific levels of education for each group separately, native whites and Mexican 1.53 group members.[8] At the very lowest levels, returns (or lack thereof) cannot be compared because less than 1 percent of native whites (but 11 percent of the Mexicans) dropped out before completing tenth grade. However, returns can be meaningfully compared at each of seven higher levels of educational achievement. None of those levels show returns differing between native whites and the Mexican group in a statistically significant way. Nor is this a case of small samples making large differences insignificant.

The sample size is large, more than 2,000 in each ethnic group, and the returns generally follow expectations. Mexican American youths may or may not judge the value of secondary schooling to be low for them; but if they do make that judgment, they are, on average, wrong. If social scientists make it, they are wrong too.

Or at least they are wrong in relative terms: the implication of the regressions is that Mexican 1.53 group and native-white incomes will increase with each level of schooling by equal proportions. Nevertheless, the residual ethnic difference in earnings from the same regression analysis indicate that at every education level Mexican 1.53 group members will earn 87 percent of what native whites earn (see again column b in table 4.4). Thus, the size of the added return for more schooling will be only 87 percent as great for the Mexican as for the native group. And of course the full earnings will be only 87 percent as great for the Mexican 1.53 group member as for the native white. This differential is greater than the advantage that a metro Californian in either group gains by completing high school rather than leaving as an eleventh grader. Thus a Mexican 1.53 group member who completes high school will earn modestly less than a native white who left school after the eleventh grade. At this key threshold, that teens can readily observe, the news is not good. It is worth stressing parenthetically that this sort of result does not emerge at higher levels of schooling: Mexican 1.53 group members who complete some college do slightly better than native whites who only complete high school, and Mexican 1.53 group members who complete a four-year college do vastly better than native whites who gain only a high school diploma.

GENDERED PATTERNS AND FAMILY STRUCTURE

The gendered dynamics of the workplace are well known from countless observations: an occupational structure highly segregated by gender, three young men for every two young women working full-time, and those men earning $1.25 for every dollar earned by those women. It is within this broader pattern that we can explore some additional ethnic and racial differences that are no less striking.

When the comparison is across group, Mexican 1.53 men and women fare about the same compared to native whites of the same sex: in 2000, the ethnic wage ratio was .75 for men, and .77 for women (table 4.6). Education accounts for 12 points of the 25-percentage-point ethnic gap among the men and 15 points of the 23-percentage-point ethnic gap among the women. Among blacks too the role of education has about the same effect on male and female earnings. The crucial difference between the black and Mexican gender patterns is that among blacks, women earn more than men compared to native whites of the same sex. Thus the black-white

Table 4.6   Determinants of Full-Time Earnings

	Percentage of Native-White Earnings Controlling For:	
Group	Place, Age	Place, Age, Education
Men		
Mexican 1.53 group	75	87
Native blacks	77	83
Women		
Mexican 1.53 gruop	77	92
Native blacks	84	92

Source: IPUMS datasets for 2000 census.

earnings ratios are .77 for men and .84 for women, and with education taken into account, .83 and .92. As a result of these patterns, the residual (unexplained) earnings gaps from native whites are about 8 percent of native-white wages for both Mexican 1.53 and black women, about 13 percent for Mexican 1.53 men and about 17 percent for black men.[9]

Nevertheless, Mexican-black earnings differences among full-time workers, whether for men or women, can take us only so far. We have looked at the family and employment differences between these groups (see chapter 3), and their effect on earnings must somehow be taken into account here. Specifically, among men, substantially smaller proportions of blacks are working full-time (59 percent versus 70 percent among young adults) and substantially greater proportions of blacks are not working at all, compared to Mexicans (20 percent versus 10 percent). Recall, too, that a significant proportion of black young men are either in institutions or are simply missing, and some fraction of these are quite possibly dead. Among women, far more blacks than Mexicans are raising children without a spouse present (39 percent versus 16 percent), and more blacks than Mexicans are working full-time (58 percent versus 41 percent). The pressures of needing work to raise earnings in the absence of spousal income, and being unable to work because of childrearing requirements, bear down on much higher proportion of black than of Mexican women. We cannot begin to sort out here the extent to which these black patterns are caused by present-day discrimination in the labor force, especially against black men, and how much of past racial discrimination in the workplace, today sustained by cultural patterns of one sort or another. Rather, the point here is that the impact of low male labor-force attachment, unwed motherhood, and the lopsided sex ratio work together to create a distinctive set of economic outcomes among blacks that the Mexican 1.53 group does not share.

We can begin to gauge these outcomes by focusing on the familiar wage ratios in a somewhat different way (table 4.7). Shifting attention from full-time workers to all workers offers no sharply different perspective (row a). However, we can extend the ratios for all workers in several ways. Row b expresses these ratios in terms of the wages of native-white men, and because on average women earn much less then men, all the ratios for women

Table 4.7   Earnings per Person in 2000

| | | Group | | |
| | | Native | Mexican | Native |
Measure	Sex	Whites	1.53 Group	Blacks
a) All workers	Men	1.00	0.79	0.74
	Women	1.00	0.82	0.90
b) Compared to native-white men	Men	1.00	0.79	0.74
	Women	0.69	0.57	0.62
c) Adjusted to include non-workers	Men	1.00	0.76	0.63
	Women	0.61	0.46	0.54
d) Per person flowing into the group				
(rows c for men + women)/2	Both	0.81	0.61	0.59
As ratio to native whites	Both	1.00	0.75	0.73
e) Earnings in the ethnic-sex subgroup	Men	101	78	55
Per 100 women and (100 × the				
M/F sex ratio) men	Women	61	46	54
Total (per same)	Both	162	124	110
Ratio to native whites	Both	1.00	0.76	0.68

Source: IPUMS dataset for 2000 census.

Notes: Earnings ratios were derived by regressing earnings on origin group categories with controls for age (continuous var.), region, metro status, Texas, California, Texas metro area, California metro area. All figures exclude farmers and unpaid family farm workers. For row b, the male-to-female wage ratio for native-white workers (.69) was calculated from the regression model.

		NW	Mexican 1.53	NBlk
For row c, proportion working	Men	0.94	0.90	0.80
	Women	0.83	0.76	0.82
For row e, sex ratio: men per 100 women		1.01	1.03	0.88

drop by a factor of .69 (the male-to-female wage ratio among native whites). Row c adjusts the ratios in row b to take account of the nonworkers in every group. Among women these are more plentiful than among men, and among black men more plentiful than among other male groups. These adjusted ratios can be seen as a summary of the mean per capita earnings flowing into the group from each person in a particular ethnic and gender category, recognizing that some of these people bring in no earnings. Row d presents these results averaged across gender, then expresses them for the Mexican 1.53 group and blacks relative to native whites: ethnic ratios of .75 and .73 respectively. The result of the adjustments thus far is not so great, although it does emphasize that extending the analysis to include the nonworkers and taking account of lower wages for women workers does tend to undercut the apparent modest disadvantages at first seen for Mexicans compared to native blacks before education was taken into account: .77 versus .75 for men and .84 versus .77 for women. However, thus far the adjustments express income flowing into the group assuming that the sex ratio in each group is even. But we have seen that the sex ratio among blacks is grimly uneven. Taking that factor into account in row e shows the Mexican 1.53 group notably better off, earning 76 percent of native-white wages whereas blacks are earning 68 percent. Earnings in the groups expressed in this way imply that blacks are earning 89 cents for every dollar that Mexican 1.53 group members earn (that is, .68/.76 = .89).

In row e the result is expressed per 100 women in each group and the number of men that the male-to-female sex ratio tells us are in the group per 100 women. This formulation differs from the preceding by shifting from a per capita approach to earnings to one which stresses, in essence, potential family units (limited to group members). To put it another way, in row e the number of black men counted in producing male earnings has been lowered by the disappearance of about one black man in ten—quite apart from the fact that 20 percent of those counted have no earnings. If we are concerned only with how well the earnings of the men support those same men, then the absence of a tenth does not matter. But if the earnings of the black men are thought of as producing part of the well-being of both men and women (and indeed children), then the absence of one black man in ten for every ten women present does matter.

The presentation thus far takes into account male labor-force attachment and the lopsided black sex ratio, but deals only indirectly with family arrangements, assuming only that it matters for women how much men in the group are earning. We can now observe the interconnections between family arrangement and economic outcomes somewhat more directly by turning briefly to information on total family income available in the census—all income streams flowing to a family from all sources and all earners. The comparisons in table 4.8 are crude, but simple and powerful neverthe-

Table 4.8   Determinants of Total Family Income, by Origin

Family Type and Group	Percent of Native-White Total Family Income Controlling for:		
	Place, Age	Place, Age, Education	Place, Age, Education, Family Structure
Men present			
Mexican 1.53 group	87	102	100
Native blacks	72	78	82
Women present			
Mexican 1.53 group	80	98	95
Native blacks	57	64	81

Source: IPUMS datasets for 2000 census.

less; all the comparisons control for the usual geographic and age factors. The first set of figures describe the income of all families in which a young-adult male lives; the second set includes all families in which a young-adult female lives. There is obviously huge overlap between the two sets of families; moreover no account is taken for the number of earners in each family. Yet crude though they may be, they are remarkable in reflecting the power of the family structure variables on black women in particular. In families with men, the Mexican 1.53 group ends up with 87 percent, and the black families with 72 percent as much income as the native-white families—perhaps reflecting, in addition to the factors measured in table 4.7, higher proportions of black men living in families with fewer other earners than is true for the Mexican group. But the most striking difference is among families with a young-adult woman: the Mexican families end up with 80 percent and the black families with 57 percent as much income as the native white. Moreover, when the educational attainment of the man or woman, in families with men or women respectively, is taken into account, the Mexican group's family income for both types of families is at virtual parity with the native-white families, with 98 percent or more of the latter's income. By contrast, for black families, the educational control reduces the great gaps by only a few percentage points, leaving the vast majority of the difference between native-white and black family income unexplained.[10]

We can now confirm that these remaining differences between blacks and others are associated with family arrangements. Some simple additional controls are added to the regression model—whether or not the individual is married and whether or not he or she has children.[11] These factors explain none of the family income advantage of native whites over Mexicans—and relatively little of the black-white difference in families with a man present. However, these same family structure variables explain much of the difference in total income available to black and white families with a woman present. The black-to-white income ratio for women's families rises by 17 percentage points to 81 percent, twice as large a gain as achieved when controlling for black-white educational differences.[12]

In sum, a comparison of full-time workers will reveal blacks and the Mexican 1.53 group at about the same level of economic well-being, but this perspective is incomplete, even when extended to part-time workers or to women workers. When men and women workers are considered together, when account is taken of missing black males, and when the income available to family units is considered, especially to women's families, advantages of the Mexican 1.53 group over native blacks appear. Thus this section has highlighted what appear to be the economic consequences of the risk factors that chapter 3 showed are more prevalent among blacks than in the Mexican 1.53 group.

CONCLUSION

THEMES OF upward mobility and immigrant absorption are at the heart of American social history. This alone would be enough to spur inquiry as to whether the future absorption of immigrants and their offspring will be like its past. But in addition to this general curiosity, there are credible reasons to think that conditions have changed—economic conditions in the host society and the nonwhite origins of the new immigrants in particular. My approach to this question has focused on the low-skill immigrant worker, the Southern, Central, and Eastern Europeans (non-Jews) of 1890 to 1914, and the Mexicans of our own time. I compare the economic starting position of the immigrant generation, the schooling of their American-born children, and the economic outcomes of those American-born children when they reached adulthood.

The starting position of the immigrant generation has been thought very much worse now. I argue that the data on which this conclusion rests were flawed and suggest new measures, which indicate that the starting positions of the SCEN and the Mexicans have not differed nearly as much as had been supposed. Still, the situation for the SCEN grew progressively better over time, because American wage inequality was declining over the first half of the twentieth century. By contrast, the situation for the Mexicans has been deteriorating because American wage inequality has been rising over the past three decades. At their most distant points (I explain the specifics below), the SCEN were earning about 63 to 72 percent of what native whites were earning and the Mexicans of 2000 earned about 51 percent of what native whites averaged that year.

The greater contrast between past and present appears in the next generation. Mexican second-generation educational attainments lag further behind those of today's native whites than the SCEN's did behind those of yesterday's native whites. And, while it is hard to be sure, it does seem that the lag cannot be fully explained in terms of the differences observed in immigrant-generation wage differences. Finally, educational handicaps matter more for wages today than they mattered in the 1940s and 1950s, when the SCEN were lagging modestly in educational attainment. Today's Mexican second generation, compared to yesterday's SCEN, lags more in terms of years of schooling completed and pay more in terms of earnings for each of those years. Moreover, there is a fairly significant additional lag in Mexican earnings that does not seem to be related to levels of schooling. It could be due to any number of unmeasured or poorly measured factors, but discrimination is certainly one possible factor.

All this places Mexican immigrants, and especially the Mexican second generation, as progressing, but progressing more slowly than the SCEN did in their time. It does seem reasonable to suggest, with two recent observers (Bean and Stevens 2003) that though grim views of eternal poverty seem off the mark, it may be that the Mexican second generation will move up more slowly than did the SCEN, perhaps taking four or five generations rather than three or four to reach parity with the native-white mainstream.

Given this slower pace, the question of how the Mexican second generation today is faring compared to blacks of our own time is relevant. Mexican Americans are dropping out of high school at much higher rates than blacks, but in terms of other social behaviors that often lead into economic trouble, their rates are well below those of blacks (chapter 3). Earnings for full-time workers typically will not capture these problems; and so among such workers, men are faring about the same in both groups, and black women somewhat better (ignoring, in both cases, differences in schooling). Nevertheless, when whole families are taken into account it does appear that the Mexican second generation is in fact somewhat more favorably situated economically. I suspect that a modest exertion of social will would accomplish the most good by trying to boost high school graduation rates among the Mexican second generation (chapter 4). A fuller overview of findings follows.

I argued that we do well to restrict the comparison of past and present not only in terms of immigrant peoples but also in terms of birth cohorts. Critical to the SCEN experience was a massive immigration in a relatively short time, followed by a suddenly imposed restriction. The result was little noticed but had profound results for the characteristics of the next generation. Most of those born after 1925, although numerous, were only a small proportion of the SCEN second generation, and not representative of the group born earlier. Large majorities had one SCEN immigrant parent and one American-born parent, or parents who themselves had arrived in the United States either as young children prior to 1914 or after the great wave of immigration. Any of these situations would have affected the socioeconomic assimilation of both generations in ways that would distort our con-

117

clusions. The Mexicans of our own time have arrived since 1965, and their children are the first group of second-generation members since the resumption of American immigration. The interaction of immigration, restriction, and resumption of immigration operated on this group too, but in radically different ways, to produce both long-term and recent swings in the size of the second generation, and in the proportion of second-generation members with one parent born in the United States. Despite the vast literature on historical immigration, it is remarkable how little work has been done on the social composition of the generations, or on the timing of second generations. I hope therefore that these findings also serve as a contribution to the population history of the second generation.

I argued for the value of the ethnic wage ratio as a means of making reasonable comparisons in economic condition. The key feature of the ethnic wage ratio is that it compares the average immigrant-group wage in each period to the average native-white wage. Thus comparing the ethnic wage ratios of then and now gives us a comparison of relative immigrant well-being across time.

Christopher Jencks (2001) had convinced me of the power of this approach when he contrasted ethnic wage ratios for low-skill immigrants in 1910, based on the work of George Borjas, with ethnic wage ratios for Mexicans today. He found the earlier ethnic wage ratios far higher than those contemporary Mexicans endure. But if the ethnic wage ratio is the critical measure, the problem is that good national wage data are available only from 1940, yet we need them for 1910. The early censuses tell us each worker's occupation, but do not report income. One way scholars have worked around this problem is to estimate the average wage in an occupation for 1910 from contemporary surveys and business records and to assign that wage to all workers in an occupation. While I am impressed with Jencks's method, I am skeptical of the particular wage estimations on which his conclusions rested. I thought that estimating a mean wage for each occupation hid important differences between native and immigrant wages within occupations. As it turns out, I now believe there is a problem of this type but it is secondary (see appendix). The larger issue with the estimates Jencks was using, however, is that they were inaccurate for 1910 wages generally, not merely for studying ethnic differences. Recent findings by economic historians on American wage inequality across the twentieth century have been made since Borjas exploited those wage estimates (Goldin and Margo 1992; Goldin and Katz 2001). The new findings establish much higher levels of wage inequality for 1910 than those earlier wage estimates capture. The same recent findings on levels of wage inequality provided a basis for a new set of wage estimates for 1910 and 1920 (also detailed in the appendix).

Thus I reject the specific contrast Jencks believed existed between the

1910 and 2000 ethnic wage ratios, based as it is upon faulty wage estimates for the earlier year. But an even more fundamental point emerged. Comparisons of immigrant wages then and now cannot be meaningfully limited to snapshots from only two moments—such as 1910 and 2000—frozen in time, because the nature of wage inequality changed so much across the decades. During most of the first half of the century wage inequality declined over decades, and during the past three decades it rose. The two low-wage immigrant groups we are tracking therefore experienced different effects from the swings in American wage inequality during the course of their work lives. The SCEN largely profited from the earlier declines in wage inequality, notwithstanding the Great Depression years. The Mexicans, however, have largely lost out in the recent increases in wage inequality.

Clearly, we cannot rely on comparisons from single points in time. We need instead a series of snapshots across the decades. The first pair can be of the 1910 SCEN and the 1970 Mexicans, the latter being a rough substitute for the parents of the Mexican young-adult second generation observed thirty years later in the 2000 census. The SCEN immigrants did not have an advantage over the Mexicans of today; indeed, the former probably faced a moderate disadvantage (among men thirty-five and older, the 1910 ethnic wage ratios hover between .54 and .60; the 1970 ratios between .66 and .70; summarized in figure 2.2). The next snapshot might reasonably be taken when second-generation members had reached age fifteen, a time when their parents' well-being is especially determinative for the children's future direction. By this time, the ethnic wage ratios for the SCEN had improved and those for the Mexicans had worsened, with the result that the SCEN were almost certainly better off than the Mexicans relative to the native whites of each period. Nevertheless, even in this second comparison, the SCEN immigrant generation's advantage over the Mexicans of the later period was moderate at most and possibly trivial: given ethnic wage ratios standing at between .63 and .72 for the SCEN and .60 for the Mexicans, summarized in table 2.2.

Finally, a third snapshot should be taken of the most recently arrived Mexican immigrants of 2000. They are only now creating the families in which the future Mexican second generation will grow up, coming of age around 2030. These immigrants have arrived after the full three decades of increasing American wage inequality, and the contrast between them and the SCEN is therefore the sharpest. This is the comparison that Jencks had in mind. Nevertheless, my estimate is that, in this comparison, the Mexican immigrants of 2000 are clearly but not greatly disadvantaged compared to the SCEN of 1910: the ethnic wage ratio for 2000 measured as .51 and the 1910 ratio, as noted, .54 to .60.[1] Yet recall that these SCEN workers would progress over the coming decades to better circumstances in the fol-

119

lowing years: captured, in ethnic wage ratios of .63 to .72 when the next generation was about fifteen years old, as mentioned. Thus a serious gap begins to show in favor of the well-being of the SCEN immigrants: .63 to .72 versus .51. Still, even that serious gap is not the massive one Jencks had been concerned about: ethnic wage ratios of .88 then, .46 now, based on the biased earlier wage estimates for 1910.

Finally, one important feature of relative levels of well-being then and now is not captured in the ethnic wage ratios, namely the rise in real wages over time. We need to supplement the comparison of immigrant well-being relative to native-white well-being in each period with a direct comparison of immigrant economic well-being then and now. This latter perspective is especially relevant to the costs of an extended education over time. A full examination of education's costs and benefits then and now are well beyond the scope of this book, but the long-term rise in real wages must be part of any consideration of this theme, and especially to the fear argument that today's ticket out of poverty, in the form of a four-year college degree, is prohibitively high. I argue first that this formulation lays too much stress on an education that two-thirds of today's young native whites will not attain. Second, at lower educational levels—high school graduation, community college attendance—the direct costs of education are low. Third, the exclusive focus on the high costs of attending a four-year college only highlights nominal costs and ignores changes in real wages, which are far higher today than they were in 1910, or even in 1940, for low-skill immigrants (notwithstanding recent erosion; summarized in figure 2.3).

Part of our story concerns the immigrants, much is worked out in the second generation, SCEN then and Mexican now. In discussing the contemporary second generation I also compared Mexican-American and native-black young adults today. A long line of studies has compared immigrants starting in low-skill work, and especially their American-born children, to native blacks. Usually the goal is to understand why the fates of the groups have differed so radically—why the second-generation children of low-skill European immigrants successfully moved up and blacks did not (Handlin, 1959; Thernstrom 1973; Lieberson 1980; Perlmann 1988; Barrett and Roediger 2002). From this perspective, the segmented assimilation theory can be thought of as proclaiming that a new social reality is taking shape (Portes and Zhou 1993). The theory predicts that the old pattern of immigrant improvement and blocked advance for blacks is a thing of the past. The new reality is not that blacks will finally enjoy the fate of the European immigrants of old (at least ghetto blacks will not). Rather, the theory predicts that the children of new low-skill immigrants will not move up as in the past, but come to resemble inner-city blacks, not least because this new second generation is also racialized as nonwhite.

My first concern is to argue against two forms of analysis that I think are hopelessly misleading. The first approaches educational attainment by treating all Hispanics, or all Mexicans, as a single group—ignoring the huge proportion of Mexican immigrants educated in the home country. We cannot take the very low levels of Mexican educational attainment as indicative of what is happening to the U.S.-born second-generation Mexicans in American schools, especially when dealing with adults. The second analysis seeks hints of future developments by noting that there is little difference between the economic well-being of today's second- and third-generation Mexicans of the same age. The assumption is that the future children of today's Mexican second generation will resemble today's third generation, and hence advance only minimally economically. But this second approach ignores both familial and national histories, treating the context in which past and present Mexican second generations grew up as identical.

Instead, we can learn a great deal from the actual educational attainments of the young-adult Mexican second generation from the 2000 census and CPS datasets from the same period (in the census by focusing on a proxy group). To compare across time, we obviously must consider the giant shifts in average length of schooling. We would not get very far by comparing only absolute levels of schooling completed six or eight decades ago to those completed today. To get around this problem, I exploit the same logic as used for wage comparisons: a measure of how the second generation schooling in each period compares to the schooling of the native whites during the same period. On this measure, the Mexican second generation today appears to lag further behind native whites of today than the SCEN second generation of the past did behind the native whites then (summarized in figures 3.3 and 3.4). These differences are larger than we would have expected given the economic standing of their immigrant parents in both periods (summarized in table 3.2).[2] Perhaps greater parental educational handicaps, or the prevalence of undocumented status among the Mexican immigrant parents, help to explain the lag. The elevated Mexican high-school-dropout rates are especially striking—are notably higher, indeed, than those of blacks (summarized in figures 3.5 and 3.6).

So far the analysis seems consistent with the segmented assimilation theory's expectations: low outcomes in the second generation that are not simply the result of the low class position of the immigrant generation. The theory would explain the outcomes by the prevalence of a dysfunctional young-adult minority cultural pattern arising within the punishing contexts of parental class origin and American discrimination against nonwhites. To explore this possibility, I compare contemporary Mexican and black young-adult social patterns—specifically, the prevalence of other dysfunctional social behaviors in the two groups, behaviors that the cultural complex the theory posits might encourage. These behaviors include young unwed child-bearing for women and low labor force attachment, high incarceration rates, and high rates of disappearance for men. But whereas dropping out of high school is notably more prevalent among the Mexican second generation than among the blacks, these other behaviors are notably less prevalent. I therefore suggest an alternative explanation, one that seems more similar to the social patterns of the older SCEN second generation than to the patterns of blacks today—involving men leaving school early to take up work, and women to take up work or homemaking. Such behavior today, however, has more serious implications for wages than it did in the past.

Comparing second-generation wages then and now shows that in both periods the second generation did progress beyond the relative standing of the first—that is, the ethnic wage ratios are higher in the second generation than in the first (summarized in figures 2.2 and 4.1). Nevertheless, today young Mexican second-generation men are earning just about 75 percent of what native whites in the same locales earn. By contrast, the earliest second-generation SCEN, which fared the worst of all SCEN cohorts, earned 84 percent of what the sons of native whites earned in 1940. Moreover, no other ethnic wage ratio for the three SCEN second-generation cohorts placed them below 91 percent of the native-white comparison wage from 1940 to 1960. By 1960, all three cohorts were earning from 94 to 96 percent of the sons of native-white earnings. The wide range in SCEN outcomes over time, from 84 percent to near parity, emphasizes the changing situation of immigrant groups and of the wage context generally. Nevertheless, even at the lowest SCEN ratio, the second-generation advantage then over the Mexican relative position today is not inconsequential.

Part of the reason the wage handicap is greater for today's second generation is the group's relatively lower educational attainment. Larger differences in educational differences also matter more today than they would have mattered in the 1940 to 1960 period. The increased American wage inequality today is expressed partly through higher rewards to the better-educated, and partly through higher returns to schooling (these educational effects are summarized in table 4.1). However, the ethnic wage difference created by both factors operating together explains only about half of the entire second-generation Mexican wage handicap today. The rest of the wage handicap remains unexplained. By definition, we cannot "explain" this residual ethnic difference in wages with the variables available to us. Part of the problem involves measurement error in those variables. And part involves other variables. In particular, we were not able to capture fairly standard information about family origin at the individual level, especially father's and mother's wages and education; nor could we determine whether a Mexican-immigrant parent was an undocumented worker. And although we can measure the second-generation member's length of schooling, we have no measure for school quality. Still less can we capture illusive factors such as ethnic group differences in information about good jobs. Beyond all these, the residual might reflect a higher level of discrimination against the Mexican compared to the SCEN second generation, or distinctive group cultural norms of one sort or another.

The existence of a residual wage difference might appear to dovetail nicely with a version of the segmented assimilation hypothesis. Thus the theory would marshal the interactions of class, racial discrimination, and inner-city youth culture to explain why the advance over the first generation now has been more restricted than that of earlier second generations. This might be called a weak-hypothesis version of the theory, because it entails progress from first to second generation today (on average). A strong-hypothesis version might predict no rise, or even a decline. In any case, I argued against this particular causal explanation in connection with educational attainment—other dysfunctional social behavior is less prevalent than the theory would predict.

Nevertheless, the residual wage handicap of the Mexican second generation today, especially among the men, cannot be ignored and requires further study with other evidence than a census provides. Still, from the census evidence we learn that the size of residual wage handicaps were generally low for the SCEN (summarized in table 4.2) and probably lower still for old-line white immigrants such as the English, Germans, or Scandinavians. They were huge for blacks in the pre–civil rights era, in the North as well as in the South. One argument about the residuals is that they often reflect discrimination; as such they are a crude measure for the potential that a feedback loop will develop in the group. Lieberson (1980) used the term to refer to a tendency for a subculture of despair to develop out of a context of discrimination: eventually that subculture will have some independent force. The classic example, of course, has been racial discrimination against American blacks across the pre–civil rights era. But if the magnitude of the residual wage handicap is taken as the measure of the potential for a feedback loop to develop, we should remain skeptical that the much-smaller residuals endured by Mexicans of today will produce one as well. On the other hand, the combination of the residual wage handicap and the education-related wage handicap leave the Mexicans earning 75 percent of the native-white wage. We have little basis on which to predict what levels of discrimination and other hardships together might produce a particular cultural pattern, particularly in a changed social and political culture. It seems reasonable, then, to not dismiss the potential for a feedback loop simply because conditions that once produced it were worse than today's. My hunch is that the Mexican differentials will not produce such a feedback loop, one that will be prevalent in the group. Nevertheless, the segmented assimilation theory's expectation that a feedback loop will be prevalent can also find support in the earnings ratios.

In comparing the young-adult earnings among Mexican Americans and native blacks today, the conventional use of the wage ratios, even when extended to consider full-time women workers or part-time workers, does not fully capture the differences. The risk factors more prevalent among blacks take their toll here and must be factored in: childrearing out of wedlock for women, lower labor force attachment, higher institutionalization, and disappearance for men. When they are, and particularly when the focus changes from individual to family, it appears that the Mexican second generation of today fares better than native blacks. The advantage is no doubt smaller than it was for the SCEN second generation in its time.[3] If the question is whether the Mexican second generation's well-being is like the SCEN second generation's of then or like the blacks of today, the answer in terms of earnings seems to be somewhere in the middle.

Because the Mexican second generation is faring less well in relative terms than its SCEN counterpart, I find it reasonable to join Bean and Stevens (2003) in suggesting that Mexican economic assimilation may take more time—four or five generations rather than three or four. The segmented assimilation hypothesis can be interpreted to predict a more dire outlook, namely a stagnation and even a downward slide. For the theory to be compelling, this outcome would have to be true not merely for some small fraction of the ethnic group but rather for enough Mexican Americans to make the description of stagnation or downward slide true for the mean ethnic wage. As I mentioned in connection with feedback loops, we cannot rule out such a prediction, but it does seem less likely than upward movement at a slower pace than in the past. Evidence for the latter alternative is the similarity of first-generation starting positions then and now, the progress made between first and second generations now, and the general absence of other measures of dysfunctional youth culture in the second generation today compared to levels prevalent in the native-black population.

The wider context—increasing wage inequality—plagues most American workers, not only the Mexican immigrants and their children. If this trend could be reversed, it would transform the dynamics we have reviewed and much else in American social life. How such a reversal might be accomplished within existing economic and political constraints is a central challenge of our time. Further restricting Mexican immigration, of course, would reduce the magnitude of the problem that concerns us here, but might well be impossible, and in any case would involve great readjustment for the American economy, to say nothing of the lives of potential immigrants. So too, legalizing great numbers of undocumented Mexican immigrants, now and in the future, would reduce the income handicaps at least for this group, by improving their standing in the job market.

A simpler policy challenge lies in the elevated Mexican high school dropout rates. As I argued, these create an important part of the Mexican second-generation wage gap. Erasing the considerable difference between Mexican and black high school dropout rates, even without reducing both rates further to equal those of native whites, would have direct effects on Mexican earnings. Moreover, it would almost certainly stimulate large additional earnings increases, because as more young people graduate from high school more can consider entering a two-year or four-year college (table 4.5). It may seem puzzling to refer to increasing high school graduation rates as a simple challenge in any context. Perhaps it is only simpler than the other challenges I mentioned. Still, boosting high school graduation rates is the sort of policy intervention that American society has confronted from time to time (Krug 1964; Covello 1967; Perlmann 1985; Hampel 1986; Katz 1987). The results were hardly an unambiguous success; but at least the modes of social and political mobilization for such efforts are familiar and consistent with much else in contemporary American life. And finally, if the second-generation Mexican earnings inequality related to schooling were addressed, at least some of the unexplained earnings inequality, the residual inequality, might dissolve as well. Surely some of that residual inequality arises out of the interactions of the group's school attainments with discrimination and with power, perceived and real, over the social environment.

APPENDIX

THIS APPENDIX concerns three major subjects. The first (itself subdivided into numerous subtopics) concerns the estimates of wage ratios for 1910 to 1920 introduced in chapter 2 of this volume. The second subject is the Mexican 1.53 group used in chapters 3 and 4 as a proxy for the "true" second generation. The third subject (discussed in chapter 3) is the ethnic variation in the way those who left school after twelfth grade described their educational attainment.

ESTIMATING ETHNIC WAGE RATIOS FOR 1910 TO 1920

The federal census has collected occupational data since the mid-nineteenth century, but wage data only since 1940; accordingly, national wage studies that deal with the period prior to 1940 and exploit census data must rely on estimates from the occupational data.

A CRITIQUE OF PAST ESTIMATES

George Borjas's estimates have been especially important for the discussion of immigrant well-being in 1910. Borjas exploited a scale that presented a mean nationwide wage for each occupation (Jencks 2001; Borjas 1994). He then applied the mean occupational wage to each person found to work in that occupation in the 1910 census microdata sample. Finally, he computed a mean of these occupational means for each ethnic group. The occupational-wage scale on which this procedure rested was the creation of still-earlier work by two other social scientists, Samuel Preston and Michael Haines (1991); they had culled the wage data from a variety of government surveys, mostly from around the year 1900.

Borjas (1994) tested the adequacy of using an occupational (rather than an individual) wage as best he could, using 1940 census data; for that year both income and occupation were available in the census. He therefore computed a 1940 occupational wage and applied it to every worker in a given occupation. He then calculated a mean wage for members of each relevant ethnic group, using first the occupational and then the individual wage. The estimated and actual results were close.[1] However, in this test, both measures came from the same source, namely the 1940 individual-level wages. Borjas was testing the adequacy of substituting the occupational for the individual wage, but could not test the adequacy of the specific wage scale he was using for 1910—the Preston-Haines occupational wage scale.

I do not reject the use of an occupational wage as a substitute for the individual wage, but I do argue for two modifications in the way the occupational wage estimates are constructed. First, I show that the Preston-Haines scale is inadequate for present purposes and offer an alternative way to construct an occupational wage scale for 1910 and for 1920. Second, I show that the occupational wage, a national mean, cannot be applied without modification across ethnic groups, because the occupational wage masks systematic and measurable ethnic differences—for which we can adjust.

Recent work by Goldin and Katz (2001) and Goldin and Margo (1992) on the American wage structure between 1890 and 1950 now permits an additional test of the Preston-Haines scale. Goldin and her colleagues report a first great compression concentrated during the 1910 to 1920 decade, and the rough equivalence of wage inequality in the mid to late 1920s and in 1940. From this finding we can draw an expectation that an adequate wage scale for 1910 should reveal levels of wage inequality that are substantially greater than those a 1940 wage scale would reveal.

Before undertaking that test, I needed to be sure that occupational wage scales could in fact capture the compressions and decompressions of the American wage structure. That is, do "good" occupational wage scales, drawn directly from the census wage and occupation questions in the same year, reveal those post-1940 shifts in wage inequality? I therefore computed measures of wage inequality directly from the actual wages and from occupational wage scales that I constructed, using the decennial census datasets for 1940 through 1970 and for 2000 (figure A.1). For each census, I first calculated the ratio of wages for workers at the 90th and 10th percentiles of wages, using individual wages and then using the occupational wage. I also calculated both ways the ratios of wages for workers at the 75th and 25th percentiles of wages—that is, across the interquartile range (IQR). The less extreme IQR comparison is important because the SCEN immigrant and native-white workers were never as far apart as the 90th and 10th percentile positions. I therefore wanted confirmation that even less extreme

Figure A.1   Measures of Wage Inequality, 1940 to 2000

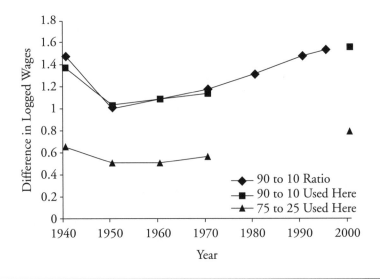

Source: IPUMS datasets for 1940 to 1970 and 2000 censuses, 1998 to 2001 CPS datasets and Katz and Autor (1999).
Note: The 90 to 10 ratio, from Katz and Autor is also shown in figure 2.1, in text. The series "used here" make no deletions for extreme scores and is limited to male workers twenty-five to sixty-four.

shifts in wage structure showed up in measures that relied on the occupational wage scale. Included from each census dataset are male nonagricultural employees between twenty-five and sixty-four years of age who reported working more than thirty-nine weeks in the preceding year.[2]

The series based directly on individual wages at the 90th and 10th percentiles reveals the key features that Goldin and Margo (1992) and Goldin and Katz (2001) discuss—the compression from 1940 to 1950, the slow rise to 1970, and the sharply increasing inequality by 2000. The series based directly on individual wages at the limits of the IQR also tracks roughly the same narrative. The series based on the occupational wage also track the changes in the wage structure quite well (figure A.2). Ratios based on occupational wage are less extreme than those based on actual wages in both the 90 to 10 and the IQR comparison; nevertheless, patterns of compression and decompression show up clearly. In short, the occupational wage scales, derived from the same source as the individual wages, pass the first test: they are sensitive enough to reflect the 1940 through 2000 stages of wage compression and decompression.

Figure A.2   Adequacy of Occupational Wage in Census Data, 1940 to 2000

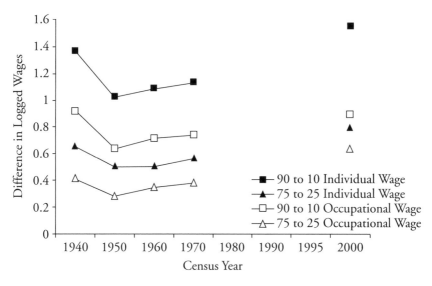

Source: IPUMS datasets for 1940 to 1970 and 2000 censuses.
Note: The 90 to 10 and 75 to 25 wage ratios are each calculated in two ways from the census data for each year. Individual wage: Calculations are made directly from the wages individuals reported (these series are identical to those labeled "used here" in figure A.1). Occupational wage: the ratios are calculated after the occupational wage (the mean wage for each occupation) was assigned to each worker in a given occupation.

We can therefore turn now to the Preston-Haines scale and ask whether it also reflects that history faithfully. Specifically, it should show that wage inequality was substantially more unequal in 1910 than in 1940, because much of the first compression occurred between those dates, indeed between 1910 and 1920. And whatever the turbulence of the Great Depression, the wage structure again reflected the effect of that first great compression by the 1940 census. To emphasize, the ratios involved in all these tests of the occupational wage, including the test for 1910, are based on all American workers who meet sex, age, and employment conditions mentioned—the tests do not involve classifying workers by ethnic or nativity characteristics at all. In the 1910 and 1920 datasets there is no way to restrict the sample by the number of hours worked each week, as I had restricted the later samples. Consequently, I calculated 1940 results two ways, with and without the restriction limiting the sample to those working at least thirty-five hours per week.

The Preston-Haines scale fails the test: far from showing much greater inequality in 1910 than in 1940, the 90th to 10th and the 75th to 25th wage ratios based on the Preston-Haines scale are both lower than the comparable ratios for 1940—the 90th to 10th is much lower and the 75th to 25th on that scale is slightly so (figure A.3). To belabor the analytic point, the problem uncovered here is not the use of an occupational wage scale per se; such scales did capture expected shifts in wage inequality when the scales had been constructed from wage information in the census datasets themselves. Rather, the problem with the Preston-Haines wage scale must lie in the representativeness of the old survey data from which that wage scale was constructed.

Why does the scale fail? We know little about the biases in any of the old surveys on which it rests. The most important of these surveys was an 1899 cost of living study, which focused especially on wage workers in industrial occupations. The researchers conducting the survey apparently

Figure A.3   Inadequacy of 1910 Occupational Wage Scale

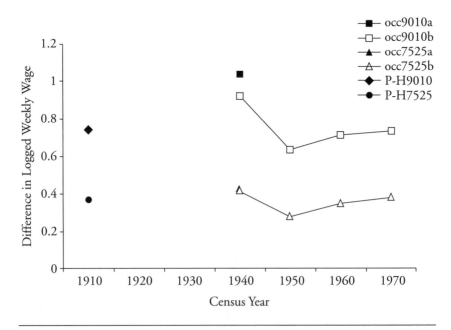

Source: IPUMS datasets for 1910 and 1940 to 1970 censuses and Preston and Haines (1991, for P-H scale).

Note: On the 1940 to 1970 b series, see figure A.2. Workers in the b series are restricted to those working at least thirty-five hours per week; because the 1910 census did not ask about hours worked per week, the 1940 data are also recalculated (in the a series) without the restriction for hours.

dispatched canvassers to places in which industrial workers were highly concentrated within thirty-three states; there the canvassers selected families to study. We know nothing about how these families were selected.[3] However, we do know that these researchers tried to study a population that was not representative of all industrial workers, and still less of all workers. Interested as they were in the cost of living of families, the survey's organizers appear to have excluded single adults, and were most interested in two-parent families with children. Moreover, the report's discussion of wages by occupation refers only to the wages of the family head. Hence among the 25,440 families surveyed, only 862 families were without a husband, 419 families without a wife, and 3,992 families without children. In short, younger, unattached men are bound to be underrepresented; and if the scale was meant to cover the wages of all workers in the economy, then women and children are surely drastically underrepresented too. How this bias plays into the national average wage for each occupation depends on the occupation's age and sex profile. My suspicion is that the survey is unrepresentative in various ways; the restriction to family heads is simply one obvious bias we know about, and quite possibly not the most important bias (Perlmann 2002).[4]

A New Occupational Wage Scale

The Goldin and Katz (2001) findings about wage structure fluctuation between 1890 and 1940 can also provide the basis for the construction of a more adequate mean occupational wage scale for 1910, and for 1920. Two especially relevant observations can be drawn from their research: wage inequality declined by as much between 1910 and 1940 as it would later decline between 1940 and 1950 and wages reported in the 1940 census were not reflecting conditions created by the Great Depression but rather had returned to conditions of the mid- to late 1920s. I created the new occupational scales based on those two observations. I created a 1910 occupational-wage scale from 1940 and 1950 individual-level census data so that the wage for each 1910 occupational category is equal (in constant dollars) to the 1940 wage times the ratio of the 1940 to 1950 wage. I first computed 1940 and 1950 occupational wage scales from the decennial census wage data for those years. Next, I used a standard adjustment for inflation so that both scales were stated in 1909 dollars.[5] Then the 1910 wage scale is estimated for each occupation as w10 = w40 x (w40/w50), where w10, w40 and w50 refer to the 1910, 1940 and 1950 occupational wage respectively (expressed in 1910 dollars). I created a 1920 occupational-wage scale by using the 1940 occupational wage scale in constant dollars.[6]

I first use the method to calculate the 90th to 10th and IQR (75th to 25th) percentiles, as in the earlier exercise. Figure A.4 confirms that when

Figure A.4   New 1910 to 1920 Occupational Wage Estimates in Context

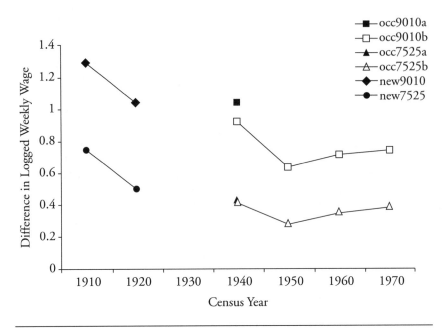

Source: IPUMS datasets for 1910 to 1920 and 1940 to 1970.
Note: On the wage ratios for 1940 to 1970, see notes to figure A.2. The new occupational wage scales for 1910 to 1920 were constructed: w10 = w40 × (w40/w50) where w10, w40, and w50 are the 1910, 1940, and 1950 occupational wages respectively—the 1950 wages first having been adjusted downward for inflation since 1940. See note to figure A.3 for explanation of the a and b series.

these estimates are made, the wage ratios for the high and low earners in 1910 are much more unequal than the comparable ratios in 1940, and that the 1920 ratios are at about the same level as the 1940 ratios. Of course, because the 1910 and 1920 occupational scales were constructed to produce such a result, figure A.4 simply confirms that the ratios are acting as they were constructed to do.

Applying the ethnic wage scales to the 1910 and 1920 occupational data produces ethnic wage ratios in the .6 to .7 range, depending on the age range and census year. I will argue that these ratios are upwardly biased in ways we can correct. However, first consider how the occupational wage operates when applied to broad occupational strata of 1910 (figure A.5). Each stratum is scored in terms of the ratio of mean wage in each stratum compared to mean wage for unskilled workers, which is set to 100. The results are shown using the Preston-Haines scale, the 1940 scale, and the

Figure A.5   Comparing Occupational Wage Scales Applied to 1910 Data

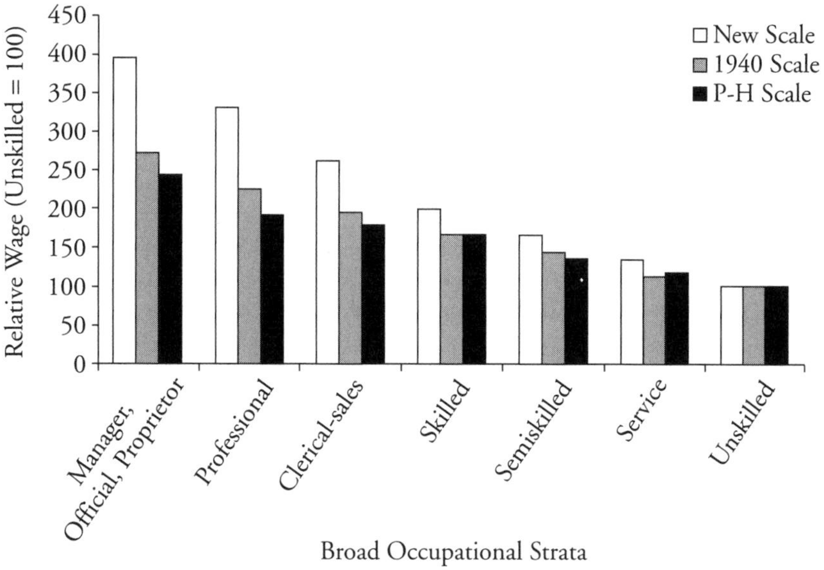

Source: IPUMS datasets for 1910 census and Preston and Haines (1991, for P-H scale).

new 1910 occupational scale. The difference between the first two is modest, and found only in white-collar occupations. On the other hand, the new 1910 scale differs from the other two throughout; but the difference is especially striking for white-collar workers, reflecting the higher returns for schooling in 1910.

ADJUSTMENTS FOR ETHNIC WAGE DIFFERENCES WITHIN OCCUPATION

This method ignores possible ethnic differences in wages within each occupation; to the extent that these systematically favored native whites over the SCEN, it overstates the ethnic wage ratio that is estimated from the occupational wage. We cannot measure the impact of all possible ethnic differences within occupation. There are, however, two sorts of wage differences not captured adequately with the occupational wage whose true magnitude we can estimate. We can then adjust the ethnic wage ratio estimated from the occupational wage for these differences.

133

GEOGRAPHIC LOCATION The first sort of undetected wage difference involves differences in wages across regions, and especially between metro and nonmetro areas. The SCEN were concentrated in northern cities; the native whites were not. Wages were higher for everyone in those cities; consequently, if we ignore geographic location, we compare SCEN immigrants situated predominantly in high-wage areas to native whites situated predominantly in lower-wage areas. (I discuss the logic of imposing the controls for place of residence in a later section of this appendix.)

By definition, the occupational wage fails to take into account the wage difference associated with region and metro status. Only geographic differences in occupational distributions are captured when geographic controls are imposed on occupational wage data; consequently imposing the controls make little difference when the occupational wage is the basis of the ethnic wage ratio. By contrast, in 1940 and 1950 census data the geographic controls have considerable effect when imposed on individual-level wage data (table A.1). It seems reasonable to assume that the ethnic wage ratios for 1910 and 1920 would become as much more unequal as they become in 1940 and 1950 were we able to account for geographic differences in those early years with wage data sensitive to geographic locale—namely, some 6 to 10 percentage points more unequal.

Generally, the ethnic wage ratios for the older years, involving the SCEN immigrants, varied more by geographic location than the wage ratios for Mexicans since 1970 did. I discuss the significance of the heavy concentration of the contemporary Mexicans in Texas and California in chapter 4. The major geographic factor affecting wages, however, at least in the period since 1940, was in any case metro status, not region—indeed much of the regional effect was a function of greater urbanization in some regions—and the contemporary Mexicans are highly concentrated in metro areas.

EDUCATION Ethnic educational differences among workers within the same occupation would also systematically bias the ethnic wage ratio estimated from the occupational wage. Consider first a vivid example of these educational differentials—the proportion of illiterates among laborers in 1910. One need not have an inflated view of the value of literacy to think that a literate laborer could carry out more functions than an illiterate laborer, and may have earned more as a result. Among male, young-adult SCEN laborers in 1910, 38 percent were illiterate; among comparable native whites, 5 percent were.[7]

Despite this example, we need to know how prevalent ethnic literacy differentials were across all occupational levels, and also how much difference such ethnic literacy differentials made to wages within the same occupation. And finally, going beyond mere literacy, the same two questions must be asked about higher educational attainments. We cannot answer

Table A.1   Ethnic Wage Differences Associated with Region and Metro
             Status (in Log Points)

| Census | Birth Cohort | Age at Census | Increase in SCEN Coefficient When Geographic Controls Are Added to the Regression Model | | |
			Regressing Occupational Wage a	Regressing Individual Wage b	Difference in Increase c
1910	1876–1885	25–34	−0.01		
	1846–1855	55–64	−0.01		
	1846–1885	25–64	−0.01		
1920	1856–1895	25–64	−0.01		
1940	1886–1895	45–54	−0.02	−0.11	−0.10
	1876–1885	55–64	−0.01	−0.09	−0.07
1950	1886–1895	55–64	−0.01	−0.07	−0.06

Source: IPUMS datasets for 1910, 1920, 1940, and 1950 censuses.
Note: Individual wage = wage reported by each individual, 1940 to 1950 censuses. Occupational wage = mean wage reported by all individuals in an occupation (men, 25 to 64). Columns a and b each report the differences in the SCEN coefficient across two regression models, first controlling only for age (continuous var.) and then for age, metro status and region.

these questions with direct evidence from 1910, of course, given the absence of both wage data and educational attainment data from that year, but we can estimate the answers more fully than it might initially appear.

We begin by showing the impact of literacy on the ethnic wage ratio in 1910, 1920, 1940, and 1950, measured by the occupational wage (table A.2, column a). The 1940 and 1950 censuses do not in fact include a literacy question, but we can create a proxy literacy measure by focusing on the individuals who reported receiving no, one, or two years of schooling. We thus isolate a group at the bottom of the hierarchy of formal schooling that covers about the same proportion of the relevant birth cohorts that reported themselves illiterate in 1910 and 1920.[8] Literacy accounts for a small but clear difference in the ethnic wage ratio based on the occupational wage in every period and age cohort. Although the literacy measure is weak, it generally shows greater returns to literacy in earlier compared to later years for the 1910 to 1950 period.[9] Note that this discussion pertains to the decline in the SCEN coefficient in the regression; the coefficient on the literacy measure is considerably larger (note to table A.2). These findings are not surprising; they simply demonstrate that the one crude measure of education available to us in the early period operates consistent with expectations—given its impact later in the century on the same and similar workers and the narrative of the changing wage structure. We do not have data on higher educational attainments in 1910 and 1920, but in 1940 and 1950 these attainments have, not surprisingly, a greater effect than mere literacy upon the ethnic wage ratio, measured by the occupational wage (column b).

For 1940 and 1950, we can also measure the impact of literacy and of educational attainments generally on the ethnic wage ratio measured by the individual wage (columns c and d). Both educational measures account for more of the ethnic wage ratio that is based on the individual wage than of the ethnic wage ratio that is based on the occupational wage. The difference (summarized in column e) is the impact of ethnic educational differences that remain undetected by the occupational wage measure, a difference of 3 to 7 log points. It seems reasonable to assume that the same processes must have had roughly comparable if not greater force in 1910 and 1920—when returns to schooling are thought to have been higher than in 1940 and 1950. Even without the preceding demonstration that literacy operates on the 1910 and 1920 ethnic wage ratios (based on the occupational wage) as expected, this assumption would be reasonable. An adjustment to the observed ethnic wage ratio based on the occupational wage in the range of at least 3 to 7 log points, seems reasonable (the range in column e).

The results of these adjustments are presented in table A.3. Column a presents the unadjusted 1910 and 1920 ethnic wage ratios (in logged form) for various age cohorts; in each case, this is the coefficient on the SCEN dummy variable when the occupational wage is regressed on ethnicity, age and geographic controls.[10] Columns b and c include the adjustment factors to account for the geographic and educational factors undetected by the occupational wage, but observable in the same age cohorts in 1940 and 1950 with the individual wage data. Columns d and e show the adjusted minimum and maximum resulting estimates in log form and columns f and g show these estimates in exponentiated form. The upshot is that in 1910, the SCEN to native-white ethnic wage ratio hovered between .54 and .67, depending on the assumptions and the age cohort involved; among workers 35 and older it never exceeded .60.

OTHER FEATURES OF THE ETHNIC-WAGE-RATIO ESTIMATION PROCESS

THE GREAT DEPRESSION AND WAGES REPORTED IN THE 1940 CENSUS

As mentioned in the text, the SCEN were more concentrated in factory

Table A.2   Ethnic Wage Differences Associated with Literacy and Educational Attainment

| | | | Decrease in SCEN Coefficient When Educational Controls Are Added to the Regression Model | | | | |
| | | | Regressing Occupational Wage Control(s) | | Regressing Individual Wage Control(s) | | Difference in Decrease All Education Levels: Column d–Column b |
Census	Birth Cohort	Age at Census	Literacy a	All Education Levels b	Literacy	All Education Levels d	e
1910	1876–1885	25–34	−0.03				
	1866–1875	35–44	−0.05				
	1856–1865	45–54	−0.07				
	1846–1855	55–64	−0.08				
1920	1886–1895	25–34	−0.02				
	1876–1885	35–44	−0.04				
	1876–1885	35–44[a]	−0.04				
	1866–1875	45–54	−0.06				
	1856–1865	55–64	−0.08				
1940	1886–1895	45–54	−0.03	−0.14	−0.05	−0.19	−0.05
	1876–1885	55–64	−0.04	−0.14	−0.06	−0.21	−0.07
1950	1886–1895	55–64	−0.02	−0.07	−0.03	−0.10	−0.03

Source: IPUMS datasets for 1910, 1920, 1940, and 1950 censuses.

Note: See note to table A.1. Columns a to d report the differences in the SCEN coefficient across two regression models, first controlling for age, metro status, and region and then also controlling for literacy or for educational attainment. In the 1940 and 1950 censuses, the literacy question was replaced by the question on grades of schooling completed. Men who had completed up to two years of schooling were coded illiterate. Literacy coefficient (oldest cohort) in successive censuses: .23, .26, .14, and .10.

[a] In United States ten years or more.

Table A.3   Estimating Actual Wage Ratios from Occupational Wage Ratios

Census	Age Cohort	Observed SCEN/NW Ratio (Occupational Wage) a	Estimated Ethnicity Adjustments		Estimate: Wage Ratio That Would Be Observed with Individual-Level Wage Data			
			Geographic Differences in Wages b	Differences in Wages Associated with Education c	Logged		Exponentiated	
					Maximum d	Minimum e	Maximum f	Minimum g
1910	25–34	−0.317			−0.407	−0.487	0.67	0.61
	35–44	−0.418			−0.508	−0.588	0.60	0.56
	45–54	−0.420			−0.510	−0.590	0.60	0.55
	55–64	−0.437			−0.527	−0.607	0.59	0.54
	25–64	−0.406	−.06 to −.10	−.03 to −.07	−0.496	−0.576	0.61	0.56
1920	25–34	−0.189			−0.279	−0.359	0.76	0.70
	35–44	−0.274			−0.364	−0.444	0.69	0.64
	35–44[a]	−0.245			−0.335	−0.415	0.72	0.66
	45–54	−0.278			−0.368	−0.448	0.69	0.64
	55–64	−0.268			−0.358	−0.438	0.70	0.65
	25–64	−0.254			−0.344	−0.424	0.71	0.65

Source: IPUMS datasets for 1910 to 1920 censuses.
[a]Resident in the United States at least ten years.

jobs than native whites; so if wages in these jobs rebounded more slowly than in higher-skill jobs, the 1940 ethnic wage ratio might reflect the differential hold of the Great Depression on SCEN wages that year. The possibility is especially important to consider because the 1940 evidence provide our earliest ethnic wage ratios based on individual-level reports rather than on estimates from the occupational wage. Indeed, all the other individual-level evidence comes from after the 1940 to 1950 great compression of wages. Moreover, the 1910 and 1920 estimates for the ethnic wage ratios from the occupational wage, which we use to capture the earlier levels of well-being of the SCEN, accord well with the 1940 evidence based on individual wage reports. That they do is a major source of confidence in the accuracy of the earlier estimates. Yet that confidence would be shaken if the 1940 estimates were too low because of the lingering effects of the depression. But the same concerns about differential wage rebounds from the depression were relevant to Goldin and her colleagues as they studied the 1940 to 1950 wage compression; after intensive review of the evidence, they concluded the contrary.

> Was 1939 a typical year for the wage structure and the returns to education and skill? After ten years of record-high unemployment, those at the bottom of the skill distribution might have acceded to extremely low real wages. If so, then the wage distribution below the median would have been abnormally and temporarily stretched by 1939. . . .
>
> Previous work has established a good case for the opposite conclusions. The wage structure in 1939 was not simply a product of the Great Depression but, rather, had been in place in the middle to late 1920s (Goldin and Margo 1992). . . .
>
> All evidence to date, therefore, confirms that 1939 is neither an oddity nor an anomaly with respect to certain measures of inequality such as the premium to skill, and the wage structure. (Goldin and Katz 2001, 41–2)

Thus, on this point too, the ethnic wage ratios for 1910, 1920, and 1940 are consistent with the Goldin and Margo (1992) and Goldin and Katz (2001) narratives of wage inequality: the 1940 levels are not the anomalous products of the Great Depression, and the shift from 1940 to 1950 levels of inequality is novel, and not a return from depression to pre-depression conditions.

THE ASSUMPTION ABOUT THE 1910 AND 1940 WAGE STRUCTURES   My method for creating the 1910 wage scale depends on the assumption that the wage structure had changed about as much between 1910 and 1940 as it changed between 1940 and 1950. The impact of making moderately different assumptions could be tested with the 1940 and 1950 census data, using the methods described in this appendix. The findings of Goldin and Katz (2001) cannot present us with a single neat figure for the average change in the entire wage structure for 1910 through 1940 compared to 1940 through 1950, even if a single measure such as the 90th to 10th percentile ratio is specified. Treating the two shifts as roughly equal in magnitude seems a reasonable approximation of what they have concluded. Readers should recall first that only large deviations from that assumption would have large effects; second that my approximation could understate the change they discuss, and third that the test of the older Preston-Haines occupational wage scale does not depend on the assumption about the precise degree of change between 1910 and 1940.[11]

THE LOGIC OF CONTROLLING FOR PLACE OF RESIDENCE   As already stressed, SCEN immigrants were much more concentrated in the high-wage northern cities than native whites were. I controlled for place of residence either directly (in the later datasets) or by estimation (in 1910 and 1920, as described earlier and shown in tables A.1 and A.3). But it is worth stepping back to ask whether place of residence should be controlled in calculating the ethnic wage ratios. Controlling highlights the wage based on what the immigrant compared to the native worker brings to the job market. Omitting the control highlights the wage based also on advantages flowing from the American place of residence. Of course, we need not choose between these approaches and can instead explore the data both ways, including or omitting geographic controls. Simplicity, however, urges a single summary measure for repeated use, and I opted for controls on two grounds. First, the major substantive questions about immigrant-native wage comparisons past and present concern changing levels of job-related skills and remuneration for those skills. So measures for these, net of any residential advantage the SCEN immigrants may have had in the early period, seemed most important; and that measure seemed necessary even if the ratio without controls were to be presented. For similar reasons, when assessing ethnic catch-up over a generation, of greatest interest will be second-generation advance *net* of ethnic geographic shifts (SCEN, Mexican, or native white). Comparisons that also measure the role of residential shifts would be more complete, but more complex and ultimately, as mentioned, spur questions about the net advance. The second reason for choosing to control for place of residence is that geographic differences in prevailing wages partly reflect differences in costs of living—such as housing and food costs in cities. So higher urban wages were at least partially wiped out by unmeasured higher urban costs—unless one were prepared to argue that these differences in costs reflect amenities from which the low-skill worker profits in a way relevant to our analysis.[12]

An estimate of the impact of the geographic controls on the ethnic wage ratios involving the SCEN can be found in table A.1, column b: seven to eleven log points, depending on census year and cohort. An increase of this magnitude would raise the estimates for the 1910 ethnic wage ratio (SCEN wage as a percentage of native white wage; shown in figure 2.2) from a percentage in the high fifties range to one in the low sixties range. The impact of geographic controls on the ethnic wage ratios in 1970 and 2000 were much lower than in the earlier years.[13]

IMPLICATIONS OF LIMITING THE SAMPLE TO NON-AGRICULTURAL WORKERS   Because wages for farmers are difficult to meaningfully compare to those of other workers, I have excluded farmers from the wage ratio, as did Preston and Haines (1991), Borjas (1994), and Goldin and her colleagues (Goldin and Margo 1992; Goldin and Katz 2001). The case of other agricultural workers is less clear; very few immigrants worked in these jobs, but another 11 percent of young native whites did so in 1910.[14] Goldin and her colleagues exclude these workers, as do Katz and Autor (1999). Once again, to exploit the similarity between my data and that of Goldin and her colleagues referring to changes through 1950, I did not include the other agricultural workers in wage ratios. Beyond the advantage of consistency with the other studies, the case for excluding these agricultural employees also rests upon the very fact that their reported wages are so low that, like farmers, it is hard to meaningfully compare any reported figure to wages of non-agricultural workers. Possible payment in kind for housing or food make the case for omission stronger. Had I included the other agricultural workers in the 1910 estimates, the ethnic ratios for that year would have been about 10 log points higher than those I report.

BIRTH COHORTS   As shown in chapter 1, the period of the SCE immigration was short, and the period in which the relevant second-generation groups were born is also fairly short. Moreover, the post-1930 birth cohorts are highly atypical of the second generation we want to study. Researchers can always find, certainly in the huge IPUMS samples, reasonably large numbers of SCE immigrants in the aged twenty-five through sixty-four labor force. But in the 1970 census, for example, all of the individuals in that age bracket would have been under twenty in 1914 and even in 1924. Even as far back as the 1940 census, the younger half of the group would have turned twenty after 1914, when the great immigration period had ended. By definition, all are unrepresentative of the young adults who arrived during the years of mass immigration. For these reasons, I focus on a narrow range of birth cohorts.

FULL-TIME MALE WORKERS   I limited all the historical comparisons to full-time workers, defined as those who had been employed for at least thirty-nine weeks of the preceding year (and in 1940 and after, at least thirty-five hours a week). Limiting the analysis to full-time male workers does not affect the conclusions about the relative well-being of the nativity groups significantly, but simplifies comparisons to the work of the economic historians.

OMISSION OF THE JEWS FROM THE RELEVANT IMMIGRANT COMPARISONS: FURTHER COMMENT   I omit the east-European Jews from the group of SCE immigrants, as explained in chapter 1. There has been some debate between Alba, Lutz, and Vesselinov (2001) and Borjas (2001) about including Jews in studies of the pace of immigrant economic assimilation since 1910. However, in that debate, the question turned on whether they should be excluded notwithstanding Borjas's goal of studying many groups at once and determining an average rate of "convergence" in ethnic behavior over generations. My goal is different: to explore the experience of the least well-off of the past immigration wave, not all immigrant groups—or rather the least well-off large group that might reasonably be compared to the situation of the Mexicans today.[15] My reason for excluding the Jews is consequently more straightforward: the other SCE groups meet that description; the Jews do not.

A PROXY FOR THE SECOND GENERATION IN THE 2000 CENSUS

Were it not for a single factor, work on the contemporary second generation would surely rest on the 2000 census; the alternative choice of aggregated CPS datasets that center on that year would be a poor substitute. Outcomes of interest are at least as richly detailed in the census as in the CPS, the census sampling design is more straightforward than that of the CPS, the census includes the institutional as well as noninstitutional population, and the census is undertaken over weeks, whereas aggregated CPS datasets involve surveys undertaken several years apart. Beyond all this, the census sample is gigantic. The CPS, although large by most standards of data collection, is tiny by comparison to the census. The public use sample from the 2000 census includes 6 percent of the American population, nearly seven million households; the 1998 to 2001 CPS datasets together cover some 150,000 households (Hicks 1997). When the CPS is sifted for small subgroups, the available number of cases quickly dwindles. For example, fewer than 200 second-generation Mexican American men aged twenty-five to thirty-four who reported earned income are found in five years of CPS surveys.

However, the single factor to which I referred almost tips the balance in favor of the CPS. Since 1980, the decennial census has failed to ask respondents where their parents were born. It is therefore impossible to identify the second generation (the U.S.-born children of immigrants) in recent censuses unless they are still living with their parents. True, in the recent censuses the native-born of Mexican origin are identified in the Hispanic-origin and ancestry questions, but their generational status remains unknown. Thus we cannot tell whether people of Mexican origin are, for example, second or sixth generation native-born.

For much work on contemporary American ethnicity, the absence of parental birthplace information makes the use of the census frustrating. However, in our case, and I believe in many other research contexts, we can nevertheless reap the great gains of using the 2000 census—because we can exploit a crucial modification introduced in another of its questions. For the first time since 1920, the census asked when an immigrant first came to the United States—in terms of single years rather than ranges of years. By using the response to this question, and the age of the respondent in 2000, we can derive the age of the immigrant at the time of immigration. From that information, we can construct a proxy for the true second generation: people born in a given country who arrived in the United States before their third birthday.

The CPS remains important, of course, because we can check numerous results on the true second generation in that dataset. Also in the CPS third or later generation Mexican Americans can be distinguished from unmixed and mixed second generations and from immigrants, whereas in the census we can distinguish only immigrants from all native-born of Mexican ancestry (table A.4).

Table A.5 shows the sample-size limitations of the CPS; the five years of datasets produce only 248 Mexican men in the true second generation born between 1966 and 1975; of these, 182 men are full-time wage workers. For the mixed second generation, the numbers are even lower, slightly over 100 for men and for women. It is these small Ns that we can avoid if the 1.53 group is a reasonable proxy for the true second generation. There are more than 2,600 sample members of men and of women in the Mexican 1.53 group and about the same number in the Mexican 1.56 group, those who arrived between their third and sixth birthdays. More than 1,800 men and 1,200 women in each group were full-time year-round workers with positive incomes. The gain for statistical confidence, which rises with the square root of the sample size, is smaller, but still important. Table A.6 shows the 95 percent confidence intervals around a rate of 30 percent (for example, high school graduation). For the 1.53 and 1.56 groups in the census, the interval would be 1 to 2 percentage points on either side of the observed rate. For the CPS true second generation, the interval would be 6 to 7 percentage points on either side.

The following analysis explores the adequacy of the 1.53 proxy for the

Table A.4   Origin Group Classifications Used in This Study for 2000 Census Data

Groups	Definitions
Mexican-origin groups	
Mexican immigrants	Mexican immigrants first arriving in the United States at age six or older
Mexican 1.56 group	Mexican born, arrived in the United States at ages three, four, or five
Mexican 1.53 group	Mexican born, arrived in the United States at ages younger than three

U.S.-born of Mexican origins	U.S.-born of Mexican origins (reported in census ancestry or Hispanic question); second or higher generation—CPS data indicates that about 65 percent are third generation or higher
	—includes, but not distinguishable:
	  i) unmixed (true) second generation
	  ii) mixed second generation
	  iii) third or later generation

Non-Mexican-origin groups	
Native whites	U.S. born; white only reported race; no Mexican origins
Native blacks	U.S. born; black racial origins reported; no Mexican origins
All others	All individuals not included elsewhere

Source: Group definitions used in this study are based on census questions on respondent's country of birth, age, year of immigration, Hispanic origin, ancestry, and race (Ruggles et al. 2005).
Note: The 2000 census allowed respondents to report more than one racial origin.

true second generation two ways. First, we focus exclusively on the census, examining a younger cohort of children, between fourteen and sixteen years of age. Because children are still found in their families of origin, we can identify both the 1.53 group and the unmixed true second generation members. How similar are their family backgrounds? Notable proportions were living with only one parent—20 percent of the 1.53 group and 29 percent of the true second generation group (table A.7, panel a). Perhaps single-parent families are less prevalent in the 1.53 and 1.56 subgroup than in the true second generation because they were more likely to have been formed before immigration, to have held up a few years, and in some cases

Table A.5   Unweighted Sample Sizes in Census and CPS, 1966 to 1975
             Birth Cohort

Ethnic Group	2000 Census		1998–2001 CPS General		1998–2001 CPS Detail		
	Male	Female	Male	Female	Generation and Parentage	Male	Female
Mexican groups							
Immigrants	81,472	60,305	2,063	1,765			
1.56 group	2,740	2,686 ⎱ →	106	107			
1.53 group	2,629	2,626 ⎰					
1.53 group, citizen	1,282	1,531					
U.S. born, Mexican origins	6,623	6,601	1,148	1,385	⎧ 2nd, nbfp	248	293
					⎨ 2nd, nbmp	165	229
					⎩ 3rd or more	735	863
Non-Mexican groups							
Native white	122,454	123,866	13,057	13,605			
Native black	18,812	22,169	1,495	2,073			
All other	127,762	131,975	3,273	3,403			
Full-time, full-year workers with positive income							
Mexican groups							
Immigrants	53,308	15,924	1,520	482			
1.56 group	1,881	1,286 ⎱ →	74	48			
1.53 group	1,867	1,264 ⎰					
1.53 group, citizen	946	794					
U.S. born, Mexican origins	4,493	3,339	804	661	⎧ 2nd, nbfp	182	164
					⎨ 2nd, nbmp	119	109
					⎩ 3rd or more	503	388
Non-Mexican groups							
Native white	94,138	66,197	9,862	6,859			
Native black	10,835	12,151	1,026	1,191			
All other	84,597	58,148	2,238	1,459			

Source: IPUMS dataset for 2000 census (6 percent sample) and 1998 to 2001 CPS datasets.

Table A.6   Confidence Intervals Around Proportions: An Example for
             Samples of Male Full-Time, Full-Year Workers in the Census
             and CPS, 1966 to 1975 Birth Cohort

Mexican Groups	2000 Census	CPS General	CPS Detail	
Immigrants	0.00	0.02		
1.56 group	0.02 ⎤			
1.53 group	0.02 ⎦ →	0.11		
1.53 group, citizen	0.03			
			⎧ 2nd, nbfp	0.07
U.S. born,	0.01	0.03	⎨ 2nd, nbmp	0.08
Mexican origins			⎩ 3rd or more	0.04
Non-Mexican groups				
Native white	0.00	0.01		
Native black	0.01	0.03		
All other	0.00	0.02		

Source: IPUMS dataset for 2000 census (6 percent sample) and 1998 to 2001 CPS datasets.
Note: Confidence intervals were calculated as twice the standard error on an observed proportion of .3 (st er = sqrt(pq/N)). CPS intervals are actually slightly larger due to sample design (Perlmann 2003a).

to have held up during years when the parents were living in different countries. In any case, it is useful to view the various comparisons separately for the single-parent and two-parent households, remembering first that single-parent households include far more mothers than fathers.[16]

The 1.53 group's parents may have completed modestly more schooling before leaving Mexico than the parents of the true second generation; yet by comparison with the American labor force, the differences are trivial. All these parents averaged only seven to eight years of school (table A.7, panel b). By contrast, the parents differ strikingly in terms of years of residence in the United States, by six to eight years (panel c). The average age of the parents of the true second generation is also greater than among the parents of the 1.53 group (panel d). Yet while the average age difference is just over two years, the difference in average length of U.S. residence is four to six years. In other words, the parents of the true second generation generally came to the United States at a slightly earlier age (confirmed in panel e), and no doubt were more likely to have come before marriage. Because the later departure did not result in longer education, we can only wonder who fared better as immigrants—those who left earlier for the United States or

Table A.7   Family Background of Mexican-Origin Youth, 14 to 16
in 2000 Census

	Youths in Two-Parent Families		Youths in Mother-Headed Families
Characteristic	Fathers	Mothers	Mothers
a) Youth with only one parent at home			
Percentage			
1.56 group	20		
1.53 group	20		
1.53 group, parent a U.S. citizen	13		
True second generation: NBFP	29		
Mixed second generation: NBMP	n.a.		
U.S. born, Mexican origins	30		
b) Parents' educational attainment (mean for grades of school completed)			
1.56 group	7.3	7.0	7.1
1.53 group	7.6	7.4	7.6
1.53 group, one or both parents are U.S. citizens	8.6	8.3	7.9
True second generation: NBFP	7.3	7.3	7.7
Mixed second generation: NBMP	8.8	10.0	n.a.
U.S. born, Mexican origins	10.0	10.1	10.4
c) Mean years lived in United States			
1.56 group	16.0	12.6	13.1
1.53 group	18.3	15.4	15.6
1.53 group, one or both parents are U.S. citizens	19.2	16.2	17.7
True second generation: NBFP	22.9	21.1	21.9
Mixed second generation: NBMP	22.3	22.7	n.a.
U.S. born, Mexican origins	n.a.	n.a.	n.a.

(*Table continues on p. 148.*)

Table A.7   (*Continued*)

Characteristic	Youths in Two-Parent Families		Youths in Mother-Headed Families
	Fathers	Mothers	Mothers
d) Mean age of parents			
1.56	41.5	39.0	40.3
1.53 group	41.7	38.8	39.3
1.53 group, one or both parents are			
U.S. citizens	42.3	39.3	41.4
True second generation: NBFP	43.8	41.1	41.9
Mixed second generation: NBMP	41.6	41.7	n.a.
U.S. born, Mexican origins	43.1	40.8	40.9
e) Mean age of parents' arrival in the United States			
1.56 group	25.5	26.4	27.2
1.53 group	23.4	23.4	23.7
1.53 group, one or both parents are			
U.S. citizens	23.1	23.1	23.7
True second generation: NBFP	20.9	20.0	20.0
Mixed second generation: NBMP	19.3	19.0	n.a.
U.S. born, Mexican origins	n.a.	n.a.	n.a.
f) Percentage of parents who do not speak English well			
1.56 group	57	70	65
1.53 group	52	67	62
1.53 group, one or both parents are			
U.S. citizens	38	57	46
True second generation: NBFP	44	56	49
Mixed second generation: NBMP	15	10	n.a.
U.S. born, Mexican origins	n.a.	n.a.	n.a.
g) Percentage of parents who are not citizens			
1.56 group	74	87	82
1.53 group	67	78	72
1.53 group, one or both parents are			
U.S. citizens	19	47	n.a.
True second generation: NBFP	60	60	57
Mixed second generation: NBMP	55	42	n.a.
U.S. born, Mexican origins	n.a.	n.a.	n.a.

Table A.7   (*Continued*)

	Youths in Two-Parent Families		Youths in Mother-Headed Families
Characteristic	Fathers	Mothers	Mothers
h) Average total family income (exponentiated from mean of logged income)			
1.56 group		31257	17396
1.53 group		33315	16706
1.53 group, one or both parents are			
U.S. citizens		37357	21588
True second generation: NBFP		36843	17762
Mixed second generation: NBMP		42481	n.a.
U.S. born, Mexican origins		44358	21305
i) Family well-being expressed as a function of poverty status (100 = poverty line; 501 = top code)			
1.56 group		163	118
1.53 group		172	112
1.53 group, one or both parents are			
U.S. citizens		195	145
True second generation: NBFP		197	124
Mixed second generation: NBMP		241	n.a.
U.S. born, Mexican origins		249	161
j) Percentage of families that do not own their home			
1.56 group		47	68
1.53 group		42	67
1.53 group, one or both parents are			
U.S. citizens		32	56
True second generation: NBFP		29	59
Mixed second generation: NBMP		26	n.a.
U.S. born, Mexican origins		27	53

Source: IPUMS dataset for 2000 census.
Note: n.a. = not available.

those who came with a longer employment experience in Mexico. In any case, differences in English language deficiencies (self-reported as "does not speak English well") are not dramatic, though they are in the expected direction (about 10 percentage points worse for the 1.53 parents; panel f). The same is true for differences in citizenship status (panel g).

How do these patterns of human capital acquisition, timing of immigration, and cultural and legal outcomes translate into economic well-being? Predictably, families of the true second generation have a higher total family income and a lower proportion who rent their homes than those of the 1.53 group. What matters is how much greater these differences are. I concentrate here on two-parent families. Patterns in the one-parent families are generally similar, but less pronounced. Income in the families of the true second generation averaged 11 percent higher than the 1.53-group—and 18 percent higher than the 1.56 group (table A.7, panel h). The poverty index, a measure of total family income in relation to the number of family members at each stage of the life cycle (Ruggles et al. 2005), shows a similar pattern (panel i). Finally, homeownership is higher by 13 percentage points among the families of the true second generation than among the 1.53 group (panel j). In general, then, the true second generation grew up in longer-resident and thus moderately better-off families than the 1.53 group did. Most important for us is how much this difference also influences the schooling and income of the next generation, the 1.53 and true second-generation children in those families. While we would expect intergenerational transmission to favor the true second generation, the magnitudes of the differences and the modest power of such transmission would also lead us to expect fairly small differences.

That is more or less what we do find. My second set of tests compare young adults (aged twenty-five to thirty-four) in the census and the CPS dataset, the 1.53 group in the former, the true second generation in the latter.[17] The major substantive difference is in education attainment. The census 1.53 group averaged modestly less schooling than the CPS true second generation, perhaps .3 to .5 of a year's worth.[18] In terms of school completion, table A.10 shows that some 6 percent more among the male 1.53 group in the census failed to graduate from high school than among the true second generation in the CPS (29 percent to 23 percent), although the difference is not quite statistically significant. The same pattern typifies the 1.56 group compared to the 1.53 group in the census. In both comparisons, longer residence in the United States is associated with more schooling, even in the narrowly defined spans involved here (table A.8, panel a). Among the women, there is a percentage point difference in favor of the true second generation (16 percent to 24 percent; table A.9) but the CPS figure is probably far off the true value due to sampling error, as I explain later in connection with citizens (see especially note 19).

Because contemporary educational issues are central to the analysis, I note this educational characteristic of the 1.53 group proxy at several points in the discussion. On the other hand, the true and proxy groups are remarkably alike in early career outcomes (percent in the full-time labor force and mean earnings), particularly among the men. While the educational differences were modestly greater, they do not appear to have translated into strong income differences at this early career stage (table A.8, panel b).

We cannot expect to have a precise measure of the gains and losses that flow from a choice to concentrate on census rather than CPS data. The comparisons made here—within census at a younger age and between census and CPS at the age of interest—should illuminate the issues at stake. To my mind, the review confirms that the advantages of exploiting the census are great and the risks relatively small—especially since the CPS results can always be consulted.

CITIZENSHIP   The census simply tells us whether an individual born abroad is an American citizen—not, for example, whether a noncitizen is undocumented or holds a green card. Nor does the census tell us when citizenship was obtained. In the sample of children aged fourteen to sixteen, 54 percent of the true second generation had at least one naturalized parent. The same was true for 43 percent of the children in the 1.53 sample. Few of the 1.53-group children, however, were citizens—less than half of those with and almost none without a naturalized parent. However, among the 1.53 group young adults (aged twenty-five to thirty-four in 2000) about half claimed citizenship, and even more among their fathers' generation (the Mexican immigrant men between fifty-five and sixty-four who had lived in the United States. for at least three decades) did so.

These differences in naturalization rates reflect the time spent in the United States, and the probability of obtaining citizenship rises with length of stay. But more is probably involved. Some age groups were more affected than others, for example, by the IRCA amnesty program, which allowed undocumented individuals to apply for citizenship if they could prove long residence prior to 1986 or short residence and agricultural employment. Nevertheless, even in cohorts who apparently would qualify for IRCA amnesty (men aged either twenty-five to thirty-four or fifty-five to sixty-four in 2000, who first arrived before 1975), the proportion of Mexicans who are citizens is much closer to 50 than to 100 percent; and even in later cohorts it is not much lower. There are many reasons why someone might not have taken up the offered amnesty. They may have had a spouse who would not qualify and would be noticed, or felt it would be disloyal to Mexico, or did not understand the procedures, or could not prove residence. Also working to reduce the distinctiveness of the amnesty years are continuing opportunities for citizenship. Despite the unavailability of the amnesty in later years, some people still qualify for citizenship—for example as relatives of earlier arrivals who became citizens, or because they

Table A.8   2000 Census and CPS 1998 to 2001: Measures for 1966 to 1975 Birth Cohort

Characteristic and Origin Groups	Census		CPS General		CPS Detail		
	Male	Female	Male	Female	Generation and Parentage	Male	Female
a. Mean grades of schooling completed							
Mexican groups							
Immigrants	8.97	9.22	9.20	9.43			
1.56 group	11.40	11.73 ⎱→					
1.53 group	11.69	12.18 ⎰	12.26	11.66			
U.S. born, Mexican origins	12.19	12.60	12.50	12.58	⎰2nd, NBFP	12.31	12.71
					⎱2nd, NBMP	12.66	12.66
					⎰3rd or more	12.53	12.51
Non-Mexican groups							
Native white	13.54	13.80	13.68	13.86			
Native black	12.47	12.92	12.81	13.02			
All others	13.31	13.47	13.45	13.62			
b. Percentage of full-time workers with positive wage income among all sample members							
Mexican groups							
Immigrants	66	26	73	26			
1.56 group	69	47 ⎱→					
1.53 group	72	48 ⎰	70	41			
U.S. born, Mexican origins	68	51	70	47	⎰2nd, NBFP	73	55
					⎱2nd, NBMP	71	48
					⎰3rd or more	68	45

Non-Mexican groups

Native white	77	54	75	51
Native black	58	55	67	58
All other	66	45	68	43

c. Mean of logged weekly wage, for regression work (full-time workers)

Mexican groups

Immigrants	5.99	5.77	5.88	5.69
1.56 group	6.24	6.08 } →	6.22	5.96
1.53 group	6.25	6.11		
U.S. born, Mexican origins	6.25	6.12	6.27	6.06

{ 2nd, NBFP	6.24	6.15
{ 2nd, NBMP	6.28	6.13
{ 3rd or more	6.28	6.00

Non-Mexican groups

Native white	6.49	6.27	6.49	6.25
Native black	6.24	6.12	6.27	6.04
All other	6.43	6.27	6.38	6.21

Source: IPUMS dataset for 2000 census and 1998 to 2001 CPS datasets.

Note: Census includes institutionalized. The institutionalized comprise non-negligible proportions among the two groups listed below. Census results for their noninstitutionalized male populations follow.

	a. Schooling	b. Percentage Full-Time Workers	c. Mean Logged Weekly Wage
U.S. born, Mexican origins	12.29	71	6.26
Native blacks	12.66	63	6.25

themselves marry a citizen (including of course a citizen of recent Mexican origin).

Within this context we can consider whether the 1.53 group who are American citizens might be a better proxy for the true second generation than the entire group. As explained, the citizenship gained by about half the group involves self-selection that may skew rather than improve the proxy. The citizenship information we can cull from the sample of adolescents in the proxy and true second-generation groups is of limited use. Still, it helps to establish that some advantages associated with citizenship are certainly the impact of self-selection. The most striking example is that the naturalized parents average about a year more of education than the parents who are not citizens (somewhat more than eight versus seven years of education). Generally, this schooling must have been obtained long before immigration to the United States. I also examined here the families of a slightly older group of adolescents, those aged sixteen and seventeen. Youths with a naturalized parent averaged about a month more of schooling—a statistically significant difference, even after controlling for a variety of other parental factors, including age, marital status, income, education, and ability to speak English. Nevertheless, an average difference of a month is not much. Living in a Californian rather than a Texan metropolitan area made a net positive difference of three months, being a girl rather than a boy made one of a month and a half. A 2.5 percent rise in total family income also had a net impact on the child's educational attainment of about a month. Of course, the net impact of parental citizenship might be higher at ages when postsecondary education is at issue, but this we cannot measure. In any case, the argument that citizenship helped the child's situation is a fairly indirect one: many aspects of parental background had a limited impact on children's life chances, and the net impact of citizenship does not appear to be an instance of a dramatically important influence.

The more important issue about naturalization is whether the citizenship status of the young-adult 1.53 group member should be taken into account (table A.9). Here differences associated with citizenship status are striking; but we must assume that some part of these difference is related to the fact that the naturalized are a self-selected group. There is, in other words, a difference between having citizenship by birth and having citizenship because a person found a way to be naturalized. And so, we cannot assume that just because the true second generation enjoy citizenship, the naturalized rather than the entire 1.53 group makes a better proxy for the true second generation.

The role of self-selection is not hard to demonstrate. First, the proportion of 1.53 group members who are naturalized differs by gender: 49 percent of men and 59 percent of women. Second, on key educational and income measures—mean years of schooling, percentage of high school dropouts, and especially earnings—the naturalized men in the 1.53 group score

Table A.9 Comparisons, Census 1.53 Group (All and Citizens) and CPS True Second Generation

	Men			Women		
	1.53		Second Generation	1.53		Second Generation
Characteristic	All	Citizens		All	Citizens	
Unweighted sample size	2,587	1,264	248	2,622	1,530	293
Percentage U.S. citizen among 1.53 group	49			59		
Mean years of education	11.70	12.42	12.31	12.18	12.65	12.71
		0.08	*0.14*		*0.06*	*0.11*
Percentage high school dropouts	27	19	23	24	18	16
		1	*3*		*1*	*2*
Percentage full-time workers with wage data	72	75	73	48	51	55
		1	*3*		*1*	*3*
Logged weekly wages of full-time workers regressed on ethnic categories: ethnic coefficients						
No controls	−0.24	−0.15	−0.25	−0.16	−0.10	−0.09
		0.03	*0.05*		*0.05*	*0.06*
Controlling age, region and metro status	−0.26	−0.18	−0.25	−0.23	−0.17	−0.11
		0.03	*0.05*		*0.05*	*0.06*
Controlling education also	−0.11	−0.07	−0.10	−0.06	−0.03	−0.02
		0.03	*0.05*		*0.04*	*0.05*

Source: IPUMS dataset for 2000 census and 1998 to 2001 CPS datasets.
Note: Standard errors in italics. All samples are limited to noninstitutional population.

curiously high. They not only enjoy higher outcomes than the those 1.53 group members who have not been naturalized; they also enjoy higher attainments than the members of the true second generation found in the CPS. The comparisons, of course, are complicated by the need to compare across two datasets, by the small CPS samples, and by the complexities in the educational attainment question in both datasets (involving two answers relevant to finishing high school; see the following section on ethnicity and high school graduation). Despite all this, it seems reasonably clear that the naturalized men in the 1.53 group are modestly but consistently more successful than the true second generation members. Just as clearly, something more than the advantages of citizenship would have to produce that difference. Admittedly, most of the differences for men are within the range of statistical confidence limits. But the consistency of the pattern suggests that the more conservative route is to avoid reliance on the naturalized group alone for a proxy.[19]

Thus when relying on the entire 1.53 group, we have a naturally occurring population, not one we know to be self-selected in a way that includes more women than men. We also have a population that scores much like the true second generation, especially in male wages. By contrast, if we limit our proxy to the naturalized 1.53 group, we find people who score consistently higher than the group we want to proxy.[20]

ETHNICITY AND HIGH SCHOOL GRADUATION IN THE 2000 CENSUS

The 2000 census asked, "what is the highest degree or level of schooling this person has completed?"[21] The question was followed by a long list of school levels from which the respondent was to choose. For grades one through eleven, the choices were listed as grades or grade ranges: first through fourth, tenth, and so forth. For postsecondary education, the choices were listed as degrees: associate degree, bachelor's degree, and so on. Those who left school after completing twelfth grade were to choose between "twelfth grade, no diploma" and "high school graduate or equivalent" (for example, GED).

These two options were meant to reflect the two ways in which the other educational responses are listed: for people who did not graduate from high school, levels refer to grades in school, and for people who did graduate from high school, levels refer to degrees from institutions. Only 3 to 4 percent of the young adults (age twenty-five to thirty-four) chose twelfth grade, no diploma. The striking point for our purposes is that blacks and American-educated Mexican American groups were notably more likely to choose twelfth grade, no diploma than native whites—9 percent of all men in the 1.53 group chose this level (table A.10, first column). There are reasons, however, to doubt these figures.

Table A.10   A Comparison of Educational Attainments for Selected Origin Groups in the 2000 Census and the 1998 to 2001 CPS (1966 to 1975 Birth Cohort)

Origin Group and Schooling Completed	2000 Census as Reported		1998–2001 CPS			2000 Census Adjusted		
	Percentage Male	Percentage Female	Ethnic Group CPS Only	Percentage Male	Percentage Female	School Level: Added	Percentage Male	Percentage Female
Mexican origin								
1.56 group								
Less than grade twelve	31	27				High school dropout	33	29
Twelfth grade, no diploma	9	7						
High school graduate	28	29					34	34
Some college	25	28					25	28
Four-year college graduate	8	9					8	9
Total	100	100					100	100
1.53 group (proxy)			True second generation					
Less than grade twelve	27	22		22	14	High school dropout	29	24
Twelfth grade, no diploma	9	7		1	2			
High school graduate	27	27		38	33		34	32
Some college	27	32		29	38		27	32
Four-year college graduate	9	12		11	13		9	12
Total	100	100		100	100		100	100
U.S. born								
Less than grade twelve	20	16		17	16	High school dropout	22	18
Twelfth grade, no diploma	7	6		2	2			
High school graduate	33	28		40	35		37	32

(Table continues on p. 158.)

Table A.10   *Continued*

Origin Group and Schooling Completed	2000 Census as Reported		1998–2001 CPS			2000 Census Adjusted		
	Percentage Male	Percentage Female	Ethnic Group CPS Only	Percentage Male	Percentage Female	School Level: Added	Percentage Male	Percentage Female
Some college	29	35		29	33		29	35
Four-year college graduate	11	16		11	13		11	16
Total	100	100		100	100		100	100
Not Mexican origin								
U.S. born, white								
Less than grade twelve	8	6	High school dropout	6	5	High school dropout	9	6
Twelfth grade, no diploma	3	2		1	1			
High school graduate	28	24		32	27		30	26
Some college	32	34		29	32		32	34
Four-year college graduate	30	33		32	34		30	33
Total	100	100		100	100		100	100
U.S. born, black								
Less than grade twelve	14	11	High school dropout	9	10	High school dropout	16	13
Twelfth grade, no diploma	7	6		1	2			
High school graduate	37	29		45	34		43	33
Some college	30	37		29	37		30	37
Four-year college graduate	12	17		16	17		12	17
Total	100	100		100	100		100	100

Source: IPUMS dataset for 2000 census and 1998 to 2001 CPS datasets.

Notes:

a. The adjustment method allocates individuals who chose twelfth grade, no diploma in the census either to high school dropout or to high school graduate. The method assumes erroneous reporting of the lower level in the census, but not in the CPS, which is conducted by trained interviewers. The adjustment method uses the following formulas to allocate the twelfth grade, no diploma census responses for each ethnic and gender subgroup.

allocated to high school dropout $= (a + b) \times (c/(c + d))$

and

allocated to high school graduate $= (a + b) \times (d/(c + d))$

where

a and c = twelfth grade, no diploma in census and CPS respectively
b and d = high school graduate in census and CPS respectively

b. The CPS includes only the noninstitutionalized population. Limiting the census to this population would alter figures shown in the table by more than 1 percentage point only for men, and only in two groups, as shown.

Schooling Completed	U.S.-born of Mexican Origin	Native Black
Less than grade twelve	18	11
Twelfth grade, no diploma	7	7
High school graduate	32	37
Some college	31	32
Four-year college graduate	12	13
	100	100

c. *Returns to schooling for twelfth grade completers: census versus CPS.* The extent to which returns are lower for twelfth grade, no diploma than for high school graduate are shown below, with greater differences in the CPS. These results are based on a regression of logged weekly earnings of full-time workers on age (continuous var.), ethnic categories, region, border state, metro status, and seven educational levels. The table shows the coefficients on twelfth grade, no diploma (high school graduate was the omitted education category).

Sex	2000 Census		1998–2001 CPS	
	Coefficient	Standard Error	Coefficient	Standard Error
Men	-0.105	0.006	-0.192	0.040
Women	-0.104	0.008	-0.160	0.054

The 1998 to 2001 CPS included the same question about school levels, but the proportion of respondents choosing "twelfth grade, no diploma" was lower than the census proportion (table A.10, first column). Furthermore, among both minority groups large enough to compare across datasets (blacks and the U.S.-born of Mexican origin), 6 to 7 percent of sample members in the census chose twelfth grade, no diploma; but only 1 to 2 percent did so in the CPS. Fewer native whites chose that response in the CPS as well, but the difference across surveys is smaller for native whites: 2 to 3 percent in the census, 1 percent in the CPS.[22] Finally, in each group, those choosing either of the two responses is similar across the two datasets. For example, 44 percent of U.S.-born blacks chose one of these responses in the census and 46 percent did so in the CPS. Responses for other levels of schooling also closely agree in the two datasets.

Why then is there a difference across datasets at twelfth grade in particular, and why a larger difference for blacks and Mexican Americans than for native whites? The answer may lie in the CPS and census enumeration procedures. Nearly all census forms are mailed out and completed by the respondents, whereas CPS forms are completed by paid, trained canvassers who interview respondents. Trained workers would be less likely to confuse the two responses. Despite the Census Bureau's best efforts to distinguish between them, it seems that some twelfth-grade completers read the first category, checked it off, and proceeded to the next question—without noticing that there was a second category that more accurately described their situation. Respondents most likely to make this sort of error might have been the twelfth-grade completers with a relatively poor mastery of paper and pencil tasks. And such respondents might be more prevalent among black and Mexican American twelfth graders than among native whites. The test scores of blacks generally and of high schools with high black or Mexican concentration are consistent with such a conclusion (Jencks and Phillips 1998).

The American Community Surveys for 2000 through 2002 provide modest support for this explanation. They too are mail-administered surveys and they too show higher proportions of respondents choosing twelfth grade, no diploma, relative to high school graduate, and especially high proportions among the two minority groups (not shown). Other evidence consistent with the explanation proposed here involves the returns to schooling in census and CPS for the two relevant groups, those reporting twelfth grade, no diploma, and those reporting high school graduate (table A.10, note). Returns to schooling differ by a larger amount in the CPS than in the census for both men and women. This result is consistent with the possibility that more people in the census than in the CPS who report twelfth grade, no diploma, are receiving higher returns to schooling than that educational level typically commands.

These considerations suggest that some of the census respondents who classified themselves as twelfth grade, no diploma, did so correctly and some did not. We can use the CPS data to adjust the census results: by assuming that the fraction that reported the lower level of attainment among all who reported either of the two educational levels is the same within ethno-racial groups of each sex (table A.10). I have used the adjusted figures in discussing high-school dropout rates. Note that the result of the adjustment reduces the dropout rate for all groups; the very high dropout rate reported for the Mexican 1.53 group would have been notably higher still without the adjustment. By contrast, in studying returns to schooling in the regression analyses in chapter 4, no correction was necessary, because a separate dummy variable was included for each of the two relevant educational levels.

NOTES

INTRODUCTION

1. Other commentaries on the theory of segmented assimilation are numerous; examples include Smith (2002), Alba and Nee (2003), Bean and Stevens (2003), and Jaynes (2004).
2. For more extensive praise of the IPUMS, see Perlmann (2003b).
3. Generally, given the wonders of computer power (and its falling costs), I used the largest available datasets through 1970. These typically include 1 percent of the American population (but 3 percent in 1970). In the last part of chapter 1, I used the 5 percent 1980 to 1990 datasets, and elsewhere the 1 percent. For all analyses of the 2000 census, I used all the cases from the 1 percent sample as well as all the cases of immigrants from the 5 percent sample.
4. The recent censuses have added a question on ancestry, which asks respondents to identify themselves in terms of countries or regions of origin. In one sense, this question is an advance, as it gives some information on origins that extend farther back than the parental generation. Yet the flip-side of this advance is the question's great shortcoming: it does not specify when the individual's family immigrated—two or twelve generations back—and it is also notoriously subjective in that people often mention some of their origins and not others. See Lieberson and Waters (1988) and Perlmann and Waters (2003).
5. For more detail, and a critique of CPS coding of the origin question, see Perlmann and Waters (2003, Introduction).
6. The samples included center on the year 2000, at least in terms of the number of subsamples drawn from before and after that year: one rotation each from 1998 and 1999 and two rotations from 2001. I relied on a version of

the CPS datasets originally combined by Roger Waldinger and his colleagues at UCLA and kindly provided to me by them.

7. Also, the CPS is the result of a highly complex design; see, for example, Hicks (1997).

8. Fortunately, for the first time in many decades, the census asked immigrant respondents the specific year in which they arrived in the United States, rather than ranges of years. The appendix provides a full description and evaluation of the proxy.

CHAPTER 1

1. Moreover, the story was sufficiently complex and the sample size sufficiently small, even in giant datasets, to suggest the aggregation into one group.

2. Four censuses provide useful mother-tongue data: 1910, 1920, 1940, and 1970. In identifying the SCEN, I used that data to supplement birthplace information by applying two rules to immigrants born in central or eastern Europe. First, those whose mother tongue was Yiddish or German were excluded from the SCEN (unless the German speakers had been born in Russia); and second, those whose mother tongue qualified them as SCEN were included in that group regardless of where in central or eastern Europe they had been born. Many tables and figures relating to the SCEN in this chapter may be found in an early working paper (Perlmann 2001b) with a more detailed ethnic classification.

3. Figures by country of origin are summarized in Carter, Olmsted, Wright, and Haines ([1989] 1997); and these as well as race or people data for the period from 1899 to 1924 are summarized in Ferenczi (1929). See also Perlmann (2001a).

4. In 1910 and 1920, three in ten young children of immigrants from central and eastern Europe are listed with English (or nothing) as their mother tongue. In 1940 fully six in ten are, and in 1970 five in ten. In 1910 and 1920 the question asked about mother tongue, in 1940 about the "language spoken in the home in childhood" and in 1970 about "language spoken in the home in childhood other than English." In 1950 and 1960, there was no comparable question (see variable descriptions in Ruggles et al. 2005).

5. From table 1.1. The Jews comprised 14 percent and the entire SCE group comprised 58 percent of total permanent immigration from 1899 to 1924.

6. The evidence of the 1897 census of the Russian Empire strongly suggests that the percentage of Russian Jewish immigrants who gave Yiddish as their mother tongue must have been over 95 percent; the proportion of Jews from central Europe—Austro-Hungary, Rumania, and the German Empire—who did so was lower, if still probably more than 75 percent. See, for example, Joseph (1914), Kuznets (1975), and Perlmann (2001b).

7. After World War I, when Poles were most likely to report that they or their

parents had been born in Poland, this strategy is better than for the prewar period. Poland as a state did not exist between Napoleonic times and World War I. Poles lived under German, Austro-Hungarian, and Russian rule. Consequently, both the census and the immigration authorities dealt differently with Poles across the years, and before 1920 often dealt with them incompletely. My best efforts to isolate the non-Jewish Poles from other Slavs are found in Perlmann (2001b).

8. Jews comprised about half of all Russian immigrants before World War I. By contrast, among immigrants from *other* central and east European countries, Jews comprised 10 percent or less of the group, and the impact of mistakenly classifying some Jews with the SCEN will be small so long as the Russians are isolated (Kuznets 1975; Joseph 1914). During and after World War I, the proportion of Jews among these other immigrants increases somewhat, especially from Poland, but the total contribution of these later years to SCEN immigration is small. See also below on the choice of second-generation cohorts selected for study.

9. The samples for several birth cohorts are not drawn from the census in which the cohort would have been younger than ten years old, but from the next-later census when it was between ten and twenty years of age. This approach was used for 1890 and 1930 because the relevant datasets for those years were unavailable, and for 1900 in order to increase sample size and exploit mother-tongue data.

10. I also made slight adjustments in the size of these age cohorts to take into account the mortality that might be expected across the relevant ages, centering all cohorts on ages five through nine. However, no attempt was made to take into account variations in child mortality across the immigrant groups and across time. The correction factors (derived from Bogue 1985) were: under age one, .91; ages one through four, .96; ages ten through fourteen, 1.01; and ages fifteen through nineteen, 1.02. No adjustments were made for children in 1980–2000, by which time infant and child mortality rates had fallen sharply from earlier decades.

11. Also during these years the "other southern" Europeans comprised a larger fraction of the total SCE group (about two-fifths of all SCE immigrants in the period—see Perlmann 2001b) than they had before.

12. This discussion rests on the detailed tables 6 and 7 in Perlmann (2001b).

13. The prevalence of such people is great only after an immigration declines sharply in magnitude. Before 1915 individuals who had arrived as children were always few compared to individuals from the same birth cohort who arrived in a later year (but still before 1915) as adults. After completing the analysis of this issue, I discovered that others had found the child migrants important in some contemporary contexts. Borjas and Freeman (1992, 9) offer a summary.

14. Another factor that will distinguish later second-generation cohorts after mass

immigration declines: they may include more children of parents who delayed childbearing and more younger children from large families. However, these factors are less likely to make the children atypical members of the second generation in terms of assimilation.

15. A central feature of Stanley Lieberson's justly influential *A Piece of the Pie* (1980) is a comparison of the educational attainments of SCE second-generation members and northern-born blacks in the birth cohorts I have included in table 1.2. Lieberson found that black educational attainments held up reasonably well against those of the SCE until the most recent birth cohort he studied, 1926 to 1935. In that birth cohort the SCE second generation pulled well ahead of the blacks. He suggested that the large ghettos forming in the period this cohort grew up, as blacks left the South in unprecedented numbers, helped explain the shift—a shift toward more rigid discrimination in northern cities. The work in this section suggested an additional possibility, namely that the crucial cohort, 1926 to 1935, comprised a much larger share of second-generation members of mixed rather than foreign parentage. Thus, in the 1916 to 1925 cohort, three in ten had a parent with one or more of the three atypical characteristics I have been discussing; in the 1926 to 1935 cohort, the comparable figure is nearly double (58 percent). I therefore reanalyzed the Lieberson-like cohorts with the IPUMS samples, distinguishing between native-born of foreign parentage and native-born of mixed parentage. As expected, and shown in table 1.2, the mixed parentage group had higher educational attainments than the foreign parentage group. However, Lieberson's conclusions were nevertheless largely confirmed. It turned out that among the SCE second generations, the native-born of foreign parentage generally experienced greater increases in educational attainment over the preceding cohort than the native-born of mixed parentage did. For a full discussion, see Perlmann (2001b).

16. The pre-conquest numbers follow Grebler, Moore, and Guzman (1970, 43–44). The estimate of pre-twentieth-century origins is derived from Edmonston and Passel (1994, 48), who estimate that 14 percent of the 1990 Hispanic-origin population derives from immigration before the twentieth century. Because in 1990 about five-eighths of the Hispanic-origin population was Mexican, and nearly all of pre-twentieth century Hispanic immigration was, a figure of 20 to 25 percent for contemporary Mexican origin descended from a pre-twentieth-century presence seems plausible. On the gradual formalization of the border, see Ngai (2004). Figures for 1900 are from Bean and Stevens (2003, 54).

17. This paragraph, and the next, rest on Massey, Durand, and Malone (2002) and on Bean and Stevens (2003).

18. The Immigration and Naturalization Service (INS) reports have only a rough relationship to the profile of immigrants or second-generation members. Undocumented immigration in particular, but also return migration, mortality,

and (for the second generation) ethnic differentials in fertility create great differences between census and INS figures. See, for example, the convenient summary of INS figures in Alba and Nee (2003, tables 5.1 and 5.2). For a brief discussion of the timing of Mexican second generations, see Lopez and Stanton-Salazar (2001).

19. This last observation is based on the relative number of the Mexican-origin age groups birth through five, five through fourteen, fifteen through twenty-four, and twenty-five through thirty observed in the CPS for the years 1998 to 2001.

20. In the case of the SCEN, we will be working with censuses that report the place of birth of both parents; in the case of the Mexicans, most of our analysis will concern the 2000 census, from which we will select individuals brought to the United States before their third birthday. While this latter group could include some children of mixed origin, it probably includes very few indeed.

CHAPTER 2

1. Mexican origins could be claimed by native-born respondents in response to the ancestry or the Hispanic-origin question. In Census 2000, multiple responses to the race question were permitted; I classified as white respondents who listed only that race, and as black respondents who listed that race whether or not they listed any other. While the challenge of classifying multi-racials may well loom larger in future decades, when multiple responses to the race question may be more prevalent than in 2000, racial classificatory strategies for whites and blacks different from the one just described had no influence on outcomes in this study. See also appendix table A.4.

2. Given the differences between male and female labor-force participation, occupational concentration and wage levels in each period, the entire analysis of wages would have to be undertaken separately for women. Moreover, the major studies to which I relate in the discussion are limited to men. Some gender comparisons of earnings in 2000 are considered in the last part of chapter 4.

3. Borjas (1994) highlighted the slope of the line describing the association between the 1910 immigrant rankings (for example in wages) along the x axis, and the 1940 second-generation rankings along the y axis. The steeper the slope, the less assimilation was occurring.

4. The federal census only began to report on wages and income in 1940. In order to learn about earlier wage inequality, Goldin and Katz compiled such pre-1940 wage data as they could find in other sources, including evidence from a 1915 Iowa state census which did include questions on income (2001).

5. On the contemporary transformation see the helpful discussions in Danziger

and Gottshalk (1995), Katz and Autor (1999), Welch (2001), and Bernhardt, Morris, Handcock, and Scott (2001).

6. The greater part of the revision created by my new estimates is the result of the new occupational wage scale, not the adjustments for the masking of geographic and educational differences within the occupational wage. And the method used to create the 1910 wage scale must be thought of not as a precise measure but as a reasonable effort to capture the summary that Goldin and Katz (2001) offer of a long process of change in wages across the work force. For further discussion see the appendix section, "A New Occupational Wage Scale."

7. Jencks (2002) interpreted some early 1940 and 1950 data I presented in a working paper in this way.

8. Because of the considerable cross-border movement, I focus on those Mexican immigrants who report living in the United States for three decades (about 45 percent of all Mexican immigrant men aged fifty-five to sixty-four in 2000).

9. These controls are added to the standard controls imposed throughout, for region, metro status, and age. Because my interest was to control as much of the educational impact as could be observed, I was unconcerned that the dummy variables complicate the interpretation of the continuous variable's impact (in years of schooling completed).

10. For the 1886 to 1895 cohort, the comparable ratio in 1950 is .94.

11. The choice of age fifteen dates back at least to Blau and Duncan (1967) and the CPS survey they studied. See also Harding, Jencks, Lopoo, and Mayer (2005, 113–14).

CHAPTER 3

1. See, for example, U.S. Department of Education (2005; for example, chap. 1, table 9).

2. Bean and Stevens (2003, 101–4) make much the same point. Moreover, in areas that now have significant numbers of black immigrants (mostly from the Caribbean, some also from Africa), it is in fact useful to distinguish among blacks generationally too.

3. All this was occurring at a time when educational attainments generally were not changing dramatically, especially for men, so we need only focus on the ethnic shifts.

4. Note too that if we had used the inappropriate method on the earlier cohort, we would have predicted that today's children of yesterday's second generation would suffer a decline from 11.10 to 10.55 years of schooling—whereas the mean for the cohort is actually 12.52 years of schooling.

5. Also contributing to change over time is the evolution of educational attainments in Mexico. Thus immigrant starting points also shift over time. Finally, note too that the subjectivity of the Hispanic origin and related ancestry

question could influence outcomes. It is at least plausible that the more assimilated and better educated were more likely not to list Mexican origins. On this point see also Alba and Islam (2005). On the broader question of current as predictor of future third-generation behavior, see also Alba and Nee (2003, chap. 6) and Bean and Stevens (2003, 130–42).

6. Figures 3.1 and 3.2 show observed means in years of schooling with no controls for region or metro area; imposing those controls explains little of the observed difference between SCEN and Mexican second-generation outcomes during the early part of the twentieth century. The same is true of second-generation catch-up in the early period, discussed below (see also figures 3.3 and 3.4).

7. Or rather, we typically cannot do so for adults; native-born children of immigrants can be identified when they are living with their immigrant parents.

8. More precisely, in each type of family at least one parent will have been in the United States for that length of time. For example, a father may have come ahead earlier, and the mother and child later.

9. Improving economic conditions after the cohort turned fifteen, or reduced isolation of the SCEN by this time may explain the youngest cohort's success. Also the youngest cohorts low standardized educational deficit relative to their fathers' large standardized wage deficit is a function of measuring the latter in 1920 and 1940 and the former in 1950.

10. Specifically, there is no need to invoke the 1910 wage ratio or standard deviation; part of the calculation relies on 1940 data, which avoids use of the occupational wage; and the standard deviations of logged wages are almost identical in all four relevant estimates of fathers' wage handicap, so that standardizing creates only small changes in the relative magnitudes of the measures.

11. The demonstration here shows the association for means in two generations, at the *aggregate* level; this association should not be confused with the association of individual fathers and with their own sons. An extensive literature on socioeconomic mobility deals with the latter sort of association (see, for example, Featherman and Hauser 1978, 259; and Ganzeboom, Treiman, and Utlee 1991). While these latter associations have been revised upwards in recent years (Solon 1999; Bowles, Gintis, and Groves 2005), they are nevertheless lower than those discussed here.

12. Generally, among the NWNP the girls received somewhat longer schooling than the boys, while in the SCEN immigrant families, this gender pattern was reversed. The pattern of keeping adolescent girls at home (or working where they could be closely observed by family members and friends) probably owed much to premigration cultural patterns (Perlmann 1988); seventy years later, with the Mexicans, its strength appears reduced. Or at least its strength appears reduced for the top eighth or twelfth of the educational distribution who reached this educational plateau.

13. The rates for most groups are slightly higher in the census (often by about a tenth to a fifth of the CPS rate).

14. Among Mexican immigrants, a high proportion of young women are found at home even if they do not have a child (24 percent of them); this stay-at-home pattern, despite the low income of the group, probably reflects a more traditional view of women's roles than is prevalent among the American born (the pattern is noticeable, but muted, in the 1.53 group). In any case, overall about half of Mexican immigrant women are not employed, roughly twice the proportion found in the other groups.

CHAPTER 4

1. For the true second generation in the small CPS samples, these ratios are virtually identical; see notes to table 4.1.

2. The shift from 1940 to 1950 is due both to the much smaller difference between SCEN and native white schooling in the later birth cohort (twenty-five to thirty-four years old in 1950), and to the drop in the returns to schooling during the intervening decade's great compression (Goldin and Margo 1992).

3. The residual could also be deflated by inaccurate ethnic classification. For example, some parents born abroad had been brought to the United States as young children yet their own children are classified as true second generation (as discussed in chapter 1). These second-generation members typically will be more assimilated than those who grow up in the homes of immigrants who had arrived in the United States as adults.

4. Prior to 1910, Mexican long-term immigration was limited, and even after that, the numbers settling, and not forced back across the border during the Great Depression, are simply too small to produce reliable sample data, even in the large census samples. While there was a substantial Mexican-origin population throughout, the second generation was by no means a large part of the whole group (and none of the earlier censuses captured ancestry beyond the second generation).

5. Mexican immigrant data is reliable for the early period and the residuals were very high, like those for blacks.

6. In the historical comparisons, I included a continuous variable for number of grades of schooling completed, and dummy variables for high school and college graduation (and in 2000 data also for twelfth grade, no diploma). I now control for seven dummy variables and omit the continuous variable (see note to table 4.4). Indeed, including separate dummy variables for the categories I did group provides no substantive differences from the results discussed here.

7. Specifically, results are from a model in which earnings are regressed on ethnic dummies, individual age, geographic location, and educational categories.

I then calculated what the mean earnings would be for each ethnic group of interest given various proportions of the group reaching particular educational levels. Instead, I could have used separate regression models for each group, thereby obtaining returns for schooling that include all the higher-order interactions of ethnicity, schooling, and earnings. But since the returns to schooling did not differ in a statistically significant way between native whites and the Mexican 1.53 group, this strategy would have involved its own minor distortions.

8. To maximize sample size, the latter regression also includes the Mexican 1.56 group (those brought to the United States between their third and sixth birthdays); a dummy variable controls for any earnings difference between the 1.53 and the 1.56 groups, but the difference across those groups is trivial.

9. The three levels of residuals differ from each other by statistically significant amounts. Smith (2002) makes the intriguing suggestion that the "soft skills" acquired by Mexican American girls in helping their families negotiate American bureaucracies and similar social contexts may help these girls not only in the labor force but also in orienting them to a less racialized, more ethnic view of their Mexican American identity than the boys will form. The differences in residuals reported here could be seen as consistent with this process, although also suggesting that the process has but a modest impact on gender differences in wage ratios.

10. The control for education is crude, because it pertains to only one adult in the household; all the more reason, however to appreciate how much it accomplishes. Note too that the female handicap captured in the black-white ratios of table 4.8 distinguish both the Mexican 1.53 and the U.S.-born of Mexican origin from blacks. The ratios of 1.53 group and native-white family income (shown in table 4.8) are (under three types of controls) .80, .98, and .95. For the U.S.-born of Mexican origin the comparable ratios (not shown) are .80, .93, and .95.

11. Controls for the number of children in the family had only a very modest additional impact on the ethnic coefficients for blacks or Mexican 1.53 group members.

12. The three-way interaction between race, family structure and total family income is also statistically significant, so that total family income for single black women without a child reaches 86 percent of what it is for single native-white women. The black-white ratios are 80 percent for married women, and 75 percent for single women with children.

CONCLUSION

1. Actually, .56 to .60 for the age cohort used in the 2000 comparison (thirty-five to forty-four rather than thirty-five to sixty-four). The youngest adult cohort is earning 58 percent of the native white wage, whereas the youngest

SCEN cohort earned 61 to 67 percent in 1910. These figures do not reflect the full inequality that will turn up among these workers when they are older.

2. An important caveat: my evidence does not permit me to examine pairs of parents and children, in the classic manner of mobility studies (Blau and Duncan 1967; Perlmann 1988; Solon 1999). I can only compare the well-being of birth-cohort members born thirty years apart who are likely to comprise parents and children. Consequently, I cannot assess whether the combined effect of wage levels and other parental characteristics might be enough to explain the worsened educational outcomes of today's second generation compared to the SCEN second generation. For example, the Mexican immigrants of 1970 lag modestly further behind the SCEN in relative educational levels, but I could not convincingly measure how much additional influence this might have on their children's attainments.

3. This is so for two reasons. First, the SCEN earned more relative to native whites than Mexicans do now. Second, today's blacks earn more relative to native whites than blacks did decades ago.

APPENDIX

1. I constructed similar tests with the 1876 to 1885 and 1886 to 1895 SCEN and native-white cohorts in the 1940 census; the ethnic occupational wage ratio was 1.1 times the ethnic wage ratio based on the individual wage.

2. All workers were sorted by the 1950 detailed occupational category. The mean wage for workers in each occupational category in each year was then computed. The 1950 detailed occupational categories are available in the IPUMS samples for all years. I also recalculated the 1940 ratio using the occupational categories for the census of that year; the original and recalculated ratios differed by one log point.

3. The researchers reported that their sample included many black families, but did not distinguish black and white returns in the report.

4. To test the importance of the restriction to family heads, I constructed several different occupational scales based on subsets of workers. Ethnic wage ratios for older adult men in 1940 were quite similar across scales (Perlmann 2002, table 4). Finally, the Preston-Haines scale was based on wages from around 1900 but was used on 1910 census data. This factor, however, should have biased wage inequality for 1910 upward if at all, not downward—since, in the Goldin-Katz narrative, wage inequality was probably worse in 1900 than in 1910.

5. I used the Consumer Price Index (U.S. Bureau of Labor Statistics 2005) for June of each year, 1949, 1959, and 1913; I then deflated the 1913 values by .94 to estimate the 1909 value.

6. This procedure for 1920 ignores any changes in the wage structure that might have occurred between the time of the 1919 wages reported in the 1920

census and wage structure of the "mid-to-late" 1920s, found to be equivalent to the 1939 wage structure reported in the 1940 census (Goldin and Katz 2001; Goldin and Margo 1992). See also note 11.

7. A display is found in Perlmann (2002, table 1).

8. For discussion of similar efforts to create a literacy proxy from grades of schooling in this period, see Margo (1990, 6–7).

9. The Goldin-Katz narrative predicts such results for higher levels of educational attainments, except perhaps for 1920 versus 1940.

10. In both 1910 and 1920, the ratios are notably more equal in the youngest birth cohort, the only one still in the labor force in 1940, because there is more variation in the occupational and in the individual wage among more mature workers.

11. Readers may find it helpful to read Goldin and Katz's summary. "Among manual or blue-collar workers, the evidence on the entire wage structure suggests that there was a compression sometime between 1890 and 1940. Skill ratios in the manual trades pinpoint the period of narrowing around the late 1910s. Another compression of the wage structure occurred during the 1940s. Of the two, the first appears to have been twice as large in terms of the 90–10 log wage differential, although the second narrowing took place in a considerably briefer time frame. There were, as well, two periods of compression for the three white collar series presented. One occurred just before the 1920s, the other was situated, once again, in the 1940s" (Goldin and Katz, 2001, 58–59; see also 64).

12. Jencks noted, "The new immigrants prospered partly because they settled in cities sooner than [the descendants of] Northern Europeans did. Settling in cities also gave their children an educational advantage" (2001, 60). Here he deals not with measuring the relative well-being of immigrant versus native in 1910 but with explaining the rapid improvement of the former group by reference to the long-term benefits of urban settlement. I have not concentrated on this suggestion (and it was only a suggestion), which is one more reason why I control, rather than study, the wage implications of 1910 immigrant settlement patterns. Of course, folding the geographic advantage of the SCEN back in to the 1910 ethnic wage ratio would not in itself measure the suggested cross-time (and cross-generation) advantages of urban settlement.

13. Much of our recent understanding of the social and economic history of the SCEN immigration comes from local case studies; *Ethnic Differences,* on conditions in Providence, R.I., is one among many examples (Perlmann 1988). If these studies of the early twentieth century are juxtaposed with national studies of the century's end, we get a false sense of the rapidity of SCEN progress across the generations. Specifically, the SCEN immigrants are observed to have been far behind native whites in the local historical studies, whereas their descendants reached parity with the descendants of native whites in the national data from the end of the twentieth century. But many

of those descendants of native whites are descended from those not living in the high-wage urban areas of 1910 and as such not part of the 1910 comparisons based on local urban areas. Including the descendants of these more disadvantaged native whites of 1910 biased the comparison in favor of SCEN progress. Today, however, IPUMS datasets from the 1900 through 1920 censuses allow us to construct national comparisons for both periods, 1910 and 2000. And for such comparisons the reasons stated in the text for including the geographic controls are, I think, compelling.

14. At issue here are the 1950 detailed occupational categories farm manager (code 123), farm foremen (810), farm laborers (820), farm laborers, unpaid family workers (830), and farm service laborers, self-employed (840). The farmers, owners and tenants, category (100) is separate from these.

15. Chapter 1 therefore argues against including, for example, the Chinese immigrants of the past.

16. Sample sizes are large and confidence intervals narrow except among single-male-parent families.

17. One minor source of difference will be coverage: the census includes the entire population, whereas the CPS covers only the noninstitutional. For all groups except black males or U.S.-born males of Mexican origin, these differences in coverage are too small to affect results (see chapter 3 of this volume), and for these two groups a note presents the rates for the noninstitutional population only. The institutional population includes those in prisons and other correctional facilities, hospitals, orphanages, and so forth. The institutional population does not include people in other forms of group quarters, such as military camps or college dormitories.

18. Generally, the CPS cohorts fare slightly better in educational attainments than the census cohorts do—for identically defined ethnic subgroups. Perhaps .1 to .2 of a .5 difference may be due to that difference in the datasets.

19. By contrast, the naturalized women show scores on the same measures that lie between the scores of the entire 1.53 group and the scores of the true second generation; the gender difference in these outcomes might in part be related to the greater selectivity involved in male versus female naturalization rates.

20. In some research contexts, however, it might prove useful to glance at the results for the male naturalized 1.53 group, as a sort of upper bound estimate for the true second generation outcomes.

21. This form of the education question was introduced in 1990. In the censuses of 1940 through 1980, respondents were asked to select the highest grade, not a degree (or level), of schooling. For example, in 1980 the census asked, "What is the highest grade or level of school this person has ever attended?" (Ruggles et al. 2005; Mare 1995).

22. The critical comparison is the difference between census and CPS in the proportion choosing "twelfth grade no diploma" among all who chose between the two twelfth-grade categories.

REFERENCES

Alba, Richard. 1985. *Italian Americans: Into the Twilight of Ethnicity.* Englewood Cliffs, N.J.: Prentice-Hall.

———. 1988. Cohorts and the Dynamics of Ethnic Change. In *Social Structures and Human Lives,* edited by Matilda White Riley, Bettina J. Huber, and Beth B. Hess. Newbury Park, Calif.: Sage Publications.

———. 1995. Assimilation's Quiet Tide. *The Public Interest* 119(spring): 318.

———. 1990. *Ethnic Identity: The Transformation of White America.* New Haven, Conn.: Yale University Press.

Alba, Richard, and Tariqul Islam. 2005. "The Case of the Disappearing Mexican Americans: An Ethnic-Identity Mystery." Paper presented at the 2005 meeting of the Population Association of America (April 2, 2005).

Alba, Richard, and Victor Nee. 2003. *Remaking the American Mainstream.* Cambridge, Mass.: Harvard University Press.

Alba, Richard, Amy Lutz, and Elena Vesselinov. 2001. "How Enduring Were the Inequalities Among European Immigrant Groups in the United States?" *Demography* 38(3): 349–56.

Archdeacon, Thomas J. 1983. *Becoming American: An Ethnic History.* New York: The Free Press.

Barrett, James, and David Roediger. 2002. "Inbetween Peoples: Race, Nationality and the 'New Immigrant' Working Class." In *Colored White: Transcending the Racial Past,* edited by David Roediger. Berkeley: University of California Press.

Bean, Frank D., and Gillian Stevens. 2003. *America's Newcomers and the Dynamics of Diversity.* New York: Russell Sage Foundation.

Bernhardt, Annette, Martina Morris, Mark S. Handcock, and Marc A. Scott. 2001. *Divergent Paths: Economic Mobility in the New American Labor Market.* New York: Russell Sage Foundation.

Blau, Peter M., and Otis Dudley Duncan. 1967. *The American Occupational Structure.* New York: John Wiley & Sons.

Bogue, Donald J. 1985. *The Population of the United States: Historical Trends and Future Projections.* New York: Free Press.

Borjas, George J. 1994. "Long-Run Convergence of Ethnic Skills Differentials: The Children and Grandchildren of the Great Migration." *Industrial and Labor Relations Review* 47(4): 553–73.

———. 1999. *Heavens Door: Immigration Policy and the American Economy.* Princeton, N.J.: Princeton University Press.

———. 2001. Long-Run Convergence of Ethnic Skill Differentials, Revisited. *Demography* 38(3): 357–61.

Borjas, George J., and Richard B. Freeman. 1992. "Introduction and Summary." In *Immigration and the Work Force: Economic Consequences for the United States and Source Areas,* edited by George J. Borjas and Richard B. Freeman. Chicago: University of Chicago Press.

Bowles, Samuel, Herbert Gintis, and Melissa Osborne Groves, eds. 2005. *Unequal Chances: Family Background and Economic Success.* New York: Russell Sage Foundation and Princeton University Press.

Carter, Susan B., Alan Olmsted, Gavin Wright, and Michael R. Haines, eds. 1997. *Historical Statistics of the United States on CD-ROM: Colonial Times to 1970.* U.S. Bureau of the Census. New York: Cambridge University Press.

Cortes, Carlos E. 1980. "Mexicans." In *Harvard Encyclopedia of American Ethnic Groups,* edited by Stephan Thernstrom. Cambridge, Mass.: Belknap Press of Harvard University.

Covello, Leonard. 1967. *The Social Background of the Italo-American School Child.* Reprint. Leiden: E. J. Brill.

Danziger, Sheldon, and Peter Gottshalk. 1995. *America Unequal.* New York: Russell Sage Foundation and Harvard University Press.

Edmonston, Barry, and Jeffery S. Passel. 1994. "Immigration and Race: Recent Trends in Immigration in the United States." In *Immigration and Ethnicity: The Integration of America's Newest Arrivals,* edited by Barry Edmonston and Jeffery S. Passel. Washington, D.C.: The Urban Institute Press.

Farley, Reynolds, and Richard D. Alba. 2002. "The New Second Generation in the United States." *International Migration Review* 36(3): 669–702.

Featherman, David L., and Robert M. Hauser. 1978. *Opportunity and Change.* New York: Academic Press.

Ferenczi, Imre, compiler. 1929. *International Migrations,* vol. 1, *Statistics.* New York: National Bureau of Economic Research.

Gans, Herbert. 1992. "Second Generation Decline: Scenarios for the Economic and Ethnic Futures of the Post-1965 American Immigrants." *Ethnic and Racial Studies* 15(2): 173–92.

Ganzeboom, Harry B.G., Donald J. Treiman, and Wout C. Ultee. 1991. "Comparative Intergenerational Stratification Research: Three Generations and Beyond." *Annual Review of Sociology* 17: 277–302.

Gerstle, Gary. 2001. *American Crucible: Race and Nation in the Twentieth Century.* Princeton, N.J.: Princeton University Press.

Goldin, Claudia. 2000. "Labor Markets in the Twentieth Century." In *The Cambridge Economic History of the United States,* vol. 3, edited by Stanley L. Engerman and Robert E. Galllman. New York: Cambridge University Press.

Goldin, Claudia, and Lawrence F. Katz. 2001. "Decreasing (and Then Increasing) Inequality in America: A Tale of Two Half-Centuries." In *The Causes and Consequences of Increasing Income Inequality,* edited by Finis Welch. Chicago: University of Chicago Press.

Goldin, Claudia, and Robert A. Margo. 1992. "The Great Compression: The Wage Structure in the United States at Mid-Century." *Quarterly Journal of Economics* 107(February): 1–34.

Gordon, Milton. 1964. *Assimilation in American Life: The Role of Race, Religion and National Origins.* New York: Oxford University Press.

Grebler, Leo, Joan W. Moore, and Ralph C. Guzman. 1970. *The Mexican-American People: The Nation's Second Largest Minority.* New York: Free Press.

Hampel, Robert L. 1986. *The Last Little Citadel: American High Schools Since 1940.* Boston: Houghton Mifflin.

Handlin, Oscar. 1957. *Race and Nationality in American Life.* Boston, Mass.: Little Brown.

———. 1959. *The Newcomers: Negroes and Puerto Ricans in a Changing Metropolis.* Cambridge, Mass.: Harvard University Press.

Harding, David J., Christopher Jencks, Leonard M. Lopoo, and Susan E. Mayer. 2005. "The Changing Effects of Family Background on the Incomes of American Adults." In *Unequal Chances: Family Background and Economic Success,* edited by Samuel Bowles, Herbert Gintis, and Melissa Osborne Groves. New York: Russell Sage Foundation and Princeton University Press.

Hicks, Lloyd. 1997. *Annual Demographic Survey March Supplement: Source and Accuracy.* Current Population Survey (CPS). Available at: http://www.bls.census.gov/cps /ads/1996/ssrcacc.html (accessed June 9, 2005).

Higham, John. 1955. *Strangers in the Land: Problems of American Nativism, 1860–1925.* New Brunswick, N.J.: Rutgers University Press.

Hirschman, Charles, and Ellen Percy Kraly. 1990. "Racial and Ethnic Inequality in the United States 1940 and 1950: The Impact of Geographic Location and Human Capital." *International Migration Review* 24(1): 4–33.

Hourwich, Isaac A. 1912. *Immigration and Labor: The Economic Aspects of European Immigration to the United States.* New York: G. P. Putnam's Sons.

Hout, Michael. 1988. "More Universalism, Less Structural Mobility: The American Occupational Structure in the 1980s." *American Journal of Sociology* 93(6): 1358–1400.

Jaynes, Gerald. 2004. "Immigration and the Social Construction of Otherness: 'Underclass' Stigma and Intergroup Relations." In *Not Just Black and White:*

Historical and Contemporary Perspectives on Immigration, Race and Ethnicity in the United States, edited by Nancy Foner and George M. Fredrickson. New York: Russell Sage Foundation.

Jencks, Christopher. 1992. *Rethinking Social Policy: Race, Poverty, and the Underclass.* Cambridge, Mass.: Harvard University Press.

———. 2001. "Who Should Get In?" *New York Review of Books.* Part I (November 29) and Part II (December 20).

———. 2002. "Who Should Get In?: An Exchange." *New York Review of Books* (May 23).

Jencks, Christopher, and Meredith Phillips, eds. 1998. *"Black White Test Score Gap."* Washington, D.C.: Brookings Institution.

Jensen, Leif. 2001. "The Demographic Diversity of Immigrants and their Children." In *Ethnicities: Children of Immigrants in America,* edited by Rubén G. Rumbaut and Alejandro Portes. Berkeley: University of California Press and Russell Sage Foundation.

Joseph, Samuel. 1914. *Jewish Immigration to the United States from 1881 to 1910.* New York: Columbia University Press.

Kasinitz, Philip. 2004. "Race, Assimilation and Second Generations, Past and Present." In *Not Just Black and White: Historical and Contemporary Perspectives on Immigration, Race and Ethnicity in the United States,* edited by Nancy Foner and George M. Fredrickson. New York: Russell Sage Foundation.

Katz, Lawrence F., and David H. Autor. 1999. "Changes in the Wage Structure and Earnings Inequality." In *Handbook of Labor Economics,* vol. 3, edited by Orley Ashenfelter and David Card. New York: Elsevier.

Katz, Michael B. 1987. *Reconstructing American Education.* Cambridge, Mass.: Harvard University Press.

Krug, Edward A. 1964. *The Shaping of the American High School.* New York: Harper and Row.

Kuznets, Simon. 1975. "Immigration of Russian Jews to the United States: Background and Structure." *Perspectives in American History* 9: 35–126.

Lalonde, Robert J., and Robert H. Topel. 1992. "The Assimilation of Immigrants in the U.S. Labor Market." In *Immigration and the Work Force: Economic Consequences for the United States and Source Areas,* edited by G. J. Borjas and Richard B. Freeman. Chicago: University of Chicago Press and NBER.

Lieberson, Stanley. 1980. *A Piece of the Pie: Blacks and White Immigrants Since 1880.* Berkeley: University of California Press.

Lieberson, Stanley, and Mary C. Waters. 1988. *From Many Strands: Ethnic and Racial Groups in Contemporary America.* New York: Russell Sage Foundation.

Lopez, David E., and Ricardo D. Stanton-Salazar. 2001. "Mexican Americans." In *Ethnicities: Children of Immigrants in America,* edited by Rubén G. Rumbaut and Alejandro Portes. Berkeley: University of California Press and Russell Sage Foundation.

Mare, Robert D. 1995. "Changes in Educational Attainment and School Enrollment." In *State of the Union: America in the 1990s,* vol. 1, *Economic Trends,* edited by Reynolds Farley. New York: Russell Sage Foundation.

Margo, Robert A. 1990. *Race and Schooling in the South, 1880–1950: An Economic History.* Chicago: University of Chicago Press.

Massey, Douglas S., Jorge Durand, and Nolan J. Malone. 2002. *Beyond Smoke and Mirrors: American Immigration in an Era of Economic Integration.* New York: Russell Sage Foundation.

Moll, Luis C., and Richard Ruiz. 2002. "The Schooling of Latino Children." In *Latinos: Remaking America,* edited by Marcelo M. and Mariela M. Paez. Berkeley: University of California Press and The David Rockefeller Center for Latin-American Studies of Harvard University.

Myers, Dowell. 1998. "Dimensions of Economic Adaptation by Mexican-Origin Men." In *Crossings: Mexican Immigration in Interdisciplinary Perspectives,* edited by Marcelo Suarez-Orozco. Cambridge, Mass.: Harvard University Press.

Myers, Dowell, and Cynthia Cranford. 1998. "Temporal Differences in the Occupational Mobility of Immigrant and Native-born Latina Workers." *American Sociological Review* 63(February): 68–93.

National Center for Education Statistics. 2003 [2005]. *Digest of Educational Statistics.* Washington, D.C.: U.S. Department of Education. Available at: http://nces.ed.gov//programs/digest/d03 (accessed June 9, 2005).

Ngai, Mae M. 2004. *Impossible Subjects: Illegal Aliens and the Making of Modern America.* Princeton, N.J.: Princeton University Press.

Niedert, Lisa, and Reynolds Farley. 1985. "Assimilation in the United States: An Analysis of Ethnic and Generational Differences in Status and Achievement." *American Sociological Review* 50(6, December): 840–50.

Olneck, Michael, and Marvin Lazerson. 1980. "Education." In *Harvard Encyclopedia of American Ethnic Groups,* edited by Stephan Thernstrom. Cambridge, Mass.: Belknap Press of Harvard University.

Oropesa, R. Salvador, and Nancy Landale. 1997. "In Search of the New Second Generation: Alternative Strategies for Identifying Second-Generation Children and Understanding their Acquisition of English." *Sociological Perspectives* 40(3): 427–55.

Perlmann, Joel. 1985. "Curriculum and Tracking in the Transformation of the American High School: Providence, R.I. 1880–1930." *Journal of Social History* 19(fall): 29–55.

———. 1988. *Ethnic Differences: Schooling and Social Structure Among the Irish, Italians, Jews, and Blacks in an American City, 1880–1935.* New York: Cambridge University Press.

———. 2000. "Demographic Outcomes of Ethnic Intermarriage in American History: Italian Americans through Four Generations." Working Paper 312. Annandale-on-Hudson, N.Y.: The Levy Economics Institute. Available at: http://ww.levy.org (accessed June 9, 2005).

———. 2001a. "'Race or People': Federal Race Classifications for Europeans in

America, 1898–1913." Working Paper 320. Annandale-on-Hudson, N.Y.: The Levy Economics Institute. Available at: http://ww.levy.org (accessed June 9, 2005).

———. 2001b. "Toward a Population History of the Second Generation: Birth Cohorts of Southern, Central, and Eastern European Origins, 1871–1970." Working Paper No. 333. Annandale-on-Hudson, N.Y.: The Levy Economics Institute. Available at: http://ww.levy.org (accessed June 9, 2005).

———. 2002. "Poles and Italians Then, Mexicans Now? Immigrant-to-Native Wage Ratios, 1910 and 1940," Working Paper 343. Annandale-on-Hudson, N.Y.: The Levy Economics Institute. Available at: http://ww.levy.org (accessed June 9, 2005).

———. 2003a. "Mexicans Now, Italians Then: Intermarriage Patterns." Working Paper 376. Annandale-on-Hudson, N.Y.: The Levy Economics Institute. Available at: http://ww.levy.org (accessed June 9, 2005).

———. 2003b. "IPUMS" (website review). *Journal of American History* 90(1): 339.

———. 2004. "The New Race Question and the 1910 Census: The 'List Of Races and Peoples,' 1898–1910." Paper presented at U.S. Census Bureau symposium, "America's Scorecard: The Historical Role of the Census in an Ever-Changing Nation." Washington, D.C. (March 4, 2004).

Perlmann, Joel, and Roger Waldinger. 1996. "The Second Generation and the Children of the Native Born: Comparisons and Refinements." Working Paper 174. Annandale-on-Hudson, N.Y.: The Levy Economics Institute. Available at: http://ww.levy.org (accessed June 9, 2005).

———. 1997. "Second Generation Decline?: Children of Immigrants, Past and Present—A Reconsideration." *International Migration Review* 31(4): 893–922.

Perlmann, Joel, and Mary C. Waters, eds. 2003. *The New Race Question: How the Census Counts Multiracial Individuals.* New York: Russell Sage Foundation.

Portes, Alejandro, and Rubén Rumbaut. 1996. *Immigrant America,* 2nd ed. Berkeley: University of California Press.

———, eds. 2001a. *Ethnicities: Children of Immigrants in America.* Berkeley: University of California Press.

———. 2001b. *Legacies: The Story of the Immigrant Second Generation.* Berkeley: University of California Press and Russell Sage Foundation.

Portes, Alejandro, and Min Zhou. 1993. "The New Second Generation: Segmented Assimilation and Its Variants among Post-1965 Immigrant Youth." *Annals* 530: 74–96.

Preston, Samuel H., and Michael R. Haines. 1991. *Fatal Years: Child Mortality in Nineteenth-Century America.* Princeton, N.J.: Princeton University Press.

Ruggles, Steven, Matthew Sobek, Trent Alexander, Catherine A. Fitch, Ronald Goeken, Patricia Kelly Hall, Miriam King, and Chad Ronnander. 2004. *Integrated Public Use Microdata Series: Version 3.0* [Machine-readable database]. Minneapolis, Minn.: Minnesota Population Center [producer and distributor]. Available at: http://www.ipums.umn.edu (accessed June 9, 2005).

————. 2005. *IPUMS Documentation.* Available at: http://www.ipums.umn.edu (accessed June 9, 2005).

Rumbaut, Rubén G. 1999. "Assimilation and Its Discontents: Ironies and Paradoxes." In *The Handbook of International Migration: The American Experience,* edited by Charles Hirschman, Philip Kasinitz, and Josh DeWind. New York: Russell Sage Foundation.

Smith, Robert C. 2001. "Mexicans: Social, Educational, Economic and Political Problems and Prospects in New York." In *New Immigrants in New York,* edited by Nancy Foner. New York: Columbia University Press.

————. 2002. "Gender Ethnicity and Race in School and Work Outcomes of Second-Generation Mexican Americans." In *Latinos: Remaking America,* edited by Marcelo M. and Mariela M. Paez. Berkeley: University of California Press and The David Rockefeller Center for Latin-American Studies of Harvard University.

Smith James B., and Barry Edmonston, eds. 1997. *The New Americans: Economic, Demographic and Fiscal Effects of Immigration.* Washington, D.C.: National Academy Press.

Solon, Gary. 1999. "Intergenerational Mobility in the Labor Market." In *Handbook of Labor Economics,* vol. 3, edited by Orley Ashenfelter and David Card. New York: Elsevier.

Stier, Haya, and Marta Tienda. 2001. *The Color of Opportunity: Pathways to Family, Welfare and Work.* Chicago: University of Chicago Press.

Thernstrom, Stephan. 1973. *The Other Bostonians: Poverty and Progress in the American Metropolis, 1880–1970.* Cambridge, Mass.: Harvard University Press.

U.S. Commissioner of Labor. 1903. *Cost of Living.* Annual Report of the Commissioner of Labor for 1903. Washington: U.S. Government Printing Office.

U.S. Bureau of Labor Statistics. 2005. "Table Containing History of CPI-U U.S. All Items Indexes and Annual Percent Changes, from 1913 to the Present." Available at: ftp://ftp.bls.gov/pub/special.requests/cpi/cpiai.txt (accessed June 9, 2005).

Waldinger, Roger, and Joel Perlmann. 1998. "Second Generations: Past, Present, Future." *Journal of Ethnic and Migration Studies* 24(1): 5–24.

Welch, Finis, ed. 2001. *The Causes and Consequences of Increasing Income Inequality.* Chicago: University of Chicago Press.

Wilson, William Julius. 1987. *The Truly Disadvantaged: The Inner City, the Underclass, and Public Policy.* Chicago: The University of Chicago Press.

INDEX

Boldface numbers refer to figures and tables.

African Americans. *See* blacks
Alba, Richard, 142
Archdeacon, Thomas, 14
Asian immigrants, 8–9
Autor, David H., 141

Bean, Frank D., 124, 168*n*2
blacks: blocked progress in the assimilation of, 3; definition of native-born, 37; educational attainments compared to SCE second generation, 1926–1935, 166*n*15; educational attainments in 2000 census, 156–61; gendered patterns/family structure, economic impact of, 110–15; high school dropout rates, 77–83; institutionalization and missing men among young, 85–88; Mexican Americans, comparison to, 117, 121–22; residual wage differences experienced by, 97–101, 123; risky social behaviors among young, 83–88; schooling of in the early twentieth century South, 66; segmented assimilation theory and, 120; teen pregnancy and single motherhood among, 83–84; total earnings of men, 103–6; work status of young, 84–85

Borjas, George J.: catch-up of immigrants, decreasing likelihood of, 43; ethnic wage ratios, estimates of, 126–27, 141, 167*n*3; Jencks's use of work by, 4, 44, 118; Jews, inclusion of in studies of immigrant assimilation, 142; occupational wage scale for estimating 1910 ethnic wage ratio, 48–49; relative wage status of labor migrants in 1910 and 2000, comparison of, 53; research agenda of, 43–44
Bracero Program, 27

Canadian immigrants, 34–35
Census Bureau, United States, 5–6
children: born out of wedlock, 83–84; as immigrants late in an immigration wave, 20
Chinese immigrants, 8–9, 35
Chiswick, Barry, 43

citizenship status: IRCA amnesty, 27, 55, 151; undocumented immigrants, 54–55, 75; usefulness in defining a proxy for the second generation, 69, 151, 154–56

CPS. *See* Current Population Survey

Current Population Survey (CPS): educational attainments of selected ethnic groups, 1998–2001, **157–59,** 160–61; identification of second-generation Mexican Americans and, 142–43, 150–53, 155–56; parental birthplace information from, 6, 29, 67; sample size limitations of, 67, 143, **145–46**

Durand, Jorge, 27, 53

economic well-being of immigrants: comparison of past SCE and present Mexican immigrants, 2–5; comparison of past SCEN and present Mexican immigrants, 116–25; education and (*see* education; second-generation schooling); ethnic earnings gap confronted by Mexican and black men, 103–10; ethnic origins and, 8; the ethnic wage ratio (*see* ethnic wage ratios); historical comparisons of, 5; income of Mexican compared to other contemporary immigrants, 32–33; Mexican, low position of among all immigrants, 31–33; occupations, comparisons of, 38–41; the second generation (*see* second-generation economic outcomes). *See also* wage inequality

Edmonston, Barry, 166*n*16

education: distinguishing immigrants from native-born, importance of, 60–61; earnings inequality and, 106–10; estimating ethnic wage ratios, adjustments for, 134–37; high school drop out rates, 5, 78–83, 106–10, 124–25, 161; high school graduation and ethnicity in 2000 census, 156–61; levels of by selected groups and cohorts, **76;** levels of in 2000, **79–82;** of Mexican-immigrant parents, 31–32; of privileged contemporary immigrants, 2; of the second generation (*see* second-generation schooling); segmented assimilation theory and, 3, 5; wage inequality and, 53–54, 57–59, 72–75, 92–95, 117, 120, 125

Education, U.S. Department of, 61

employment among young adults, 84–85

ethnic capital, 44

ethnic earnings gap, 103–10

ethnicity: classification in governmental data, 10–12; economic class and, 8. *See also* names of national or ethnic groups

ethnic wage ratios: conceptualization of, 41–45, 118–19; education and, 53–54, 58–59, 92–95; historical context of wage inequality and, 45–48, 119–20; for immigrants, 50–55; measuring for 1940–2000, 49–50; for second-generation cohorts, 90–101, 122–24

ethnic wage ratios, estimation of pre-1940, 48–49; additional features of the process, 136, 139–42; adjustments within occupations, 133–38; critique of past estimates, 126–31; new occupational wage scale, 131–33

families: second-generation economic outcomes and, 110–15; second-generation Mexican Americans and, 144, 146–50

gender: men, analytical focus on, 37, 141–42; second-generation economic outcomes and, 110–15
German immigrants, 10–11, 13
Goldin, Claudia: wage inequality before 1940, 49, 167n4; wages, historical narrative/summary of great swings in, 5, 46, 127–28, 139–40, 168n6, 173n11; wage structure of the mid- to late-1920s, 173n6; wage structure reflected in the 1940 census, analysis of, 51–52, 139
Grebler, Leo, 166n16
Guzman, Ralph C., 166n16

Haines, Michael, 49, 126, 141
Hispanics: educational attainment of, 60–61
human capital migrants, 37

immigrants: contemporary compared to SCE, 2–3, 116–25; labor migrants, 3–4, 37; Mexican (see Mexican immigrants); place of origin among contemporary by percentage, 31; by race or people, 1899–1924, 11; remigration of, 14; second generation of (see second-generation immigrants); social mobility of, 1–5, 82–83, 95–96, 116–25; from southern, central, and eastern Europe (see SCE (southern, central, and eastern European) immigrants); undocumented, 54–55, 75; waves of, timing of arrival in, 14–17
Immigration and Naturalization Service (INS), 166–67n18
Immigration Reform and Control Act of 1986 (IRCA), 27, 55, 151
income. See economic well-being; wage inequality ethnic earnings gap

institutionalization among young adults, 85–88
IPUMS datasets, 9–10, 13, 61
IRCA. See Immigration Reform and Control Act of 1986
Italian immigrants, 2–3, 14, 20, 22–23, 30. See also SCE (southern, central, and eastern European) immigrants

Japanese immigrants, 8–9
Jencks, Christopher: ethnic wage ratio, use of for comparing SCE and Mexican immigrants, 44–45, 48–49, 52–53, 118–19; interpretation of 1940 and 1950 data, 168n7; SCE and Mexican immigrants, comparison of, 4–5; urban settlement as source of immigrant prosperity, suggestion regarding, 173n12
Jewish immigrants, 2, 10–14, 30, 142, 165n8

Katz, Lawrence, 5, 49, 127–28, 131, 139–40, 167n4, 173n11; wages, historical narrative, 46–47, 168n6

labor migrants, 3–4, 37. See also Mexican immigrants
Lieberson, Stanley, 2, 12, 97, 123, 166n15
literacy as measure of education, 54
Lutz, Amy, 142

Malone, Nolan J., 27, 53
Margo, Robert, 5, 46, 127–28, 139; creating literacy proxy from grades of schooling, 173n8
marriage: among late arrivals in an immigration wave, 20–21; patterns among Mexican immigrants, 33–35; patterns among SCE immigrants, 19–20
Massey, Douglas S., 27, 53

Mexican Americans: blacks, comparison to, 117 (*see also* blacks); culture of disaffection among young, 77–78, 83–88; earnings of (*see* second-generation economic outcomes); education of (*see* second-generation schooling); gendered patterns and family structure, economic impact of, 110–15; geographic concentration of, 101–3; institutionalization and missing men among young, 85–88; proxy used for second-generation, 67–69, 142–56; teen pregnancy and single motherhood among, 83–84; work status of young, 84–85. *See also* second-generation immigrants

Mexican immigrants: discrimination against early, 65–66; earnings of the second generation (*see* second-generation economic outcomes); economic well-being, 31–33; economic well-being: earnings and gendered patterns/ family structure, 110–15; economic well-being: occupations, 38–41; economic well-being: the ethnic wage ratio, 41, 45, 50–55; educational attainments of, 31–32, 60–61, **63**; educational attainments of second generation (*see* second-generation schooling); generational standing of second and later generational cohorts, **29**; geographic concentration of, 101–3; historical background of, 26–30, 170*n*4; history of and questions regarding the second generation, 4; institutionalization and missing men among young, 85–88; late nineteenth- and early twentieth-century, 8–9; marriage patterns of, 33–35; Mexican-born population in the United States, **28**; nu-

merical dominance among contemporary immigrants, 30–32; places of residence, **102**; remigration of, 28; SCE/SCEN immigrants, comparison to, 3–4, 116–25; second generation (*see* Mexican Americans; second-generation immigrants); teen pregnancy and single motherhood among, 83–84; undocumented status, impact of, 54–55, 75; U.S. public policy and, 27–28; wage inequality and, 5; work status of young, 84–85. *See also* immigrants

Minnesota, University of, Minnesota Population Center, 6

Moore, Joan W., 166*n*16

native-born blacks. *See* blacks

native whites: definition of, 37; economic well-being: occupations, 38–41; economic well-being: the ethnic wage ratio, 41, 45, 49–55, 59; educational attainments in 2000 census, 156–61; gendered patterns/family structure, economic impact of, 110–15; institutionalization and missing men among young, 85–88; levels of schooling attained by, 75–82; risky social behaviors among young, 83–88; teen pregnancy and single motherhood among, 83–84; total earnings of men, 103–6; work status of young, 84–85

native whites of native parentage (NWNP): earnings of, 90–92; education of, 65–66; levels of schooling attained by, 75–77

naturalization. *See* citizenship status

NWNP. *See* native whites of native parentage

occupational distribution, 1910–2000, 38–41

occupational wage scales, 49, 126–36

Passel, Jeffery S., 166*n*16
Polish immigrants, 2–3, 10–13, 22–23, 30, 164–65*n*7. *See also* SCE (southern, central, and eastern European) immigrants
Portes, Alejandro, 3, 37, 42–43
Preston, Samuel, 49, 126, 141
Preston-Haines occupational wage scale, 49, 126–27, 129–30, 132–33, 140, 172*n*4
Puerto Rican immigrants, 34–35

race: discrimination against Asians, 9; discrimination against early twentieth-century Mexicans, 9; misleading analyses of educational attainment, sources of, 61; segmented assimilation theory and, 3, 43. *See also* blacks
remigration: of Mexican immigrants, 28; from the 1890–1920 migration wave, 14
Rumbaut, Rubén, 3, 37, 67

SCEN (southern, central, and eastern European, non-Jews) immigrants, 10; contemporary Mexican immigrants, comparison to, 116–25; demographic data, availability of, 37–38; earnings of the second generation (*see* second-generation economic outcomes); economic well-being: conditions for launching the second generation, 55–59; economic well-being: occupations, 38–41; economic well-being: the ethnic wage ratio, 41, 49–55; education of the second generation (*see* second-generation schooling); geographic controls for studying progress of, case for, 173–74*n*13; history of compared to history of Mexican migration, 28

SCE (southern, central, and eastern European) immigrants: contemporary immigrants, comparison to, 2–3; economic well-being: the ethnic wage ratio, 45; history of and questions regarding the second generation, 4; the immigration wave of 1890 to 1914, **16**; the immigration wave of 1890 to 1914, timing in, 14–17; marriage patterns of, 19–20; mass immigration of 1890 to 1914 by, 1–2; percentage of all immigrants, **15**; remigration of, 14–15, 19; second generation of (*see* second-generation immigrants); selection of groups to study, 8–13
second generation: age of SCE cohorts, **25**; birth cohorts of Mexican and contemporary, **32**; birth of SCE cohorts, 17–19; conceptualization of and questions regarding, 4–5; contrast between SCEN and Mexican cohorts, 116–17; earnings of (*see* second-generation economic outcomes); economic positions for launching, 55–59; education of (*see* second-generation schooling); generational standing of Mexican-origin population, 28–30; historical experience of SCE cohorts, 24–26; immigration waves, changing composition of cohorts at the end of, 19–22; later SCE cohorts, changing composition of, 19–22; later SCE cohorts, mixed parentage among, **21–22**; Mexican, proxy for, 67–69, 142–56; numerical primacy of Mexican cohorts among contemporary, 30–32; parentage of contemporary, mixed and unmixed, 33–36; parental place of origin among contemporary by percentage, **31**; the segmented assimila-

second generation (*cont.*)
tion theory and, 3–4, 41–43,
120–21; selection of groups to
study among SCE, 8–13
second-generation economic outcomes: education and, 92–95,
106–10, 122–23; gendered patterns and family structure, 110–
15; intergenerational mobility
and, 95–96; relative starting positions, 55–59; residual wage differences in historical perspective,
96–101, 122–24; total earnings
of Mexican American men, 103–
10; wages of Mexican American
cohorts, 92; wages of SCEN cohorts, 90–92
second-generation schooling, 60;
comparison of birth cohorts
across ethnic groups relative to
native whites, 64–67, 69, 117;
distinctiveness of Mexican pattern, 88–89, 121; educational attainments, 5, 22–23, 57–59;
156–61; educational attainments
of SCE cohorts, 22–23; educational attainments of SCE cohorts compared to northern-born
blacks, 1926–1935, 166n15; ethnic educational differences, level
of schooling as measure of, 75–
77; ethnic educational differences, measuring across historical
periods, 69–75; first to second
generation catch-up, **70–71**;
high school dropout rates of
Mexican Americans, 5, 77–83,
106–10, 124–25, 161; Mexican
second generation, use of proxy
for, 67–69, 142–56; misleading
analyses: Hispanic educational attainment, 60–61, 121; misleading analyses: ignoring historical
context in comparisons of succes-
sor generations, 62–64, 121
segmented assimilation theory, 83;
the contemporary second genera-

tion, applied to, 3–5, 120–21;
the ethnic wage ratio and, 41–
43; Mexican economic assimilation, dire predictions regarding,
4–5, 124; minority subculture of
the poor, predictions regarding,
77, 83; residual wage differences
and, 97, 123
single motherhood, 83–84
Smith, Robert C., 171n9
social history, SCE second-generation
cohorts' experience of, 24–26
socioeconomic advancement/mobil-
ity: high school dropout rates
and, 82–83; immigrants and the
mythology of, 1; intergenerational, 95–96; of past SCE and
present Mexican immigrants,
2–5; of past SCEN and present
Mexican immigrants, 116–25.
See also economic well-being of
immigrants; second-generation
economic outcomes
Stevens, Gillian, 124, 168n2

teen pregnancy, 83–84

United States Commissioner of Immigration, 10–11

Vesselinov, Elena, 142

wage inequality: comparison of
SCEN and Mexican immigrants,
significance in, 116; the context
of American, 45–50; earnings
per person in 2000, **112**; education and, 53–54, 57–59, 72–75,
92–95, 117, 120, 125; estimates
for 1910, inaccuracy of, 118 (*see
also* ethnic wage ratios, estimation of); the ethnic wage ratio
(*see* ethnic wage ratios); gendered
patterns/family structure and,
110–15; historical swings in and
comparisons of immigrant well-
being, 5, 118–20; 1940–1995,

47; occupational wage scales, 49, 126–36; real wages of immigrant male cohorts, **58**; the second generation, relative position for launching, 55–59; for second-generation cohorts, 90–101, 122–24; undocumented status and, 54–55. *See also* economic well-being of immigrants

Waldinger, Roger, 3, 164*n*6

whites, native. *See* native whites

Wilson, William Julius, 97–98

youth culture: disaffection and socially risky behavior in, 77–78, 83–88, 121–22; dropout pattern of second-generation Mexican immigrants and, 5, 77–83, 121–22; segmented assimilation theory and, 3, 43